The Outer Hebrides

Guide Book

by CHARLES TAIT

THIRD EDITION (2ND REVISION)

Hebudes, Innse Gall
Sudreyar
Na h-Eileanan an Iar
The Western Isles, Outer Hebrides

ISBN 9780951785997

The Outer Hebrides Guide Book
copyright Charles Tait 2017
3rd edition, 2nd revision
Published by Charles Tait
Kelton, St Ola, Orkney KW15 1TR
Tel 01856 873738 Fax 01856 875313
charles.tait@zetnet.co.uk
charles-tait.co.uk

This book is dedicated to the memory of my step-mother,
Jean Maxwell Tait (1913-1999)

Text, design and layout © copyright Charles Tait, all photographs © copyright Charles Tait unless otherwise credited, old photographs from Charles Tait collection.
OS maps reproduced from Ordnance Survey mapping with permission of the Controller of HMSO, Crown Copyright Reserved MC 100035677.
Printing by Martins the Printers, Berwick-upon-Tweed.

ISBN 9780951785997

Front cover: Allasdale, Barra; Water Lilies, South Uist; Rodel Church, Harris; Chessman replica, Stornoway; Seilebost, Harris; Corncrake, Ness; Callanish sunset, Lewis
This page: Traigh Iar, Harris

Traigh Iar, Harris

The Outer Hebrides
Guide Book
by CHARLES TAIT

Na h-Eileanan an Iar
Hebudes, Sudreyar,
Innse Gall, Western Isles

CONTENTS

Callanish Standing Stones

The Outer Hebrides is a chain of over 200 islands to the west of northern Scotland. It extends for about 200km (130mi) from the Butt of Lewis in the north (58°31'N, 60°16'W) to Barra Head (56046'N, 7039'W) in the south. The islands are between 50km (30mi) and 100km (60mi) from the Scottish Mainland across the Minch and the Sea of the Hebrides. In area they cover 3,070km² (1,190mi²).

The archipelago was referred to by Scottish Gaels as Innse Gall, Islands of Strangers, referring to the Norsemen who held sway here for nearly 500 years. The name Hebrides probably arose from the Greek Hebudes by mistranscription. Today, the Scottish Gaelic influence is strong, however the Norse heritage remains very evident in many of the placenames and in the language.

The 2011 census recorded 27,694 people inhabiting 15 of the islands, with the majority living in Lewis and Harris (c.21,000). The main town is Stornoway with a population of about 9,000.

From Scotland, the Outer Hebrides appear as a long series of hilltops on the horizon. When approached from the east they initially appear rocky and bleak, with many inlets and small islands. In contrast, the west side has many sandy beaches and attractive bays, with relatively few high cliffs.

Ferries Connections are operated by Calmac. The new MV *Loch Seaforth* runs between Stornoway and Ullapool, while MV *Hebrides* connects Tarbert in Harris with Uig in Skye and Lochmaddy in North Uist. In the south, MV *Clansman* links Lochboisdale in South Uist and Castlebay in Barra with Oban. There are ferries between Harris and North Uist, and from Eriskay to Barra. Berneray, Scalpay and Vatersay are served by fixed links.

Air links Loganair operates air services with codeshares. From Stornoway there are daily flights to and from Edinburgh, Glasgow, Aberdeen and Inverness. Benbecula has daily connections to Stornoway, Barra and Glasgow, while Barra has daily services to Glasgow and Benbecula. Other information on operators is detailed in the See & Do Section.

The earliest written references to the islands are probably by Pliny the Elder around 70AD and Ptolemy in about 150AD. Pytheas the Greek may have visited Lewis in about 325BC during his voyage, when he established the latitude of the Stornoway area and may have visited Callanish.

The Norse sagas, which date from the 12th century, describe many events and people in the Hebrides, but it was not until the late 17th century that detailed accounts began to be made about visits to the area. In more recent times many eminent people have visited the Outer Hebrides and a number have written in various terms about their experiences.

There are a number of distinguished local authors, and there is always a good selection of local books available in the bookshops, including many in Gaelic. The library in Stornoway has a fine reference section for those wishing to consult the many books which are out of print.

The landscape is beautiful, history is evident everywhere, and there are many good opportunities to see wildlife. However the aspect of the islands which is perhaps the most important and rewarding to get to know is the local people. Do not hesitate to ask the way, or about things as you are sure to get a courteous

Loch Bee, South Uist - one of the largest of many in the Outer Hebrides

reply. Gaelic remains the first language of over 50%.

If you are lucky you might be regaled with a few good stories as well! There is a saying in the Outer Hebrides that "When God made time he made plenty of it", which describes the apparent pace of life in the islands rather well.

Maps Some of the places mentioned in this book are signposted, but many others are not. Confusingly, signposts, references in books and on maps may be in modern Gaelic or in various cartographers' spellings. Ordnance Survey references are quoted for many sites of interest.

Kisimul Castle, Castlebay, Isle of Barra

COUNTRYSIDE CODE

We are justly proud of our historic sites, wildlife and environment. Please help ensure that future visitors may enjoy them as much as you by observing these guidelines:

1. Always use stiles and gates and close gates after you.
2. Always ask permission before entering agricultural land.
3. Keep to paths and take care to avoid fields of grass and crops.
4. Do not disturb livestock.
5. Take your litter away with you and do not light fires.
6. Do not pollute water courses or supplies.
7. Never disturb nesting birds.
8. Do not pick wild flowers or dig up plants.
9. Drive and park with due care and attention, do not obstruct or endanger others.
10. Always take care near cliffs and beaches, particularly with children and pets. Many beaches are dangerous for swimmers.
11. Walkers should take adequate clothes, wear suitable footwear and tell someone of their plans.
12. Above all please respect the life of the countryside, leave only footprints, take only photographs and pleasant memories.

Notice: While most of the sites of interest are open to the public and have marked access, many are on private land. No right of access is implied in the description, and if in doubt it is always polite to ask. Also, while many roads and tracks are rights of way, not all are.

A Tour of the Main Ancient Sites

There are so many sites of interest in the Western Isles that it would take a lifetime of trips to visit them all. However even on a short stay it is possible to observe human constructions from a wide range of periods.

The early settlers have left much evidence behind them, ranging from numerous chambered cairns to standing stones. These include the well preserved cairn at Langass on North Uist, the enigmatic Steinicleit at Shader in Lewis and the spectacular standing stone settings at Callanish.

Neolithic, Bronze Age, Iron Age, Norse, Medieval and, more modern sites are scattered from the north of Lewis to Barra Head. Some are signposted, but most are not, rendering maps essential in finding them.

The most dramatic of all the Outer Hebrides monuments are the Standing Stones at Callanish. These megaliths and the adjacent smaller circles represent an immense amount of work for a Neolithic society and were clearly erected with a strong sense of purpose and reverence.

Dun Carloway is the best preserved of the many Iron Age brochs and duns in the islands. Its drystone walls have survived despite being used as a quarry for nearby blackhouses and shows the galleried structure typical of all brochs.

Langass chambered cairn is one of the best preserved of its type

Steinicleit is an enigmatic Neolithic ruin in north Lewis

Midsummer sunrise at Callanish

Dun Carloway is a well-preserved broch

Duns and brochs form a class of domestic structure often termed as Atlantic round houses. There are many throughout the islands, but the best are probably in North Uist, especially Dun Sticir, near Otternish and Dun Torchuill.

Dun Torchuill in North Uist is a ruined broch on an islet on a loch

Many are situated on loch islets and accessed by causeways. They were often occupied for long periods, from the Iron Age to Medieval times in some cases. Some sites were originally Neolithic.

There are only a few remaining castles in the islands, and Kisimul Castle on Barra is the most dramatic. The castle at Stornoway was largely destroyed by Cromwell's troops after the 17th century Civil War. The remains now lie under the old ferry pier.

Kisimul Castle, Castlebay, Barra

The Western Isles have many ancient chapel and monastic sites. Most are ruinous and remote. The best preserved Medieval church is the 16th century St Clement's at Rodel, Harris. There is a 12th century Norse chapel at Kildonan on South Uist.

St Clement's Church at Rodel in south Harris has an elaborate MacLeod tomb

Blackhouse Museum at Arnol, West Lewis

Throughout Scotland blackhouses were the standard domestic building until the 19th century. These apparently primitive dwellings with thatched roofs, were shared by their human inhabitants and livestock, much as in Neolithic times. They had a central fireplace, and the smoke escaped through the thatch.

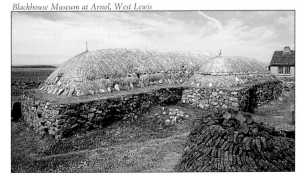

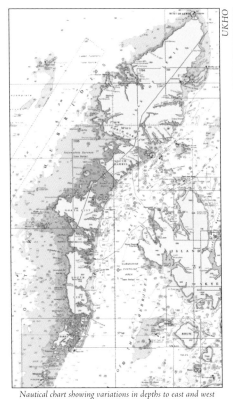

Nautical chart showing variations in depths to east and west

The wild east coast of Harris

Eoligarry Machair, Barra

St Kilda was formed by volcanic eruptions 60 million years ago

GEOLOGY The Lewisian Gneiss Complex was formed between 3100 million years ago (Ma) and 400Ma. It is some of the oldest exposed rocks on Earth. The main structures date from the Scourian event (3100Ma to 2500Ma), with significant igneous intrusion in Harris around 1880Ma.

During the Laxfordian event (1850Ma to 1600Ma) major folding and metamorphic changes took place. The South Harris Igneous Complex formed deep within the Earth's crust around 2000Ma. It includes minerals such as anorthosite, anorite and diorite, some of which have been subject to commercial extraction.

The highly indented coastline extends to about 2,100km (approx 1,300mi). The Outer Hebrides Fault Zone runs up the east coast, where the deep waters of the Minch reach over 100m close inshore. During the Torridonian Period (c.1000Ma) large quantities of sediments accumulated here.

These are evident on the surface only around Stornoway as the Stornoway sandstone beds. These form the fertile farmland here,

Torridonian Sandstone forms a beautiful reddish beach at Braigh na h-Aoidhe east of Stornoway

which is otherwise rare in the Outer Hebrides, except in areas with machair.

In contrast, the west coast is mostly bounded by the Outer Hebrides Platform. Inshore depths are 10-15m only and the 50m line is up to 70km (approx 40mi) offshore. These shallow seas have played a major factor in the build up of sand on the west coasts of the islands. The many beautiful beaches are in stark contrast to the east coasts.

The Western Isles were thinly glaciated in the last Ice Age, and were one of the first areas to be free of ice, around 12,000 years ago, due to the Gulf Stream. One of the results of this is that whereas much of mainland Scotland has risen since the melting of the ice, the Western Isles have sunk. Combined with the rise in sea level this means that much land area has been reclaimed by the sea, especially on the west side.

Glacial striations are apparent on many of the exposed rock surfaces throughout the isles. These parallel scratches, combined with the structure of the gneiss, add an extra dimension of beauty. Dramatic folds, mixtures of different minerals and ancient deformed igneous intrusions are visible in many places. Erosion, over thousands of millions of years, has exposed a fascinating and beautiful geology.

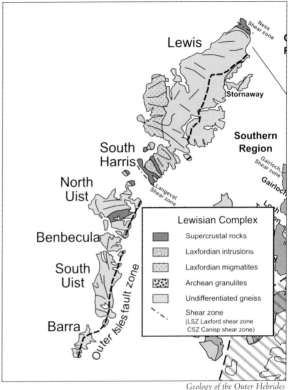

Geology of the Outer Hebrides

Lewisian Gneiss

Massive contortions at Ness

Torridonian Sandstone

Dolerite columns on the Shiant Islands

Glacial striations on Barra

Uig Bay has beautiful sands backed by extensive dunes and high mountains

Environment Lewisian Gneiss is predominant in the Outer Hebrides. These ancient rocks were formed deep in the Earth nearly 3,000 million years ago. Apart from the mountains of Harris and the east coasts of the Uists, most of the land is relatively low lying. The highest point is Clisham in Harris (799m).

There are several types of terrain, including moorland and hills, machair, sandy beaches and dunes, rocky coasts and cliffs, woodlands and inland lochs. Much of the interior of the islands, especially Lewis and North Uist, comprises vast areas of peatland, while the eastern seaboard is mostly rocky, facing the deep waters of the Minch.

In contrast the spectacular sandy beaches which dominate the western sides of the islands are often backed by large areas of dunes and machair. This forms when windblown sand has accumulated in considerable quantities inland. When fertilised with seaweed and farmyard manure, machair makes excellent agricultural soil.

The only sandy beaches on the east side of Lewis are north of Stornoway. Benbecula and Barra, as well as some of the outlying islands, also have extensive east-facing expanses of sand. The most remarkable is perhaps the Cocklestrand, or Traigh Mhor, which forms Barra Airfield and borders the shallow Sound of Barra.

Long fjord like sea lochs indent the coasts of the islands, especially in the east. The largest of these, Loch Seaforth, is one of

many such drowned valleys which have been sculpted by glaciers. These coasts are mostly rocky, with deep water close inshore. Many small islands and skerries lie offshore.

Inland, especially in Lewis and the Uists, the terrain is dotted with over 7,000 lochs. These form in hollows scooped out by ice and afford excellent trout fishing. Loch Langavat is the longest at 11km (6.8mi), Loch Scadavay the most irregular and Loch Suaineabhal deepest, at 33m.

The islands are treeless apart from the plantations in Stornoway and around houses. Commercial forestry experiments have failed due to climate. Most of the interior of Lewis is a vast area of blanket peat bog dominated by heather moorland vegetation.

Climate The climate is essentially oceanic, controlled by the North Atlantic weather systems. Most of the year a series of depressions crosses the area, with their attendant wind and rain, but anticyclones can last for weeks once established. Rainfall is relatively low, but average wind speed high.

Seilebost is one of the fine beaches of west Harris

Peat cuttings in heather moorland

Clisham and Allt Thomnaval

The average temperature of the sea ranges from 7° in January to 14° in August, making summers temperate, and winters mild. Rainfall is moderate except in the mountains. Stornoway averages 1,000mm (43in) of precipitation and 1,200h of sunshine annually. Exposure to the prevailing salt laden westerly wind inhibits the growth of trees and shrubs except in sheltered places. Gales occur more than once a week at the Butt of Lewis.

May until August are the sunniest and driest months, with June perhaps the best. In midsummer the sky remains bright all night, while in midwinter the sun hardly rises above the horizon. In these islands every season offers dramatic vistas.

Loch Seaforth is a drowned glacial valley

Saltmarsh occurs in many places where there are shallow inlets

North Uist has a maze of lochs

Tree stumps are found in peat bogs

SUNRISE & SUNSET
Solstices at Stornoway

Midsummer	sunrise	04:19, 039°
	sunset	22:34, 321°
Midwinter	sunrise	09:11, 137°
	sunset	15:35, 223°

The above times are in:
BST (UTC+1) in summer
GMT (UTC) in winter
Stornoway (58.2°N, 6.4°W)

HABITAT TYPES

Sea, Skerries, Small Islands
Coastal
Saltmarsh
Machair
Croftland
Wetland
Lochs, Ditches & Burns
Woodland & Gardens
Roadside Verges
Moorland
Montane

Gannet, Sula Sgeir

SEABIRDS The Western Isles are home to a large number of seabirds. Most of the big colonies are on relatively inaccessible outlying islands, where they can escape predators, such as rats.

Some of the best opportunities for seabird (and cetacean) watching are to be had from the various ferry crossings from the Mainland or between the islands. The Sounds of Harris and Barra are particularly good places for the binoculars. It is easily possible to see most breeding seabirds here in June or early July, often from close quarters.

There are huge colonies of Gannets at St Kilda and Sula Sgeir. These spectacular birds may be seen plunge diving off all of the coasts when fish such as Mackerel, Herring or Saithe are in.

Puffins and other auks are also common and, apart from the Black Guillemot, only breed on offshore islands. Good views may be had from the ferries, but even better sightings are to be made from small boats.

Great Skuas, Arctic Skuas and seagulls also breed, including on coastal areas of the main islands. Large numbers of

Arctic Terns as well as a few Little and Common Terns nest with varying success on sandy or shingly beaches. They may often be seen over bays and inlets diving and crying. Terns are especially prone to disturbance, predation, food availability and weather during the critical days after hatching.

Eider Ducks may be seen commonly round the coasts. The brown females herd and protect their kintergartens of ducklings. Great Skuas and Black Backed Gulls are the main predators, but Otters and seals also take ducks and ducklings. The black and white male Eiders take no part in the rearing of their offspring and form separate rafts.

The outliers, including the Monach Islands, St Kilda, the Flannans, Sula Sgeir, Rona, the Shiant Islands and the southern Barra Isles are the best places to view breeding seabirds. Although St Kilda has the biggest of such colonies, all of these islands offer spectacular opportunities for bird watching between May and late July.

Male Eider Duck, Sound of Harris

Shag on nest, near Butt of Lewis

Puffin

Leaches Petrel breed on Rona

Boat trips are available to all of these places, especially to St Kilda and Mingulay. All are very weather dependent, but offer a rich experience of seabirds, cetaceans and offshore adventure. Suggested operators are listed in the Services Section.

Many seabird species forage far and wide for food, especially during the breeding season, and can be seen passing the headlands mentioned in the

Razorbill

Arctic Tern

migrants pages. Non breeders also form rafts in bays and below sheltered cliffs.

Fulmar Petrel

Great Skua

BREEDING SEABIRDS

Arctic Skua
Arctic Tern
Black Guillemot
Black-headed Gull
Common Gull
Common Tern
Cormorant
Eider Duck
Fulmar Petrel
Gannet
Great Blackbacked Gull
Great Skua
Guillemot
Herring Gull
Kittiwake
Leaches Petrel
Lesser Blackbacked Gull
Little Tern
Manx Shearwater
Puffin
Razorbill
Shag
Storm Petrel

Corncrakes remain quite numerous in the Outer Hebrides

LANDBIRDS The Outer Hebrides is home to some ornithological treats. These include species rare elsewhere, such as the elusive Corncrake. The rasping call of the male is one of the characteristic sounds of summer on the machair croftlands.

Corncrakes can be hard to locate as they rarely fly and can throw their calls. They are most likely to be seen crossing the road, when they may pose conveniently. Corncrakes are locally common in the west of Lewis, the Uists and Barra. Though their calls are loudest in the early hours, they may be heard at any time of day during the breeding season.

The woodland around Lews Castle in Stornoway is home to a large number of passerines, otherwise mostly absent from the area. These include Blue and Great Tits, Treecreepers, Thrushes and Warblers. The walks in these woods afford many opportunities to view these species.

Dippers breed near the Creed and Bayhead Rivers and may be seen catching their insect prey under water. This unusual behaviour is also a giveaway as once seen they become quite conspicuous with their white bibs.

Passerines include the Skylark, which remains common here, as well as such species as Wheatear, Meadow and Rock Pipit, Grey and White Wagtails, Twite and the ubiquitous Starling. Reed Buntings breed around lochs where suitable habitat remains. Two of the commonest sounds of summer are the noisy Stonechat and the equally vocal Wren.

Rooks only nest around Stornoway, where there is a large rookery in the woods. Ravens and Hooded Crows are quite common throughout the area. The deep craw of the Raven contrasts with the mostly silent eagles. They nest early in the year on cliffs, ruined buildings and stunted trees. Hooded Crows are great stealers of other birds' eggs, but are often seen feeding along the shore or on croftlands also.

Red Grouse still breed in small numbers on the heather moorland. When they are flushed they rise fast and noisily. Their cryptic camouflage means that they are only rarely observed from close up whilst on the ground.

Eagles The spectacular White-tailed Eagle and the Golden Eagle both breed here. The former was reintroduced

Skylark

Wheatear

Dipper

Laurie Campbell

Laurie Campbell

RSPB

White-tailed Eagle

Golden Eagle

Golden Eagle

Common Buzzard

in Rum in 1975 and has since spread to Skye, Mull and the west Highlands as well as Lewis. They breed on remote cliffs but may be seen fishing around the coast or on larger lochs.

Golden Eagles may be seen almost anywhere in the isles and breed from the Lewis hills to Barra. Usually they are observed soaring high above, but a lucky few may be rewarded by a spectacular stoop to catch a rabbit or other prey. In early spring during their courting displays, Golden Eagles are almost oblivious to people. The North Harris Eagle Observatory in Glen Meavaig is open all year.

Buzzards are also common throughout and are easily mistaken for their larger cousins by the unwary. Peregrines nest on coastal cliffs and Merlins may be seen furiously chasing their favourite prey of Meadow Pipits. Short-eared Owls, Hen Harriers, and Kestrels are only present in the Uists due to a lack of voles in Lewis and Harris.

LANDBIRDS
Blackbird
Common Buzzard
Corncrake
Golden Eagle
Grey Wagtail
Hen Harrier
Hooded Crow
House Sparrow
Kestrel
Meadow Pipit
Merlin
Peregrine
Raven
Reed Bunting
Rock Dove
Rock Pipit
Rook
Skylark
Song Thrush
Starling
Stonechat
Twite
Wheatear
White Wagtail
White-tailed Eagle
Wren

Reed Bunting

Stonechat

Greylag Geese herding their goslings

WETLANDS abound in the Outer Hebrides, especially in the Lochs district of Lewis and the Uists. The many lochs, lochans, marshes, burns, ditches as well as areas of nearby moorland and machair provide an ideal habitat for waders and waterfowl.

The extensive flat sandy beaches, salt marshes and tidal mud flats provide ideal feeding areas for waders. They hold internationally important populations of these birds, both residents and migrants, all year round.

These include Dunlin, Golden Plover, Lapwing, Redshank, Ringed Plover, Oystercatcher, Curlew and Snipe as common breeders. A few Red-necked Phalarope nest at the southern limit of their range. Greenshank also breed, mostly in the Uig area of Lewis.

Ducks breeding here include Red-breasted Merganser, Mallard, Tufted Duck, Shelduck and the rare Pintail. Both Red-throated and Black-throated Divers nest on some of the larger and more remote lochs and lochans. Both spe-

cies are commonly heard as they shuttle back and forth with food for their broods.

Greylag Geese and Mute Swans breed here in considerable numbers. Loch Bee and Loch Druidbeg hold the largest populations. The many small roads and tracks among the lochs and waterways afford good viewing opportunities for most of the species mentioned here.

The woodlands at Stornoway are host to the only heronry in the Outer Hebrides, Grey

Golden Plover

Lapwing

Greenshank

Ringed Plover

Oystercatcher

Dunlin

Red-breasted Merganser

Grey Heron

Herons are impressive birds which are often seen fishing around the harbour. They can be observed in many other suitable places such as shallow lochs, streams and inlets throughout the isles.

Reserves The RSPB Reserve at Balranald on North Uist is a good place to view many of the species which breed around the machair lochs. The National Nature Reserve at Loch Druidibeg on South

Uist holds large numbers of breeding Greylag Geese and several species of ducks.

Shelduck

Red-throated Diver

Black-throated Diver

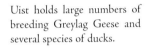

Red-necked Phalarope

WADERS AND WATERFOWL

Black-throated Diver
Curlew
Dunlin
Golden Plover
Grey Heron
Greylag Goose
Lapwing
Mallard
Moorhen
Mute Swan
Oystercatcher
Pintail
Red-breasted Merganser
Red-necked Phalarope
Redshank
Red-throated Diver
Ringed Plover
Shelduck
Snipe
Tufted Duck

Sanderling arrive in large flocks in autumn

Migration In spring and autumn the islands are in the path of migrants which breed further north and in the Arctic. Apart from these regular visitors a wide range of vagrants can turn up.

Wildfowl Large numbers of geese pass through, some of which stay all winter. Greylag, Pink-footed, Greenland White-fronted and Barnacle Geese may all be seen grazing on croftland. Whooper Swans are also regular winter visitors. The lochs are host to many migrating ducks.

The Sea The large areas of sheltered, shallow sea water

with gently shelving beaches provide good feeding areas for birds on passage or when overwintering. Cormorant, Shag and Eider Duck are all resident. They are joined in the autumn by Great Northern Diver, Velvet Scoter, Long-tailed Duck, Goldeneye, Slavonian Grebe and others.

The Shore Intertidal zones and piles of seaweed provide rich feeding areas for waders, resident and migrant. These include Purple Sandpiper, Curlew, Bar-tailed Godwit, Golden Plover, Lapwing and Dunlin.

Migration Time may bring in unusual vagrants, especially

waders or ducks from North America. They may be found among flocks of local birds or solitary. Birds from Eastern Europe are less common but may turn up after prolonged strong easterlies.

Sea Watching There are many good vantage sites for sea watching, including on Lewis, the Butt of Lewis and Tiumpan Head, on North Uist, Aird an Ruanair and on South Uist, Rubha Ardvule. Large numbers of birds can be seen on passage during peak migration times.

Huge flocks of waders are often present on nearby beaches before they move on.

Bar-tailed Godwit

Long-tailed Duck (female)

Dunlin in winter plumage

Turnstone

Goldeneye

Thrushes, finches and other small passerines sometimes make landfall in numbers near such headlands before moving to suitable feeding areas and eventually heading off again.

Woodland The gardens and woodland of the Stornoway area attract many passerines. Throughout the isles there are small plantations which are worth checking during migration times.

Raptors such as Merlin and Peregrine follow these movements. Sparrowhawk and Kestrel are less common winter visitors. Long-eared Owls are seen every year in the woods. Occasionally a conspicuous white Gyrfalcon or Snowy Owl may appear for a few days and create great excitement among birders.

Great Northern Diver resplendent in summer plumage in May

Irruptions Every few years species such as Waxwing or Crossbill arrive in large numbers. They breed in Scandinavia and Northern Russia and after a very successful breeding season they may irrupt in large numbers to Britain. Every available bush gets rapidly stripped of berries before they carry on south. For a short time every suitable bush and tree will be thronged; they especially like *Cotoneaster*.

MIGRATION TIMES

From mid March to early June
May best
From end July to early October
September best

SOME MIGRANTS

Barnacle Goose
Crossbill
Dunlin
Glaucous Gull
Goldeneye
Great Northern Diver
Greylag Goose
Iceland Gull
Knot
Long-tailed Duck
Pochard
Purple Sandpiper
Redwing
Sanderling
Turnstone
Waxwing
Wheatear
White-fronted Goose
Whooper Swan
Widgeon

Whooper Swans

Thrift and yellow lichen

FLORA The wide range of habitats found in the Western Isles has allowed a diverse flora to proliferate. July is perhaps the best month for a profusion of wild flowers on the machair. In fact any time between May and September will reward the visitor interested in botany.

Coastal habitats include sandy beaches, dunes, dune slacks, machair, exposed clifftops and rocky shores. Thrift is ubiquitous all around the coast, along with Sea Campion, Scurvy Grass, Silverweed, Yarrow, Scots Lovage and other salt tolerant plants.

Rocky shores tend to be more exposed and thus support a smaller range of plants, which are often stunted compared to the same species growing in more sheltered surroundings. Spring Squill, Grass of Parnassus, Sea Plantain, Thrift, Scurvy Plant and Mountain Everlasting as well as many lichens are a few of the plants that thrive here.

Sandy beaches and dunes also support many species. Sea Rocket, Scentless Mayweed, Sea Milkwort, Sow Thistle and Orache are widespread above the high water mark. Large areas of sand dunes have remained unexploited here unlike in other areas. Many have been stabilised by planting Marram Grass.

Saltmarshes are frequently found at the heads of shallow sea inlets which become flooded at high tides. Many plants

Lesser Twayblade

Red Campion

thrive in these zones, which are a sea of pink, blue and yellow in early summer. Thrift, Spring Squill, Sea Plantain and Silverweed are a few of the many colourful wild flowers to see here. Later, Sea Aster turns the saltmarshes mauve.

Machair forms behind many beaches where windblown sand encroaches over peat further inland. It is composed of up to 90% shells and thus the soil has a high lime content. In summer these areas are covered by a carpet of wild flowers, with up to 40 different species per square metre. Earlier, whites and yellows predominate, while later reds, blues and purples take over.

Orchids, some of which only occur in the Hebrides, are particularly common. Fragrant, Pyramidal and Hebridean versions of Marsh as well as Spotted Orchids are all present on the machair. Further inland the rare Irish Lady's Tresses grows on pasture which has been grazed and trodden by cattle.

Machair flowers

Ladies Bedstraw

Sea Plantain

Yarrow

Marsh Orchid

Pyramidal Orchid

COASTAL WILD FLOWERS

Eyebright
Goldenrod
Grass of Parnassus
Lady's Bedstraw
Mountain Everlasting
Orache
Orchids
Red/White Campion
Scentless Mayweed
Scots Lovage
Scurvy Grass
Sea Aster
Sea Bindweed
Sea Milkwort
Sea Plantain
Sea Rocket
Silverweed
Spring Squill
Thrift
Yarrow

Meadowsweet and Vetches are common roadside flowers

Blackland Inland, the cultivated blackland between the machair and the moorland, with fields for pasture and hay, also supports a wide variety of wild flowers. If reseeding has not been done recently, and the crop is harvested late in the season the displays are more spectacular.

Reduced grazing and cropping for hay or silage has resulted in many meadows becoming overgrown with rank grasses and rushes. The best wild flowers are always found where the land is well eaten by cattle and where fertiliser, especially nitrogen, has not been applied.

Roadside Verges, particularly when only cut late in the season, retain a huge diversity of species. The lack of use of crop spray in the Outer Hebrides means that roadsides present an easily visited diversity of wild flowers. Verges include habitats such as dry grassland, ditches, burns, uncultivated meadows, exposed rocks, peaty or sandy soil and many others.

Where roads are salted in winter many coastal species predominate, even well inland. Overgrazing by sheep or deer in the past tended to decimate roadside flora, but this has become less severe as ovid munching has decreased. Roadsides are particularly good places for orchid hunting since most have never been cultivated. Disturbance due to roadworks also frequently creates conditions where long dormant seeds may suddenly be stimulated into germination.

Woodland Although there are few areas of natural woodland today there is evidence that trees were more widespread in the past. Many tree stumps have been found underneath peat cuttings. This suggests that climate change to wetter conditions encouraged the expansion of peatbogs, which engulfed the woodland.

The legend is that the Vikings burnt all the trees, however it is more likely that cutting for fuel and timber combined with the grazing of domestic animals preventing regeneration

Machair wild flowers in June

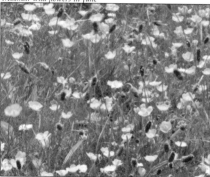

Primrose

Gorse, or Whin, flowers from winter to midsummer

Wild Thyme

The River Creed at Stornoway runs through the woodlands of Lews Castle

wiped out most of the woodland. Small islands on sheltered lochs are nearly always covered with trees and bushes, suggesting that protection from sheep and deer would allow woodland to thrive in some places.

The only large wooded area is around Lews Castle at Stornoway. This was planted in the mid-19th century on imported soil and includes a large variety of exotic species. Experimental plantations of forest were planted in several places, and while not perhaps commercially viable some are now managed as a recreational resource. Insect pests killed many of the exotic conifers.

Kidney Vetch

Hebridean Spotted Orchid

Spotted Orchid

WILD FLOWERS
ROADSIDE & MEADOW

Buttercups
Coltsfoot
Common Twayblade
Daisies
Foxglove
Fragrant Orchid
Frog Orchid
Hawkweeds & Dandelions
Heath Spotted Orchid
Hebridean Spotted Orchid
Kidney Vetch
Knapweed
Lesser Butterfly Orchid
Lesser Celandine
Lesser Twayblade
Meadowsweet
Northern Marsh Orchid
Plantain
Primrose
Pyramidal Orchid
Scabious
Thistles
Vetches
Whin

White Water Lilies occur on many lochs

Lochs are prominent in the landscape of the Outer Hebrides, especially in low lying areas of North Uist, South Uist and the parish of Lochs in Lewis. About 25% of Scotland's 30,000 lochs are situated here.

Machair Lochs are generally alkaline and relatively high in nutrients due to the shell sand and windblown salt spray. They are also affected by runoff from surrounding cultivated land. They are often

surrounded by Yellow Iris and Marsh Marigolds with many orchids in the surrounding damp meadows.

Dubh (G Black) Lochans are common in hollows in peaty areas. Stained dark brown by the peat, they tend to be acidic and dystrophic, or low in Oxygen. They are also affected by windblown salts and so tend to be richer in nutrients than similar bodies of water inland.

Many of these lochs are covered by White or Yellow Water Lilies and Bogbean thrive around the edges. The surrounding marshes hold insectivorous Sundew and Butterwort as well as Bog Asphodel and many mosses.

Moorland The moors are mostly covered with blanket peat, often several feet deep. Heather, Bell Heather, Cross-leaved Heath, Woodrush and Cotton Grass add colour to the drier areas during the summer.

These bogs form over hard, impervious rocks when rainwater does not drain away, resulting in a very high water table. This prevents breakdown of plant material, especial Sphagnum Moss, which builds up to form peat. The underlying and undulating Lewisian gneiss has thousands of hummocks and hollows. As a result the higher areas are drier and the lower areas wetter.

Small shrubs such as Bog Myrtle, Dwarf Willow and Juniper grow in some places, especially where protected from grazing. Depending on exposure they may be very small or even prostrate.

Lichens grow everywhere in the Western Isles, from the most exposed seashore to the highest peak. There is a profusion of colours and forms, depending on the chemistry of the rocks, exposure, salinity and humidity.

Orchid

Bog Asphodel

Yellow Iris

Bogbean

Sundew

Butterwort

Bog Cotton

Cross-leaved Heath

WILD FLOWERS WETLAND LOCHS & MOORLAND

Bell Heather
Bog Asphodel
Bog Cotton
Bog Myrtle
Bogbean
Butterwort
Cross leaved heath
Dwarf Willow
Heather
Juniper
Lichens
Lousewort
Marsh Marigold
Mosses
Orchids
Sphagnum Moss
Sundew
White Water Lily
Woodrush
Yellow Iris
Yellow Water Lily

Common or Harbour Seal

FAUNA The Western Isles are home to only a small number of indigenous mammal species. At the end of the last Ice Age there was probably no land bridge to Scotland, due to the depth of the Minch. Thus native species are limited to Grey Seals, Common Seals and Otters.

Grey Seals come ashore to pup and mate on many of the outlying islands, especially the Monachs and Rona, in autumn. The pups are white when born. They moult and go to sea after about a month ashore.

Common Seals have their pups in early summer. They can swim almost immediately and can be seen with their mothers being taught to hunt and dive. Also known as Harbour Seals, they haul out on sheltered rocks, often in large numbers.

Otters are elusive, but not uncommon. They are generally seen early or late in the day along rocky shores. Ferry terminals, old piers and breakwaters are often good places to look. Spraints and tracks are much easier to see than the animals themselves.

Cetaceans The Hebridean waters are home to several species of cetaceans which may often be observed from the ferries. Bottlenose, Risso's, White-beaked and White-sided Dolphins are quite common. Porpoises are also present and usually seen in groups.

Whale species include Minke, Killer, Pilot, and occasional Sperm and Humpbacks. Large pods of Pilot Whales are often seen offshore, while groups of young male Sperm Whales sometimes appear. Killer and Minke Whales follow the shoals of Herring and Mackerel in summer.

Tiumpan Head on Lewis is a good place from which to watch Risso's Dolphin, of which there is a resident population. In summer, White-sided Dolphin may also be seen. The water depth of over 100m close inshore means that other cetaceans may be present. All whale watching needs patience, a sharp eye, good light and a relatively calm sea. Photography needs a very fast reaction time!

Grey Seal

Otter

Risso's Dolphin

Minke Whale

Basking Shark, a species formerly hunted to near extinction here, may also be observed. They are increasingly present offshore in summer and are best seen from boats and ferries.

Basking Shark

Land Mammals All land mammals were introduced by people. There are three sub species of Field Mouse, the Hebridean, St Kildan and Barra varieties. Voles are only present on the Uists.

Red Deer may often be encountered on the hills, especially in the Uists and Harris. Rabbits are common. They do much damage to crops and destabilise sand dunes. Mink, which have escaped from farms, and Hedgehogs, which were recently introduced cause much harm to

Red Deer

ground-nesting birds, and are the subject of culling programmes. Hares are also present in small numbers.

Bottlenose Dolphin

FAUNA
Otter
Red Deer
Vole (only on the Uists)
Grey Seal
Common Seal
Bottlenose Dolphin
White-sided Dolphin
White-beaked Dolphin
Porpoise
Pilot Whale
Killer Whale
Risso's Dolphin
Minke Whale
Sperm Whale
Basking Shark

Callanish summer sunset

HEBRIDEAN CHRONOLOGY

BC	
c.10000	Ice retreats
c.6000	Grassland, hazel-scrub, ferns cover islands
	First people arrive??
c.3900	First known settlers
	Vegetation becoming more open
3800	Climate deteriorates
3500	Allt Crysal settlement
3200	Eilean Domhnuill house
3150	Shulishader axe
c.3000	Chambered Tombs being used
c.2900	Callanish Stones
2700	*Start of Great Pyramid Age*
2600	Not many trees left
c.2500	Callanish cairn
c.2000	Chambered cairns sealed up
	Bronze age, Beaker pots
	cremations, cist burials
1500	Peat bogs developing
1159	Hekla erupts in Iceland
c.800	Callanish abandoned
700	Iron Age round houses
600	Oldest Broch deposits
c.325	Pytheas circumnavigates Britain
214	*Great Wall of China constructed*
100	Brochs at peak
c.55	Diodorus Siculus mention
AD	
33	*Death of Christ*
43	Roman invasion
c.70	Pliny the Elder
83	Agricola's fleet visits Orkney
c.100	Brochs abandoned
c.150	Ptolemy refers to *Ebudae*
c.500	Irish monks arrive
c.620	Cille Bharra established
632	*Death of Muhammad*
700s	Norsemen appear in West
793	Major Viking raids begin
795	Iona first attacked
800s	Norse migration
871	Onund Wooden Leg in Barra
c.872	Harald Fairhair King of Norway
	Sigurd of Moere Earl of Orkney
955	Earl Sigurd the Stout baptised
1000	Leif Erikson discovers America
	Earl Gilli governor
1014	Battle of Clontarf
	Thorfinn becomes Earl
1065	Earl Thorfinn the Mighty dies
1066	*Battle of Stamford Bridge*
	Battle of Hastings
1079	Kingdom of Man & the Isles
1098	Magnus Barelegs expedition
1156	Isles partitioned
	Somerled takes Inner Hebrides
	Earl Rognvald to Holy Land
1171	Sweyn Asleifson killed Dublin
c.1200	Teampall na Trionaid founded
1231	Last Norse Earl dies
	(John Harraldson)

1263	Battle of Largs, King Haakon dies
1266	Treaty of Perth
1275	Battle of Ronaldsway
1300	Dutch already fishing Herring
1354	John of Islay Lord of the Isles
1350s	Borve Castle Benbecula built
1398	Henry Sinclair visits America??
1468	Impignoration of Orkney
1492	*Columbus reaches America*
1493	Lordship of Isles forfeit
1506	Stornoway Castle captured
c.1520	Rodel Church built
1540	King James V visits
1547	Alasdair Crotach buried Rodel
1550s	Cromwellian garrison
1598	Fife Adventurers
1601	Battle of Carinish
1603	Union of the Crowns
1607	Stornoway Burgh of Barony
1653	Cromwellian fort built
1666	*Great Fire of London;*
	Newton gravity of situation
c.1700	Martin Martin visits
1707	Treaty of Union
1715	Jacobite rising
1721	Kelp-making introduced to isles
1722	Flora MacDonald born
1727	Smallpox epidemic on Hirta
1741	Tigh Chearsabhagh built
1745	Bonnie Prince Charlie arrives
	First emigrants leave Barra
1746	Battle of Culloden
1760	Sheep farming introduced
1764	Sir Alexander MacKenzie born
1770	Grass, clover and turnip seeds
	introduced, farming reforms
1776	*American Declaration of*
	Independence
1786	John Knox visits
1789	Eilean Glas lighthouse
c.1800	Crofting system introduced
1816	Stornoway Old Pier renovated
1820s	Start of large scale clearances
1830	Collapse of Kelp Boom
	Mermaid sighted
1831	Lewis chessmen found at Uig
1833	Barra Head lighthouse
1840s	Potato blight
1841	Fudaigh Mor cleared
1842	Harris Tweed invented
1843	Disruption in the Kirk
1844	James Mathieson buys Lewis
	Regular steamer to Stornoway
1850s	Many evictions
1851	Major clearances on Barra
1852	Arnish Point lighthouse
1853	Annie Jane shipwreck
1860	Herring fishing gets important
1862	Butt of Lewis lighthouse
1865	Stornoway Harb. Commission
1867	Callanish cleared of peat
1869	Castlebay major Herring port
1872	Education Act 1872

1874	Bernera Riot
1880s	Canadian Prairies available
1880	Steamer pier Lochboisdale
1884	Napier Commission
1886	Crofting Act
1887	Pairc Deer raid
1888	Aignish Riot
1897	Government purchases land
	Kyle Railway opens
	Golden Road on Harris
1900	Flannans lighthouse mystery
1901	Railway reaches Mallaig
1904	Loss of *SS Norge* at Rockall
1906	Vatersay raid
	Harris Tweed Trade Mark
1910	Adabrock bronze hoard found
1912	Mingulay evacuated
1915	First Great Skuas breed
1918	Leverhulme buys Lewis
	U-boat shells Village Bay
1919	*Iolaire* shipwreck
	Coll & Gress raids
1920	N Zealand Wild White Clover
	Hattersley Loom
	Bragar Blue Whale
1920s	Pentland Road built
1923	Stornoway Trust
1930	St Kilda evacuated
1934	Rocket Post to Scarp
	First air services start
1936	Scheduled air services to Barra
1937	End of Herring boom
1938	Work on South Ford link starts
1939	World War II
1941	*SS Politician* grounded
1942	Monachs evacuated
1948	filming of *Whisky Galore*
1953	Great Bernera Bridge
1957	Rocket Range South Uist
1959	*Russia launches first satellite*
1960	North Ford causeway built
1965	Arnol Blackhouse last inhabited
1967	Loganair starts inter-island service
1969	*First landing on the Moon*
1973	MV *Suilven* start of roro
1974	roro service to Lochboisdale
1975	Islands Council formed
1987	St Kilda World Heritage Site
1990	Vatersay causeway opened
1993	Harris Tweed Act
1997	Scalpay Bridge
1998	First unmanned aircraft to cross
	Atlantic lands at Rocket Range
1999	Berneray Causeway opened
2001	Eriskay Causeway opened
2002	1ˢᵗ edition of this guide
2003	Land Reform (Scotland) Act
2005	Gaelic Language Act
2008	RET introduced on ferries
2009	Sunday ferries to Stornoway
2011	Peter May first of trilogy
2015	3ʳᵈ revised edition of Guide Book
2016	New Museum nan Eilean opens

Moonset over Callanish at the major lunar standstill

After the last Ice Age ended about 12,000 years ago, Mesolithic nomadic hunters arrived in Scotland. Many sites attest the presence of these people, but evidence in the Outer Hebrides remains sparse. Most probably this is because relative sea level was 5-10m lower then than today. As a result, much land and archaeological evidence, has been lost to the sea, especially off the shallow west coasts.

By 4000BC, Neolithic farmers were settled in the area and for over 1,500 years their culture flourished. The houses, tombs and standing stones they built are among the most spectacular Neolithic monuments in Britain.

The Bronze Age succeeded the Neolithic and left behind burnt mounds, middens and ruins of small houses. Individual burial in stone cists or barrows became the norm, either as cremations or inhumations. This period was marked by a deterioration in climate and the appearance of

bronze tools and weapons as well as Beaker style pots.

About 700BC larger round houses started to appear and later the spectacular brochs, some with large settlements around them, were developed. Iron tools and weapons were revolutionary at this time. The Outer Hebrides remained peripheral, but later as part of the Pictish Kingdom, they started to experience more outside influence.

In the 8th century the Norse began to appear. Large scale migration took place during the 9th century, followed by the *Golden Age of the Vikings*. The Norse domination lasted for nearly 500 years and this influence can still be seen in many placenames today.

Orkney was a vital strategic base during Viking times. The exploits of the Earls and their supporters are related colourfully in the *Orkneyinga Saga*. The Hebrides are frequently mentioned in this and other sagas.

Medieval times saw a small influx of Lowland Scots, but the Western Isles long remained remote. After the Jacobite rebellions major political changes brought them much more into the mainstream. During the 19th century the notorious clearances removed thousands of native inhabitants, and created the crofting landscape of today.

The region was opened up with the advent of steam power in the 19th century when sea transport became more reliable and railways were built to ports such as Oban. During the later 19th and the 20th century Herring fishing, two World Wars, improvements in agriculture and North Sea Oil were all significant.

Recently an influx of immigrants from the mainland has slowed the population decline. Wind, wave and tidal power generation are likely to make an impact on economic development in the near future.

Bharpa Langass on North Uist is well preserved

NEOLITHIC AGE The first settlers to the Western Isles were probably Mesolithic hunter-gatherers around 7000BC. However, the earliest substantial remaining structures are the many prominent chambered cairns, domestic sites and standing stones built by settled Neolithic farmers.

The introduction of agriculture brought with it a different lifestyle involving animal husbandry, as well as the planting and harvesting of crops. Natural resources such as fish, crustacea, molluscs, wild animals and plants were still exploited but no longer as the main source of food.

Everything that is known about Neolithic people has been gleaned from archaeology. The language and beliefs are unknown, but the many artefacts cast light on their way of life. These include human and animal bones, pottery, beautifully carved objects as well as stone and bone tools. In recent years Neolithic art has become much more prominent.

Chambered cairns are found throughout the islands, and are particularly numerous in the Uists. Most are prominently sited on hilltops or ridges above good agricultural land. They are monuments to the dead characteristic of

Neolithic times which occur throughout the Atlantic coast of Europe.

These monumental structures are stone built and were used for funerary and ritual purposes. They were constructed from around 3500BC and some remained in use for a millennium. The large scale of many suggests that society was organised and successful before being able to spare the time and effort to create such structures. Most are ruinous, having been used as quarries over the years, or cleared out in the 19th century.

Chambered cairns typically have a central chamber with

Heel shaped cairn, Barra

Bharpa Langass showing entrance to passage

an entrance passage. While most in the Western Isles are round, other variations include heel-shaped and long cairns. Some have several cells off the main chamber and many have a forecourt which may be enclosed by horns.

Massive stones are a feature of these cairns. Externally they are often surrounded by a kerb of massive uprights, with especially impressive megaliths at the entrance. Internally they are frequently divided by large upright stalls. The walls and corbelled roofs are usually built with very large slabs. Although most are now ruinous piles of stones one can imagine the labour and craftsmanship that went into these structures.

Bharpa Langass on North Uist is the best preserved

Dun Bharpa, above Craigston, Barra, is well preserved with impressive kerbstones

chambered cairn in the Outer Hebrides, with an intact chamber and passage. There are many other impressive cairns to visit throughout the archipelago. Unfortunately few are signposted but finding them and admiring the view is all part of the pleasure in visiting these enigmatic monuments.

NEOLITHIC TIMELINE	
BC	
c.11000	Ice in retreat
c.7000	First evidence of arrival of
	Mesolithic hunter-gatherers
c.3500	Settlement at Allt Chrisal
c.3150	*Unstan Ware*
	Carinish hearth
	Shulishader axe
	Grooved Ware
c.3000	Chambered Tombs
	Callanish stone ring
c.2000	Callanish tomb
	Chambered tombs finally
	out of use and sealed up

NEOLITHIC SITES TO VISIT

Lewis		
	Callanish	84
	Carn a' Mharc	80
	Garrabost	78
	Steinicleit	94
	Clach an Truiseil	94
Harris		
	Northton	118
North Uist		
	Bharpa Langass	140
	Pobull Fhinn	140
	Carinish	142
	Clettraval	137
	Unival	138
	Loch Olabhat	137
South Uist		
	Reineval	159
	Loch a Bharp	161
Barra		
	Allt Chrisal	178
	Dun Bharpa	172

Reineval chambered cairn, South Uist

Bharpa Langass entrance passage from inside

Neolithic house at Allt Chrisal, Barra

SETTLEMENTS In contrast to the large number of chambered cairns, there is very little visible evidence of domestic settlement in the islands. Several sites have been excavated, notably Eilean Domhnuill at Loch Olabhat on North Uist, which is one of many islets connected to the shore by a causeway. Machair sites at Udal on North Uist and Northton on Harris have also been studied.

These excavations yielded a large amount of material and information about life in the Neolithic and have revealed substantial footings and hearths of buildings.

Grooved Ware pottery, quite similar to that from the same period in Orkney, was found, suggesting the existence of cultural links. "Ritual" carved stone objects and polished stone axe blades were also present. A

complete stone bladed axe with a beautifully carved Hawthorn haft was found at Shulishader on Lewis in peatworkings. The wood dates from 3150BC.

In peaty areas the generally acidic soil conditions do not allow for the preservation of bone and most organic objects, but in the alkaline machair areas preservation is much better, especially in waterlogged conditions. Since so much of the land area is cov-

Polished stone axe

Neolithic Grooved Ware pottery

ered by blown sand or blanket peat, it seems likely that much remains to be discovered.

The Neolithic period was characterised by the gradual removal of trees and scrub, which had re-established after the melting of the ice. Land clearance for agriculture, combined with grazing preventing regeneration were major factors. Wood was also consumed in the construction of buildings, in the making of tools and boats as well as for fuel.

The Neolithic farmers kept cattle, sheep, goats and pigs. They also hunted deer, seals, dolphins and small whales. Shellfish, fresh water fish, deep water species, such as Cod and Haddock, as well as birds all featured in the diet. Six-rowed Barley or Bere was grown as well as some Wheat.

Although there is no artefactual evidence about their boats, it is obvious that they had sea going craft. These were capable of fishing offshore and of carrying people, goods and animals substantial distances. Most likely their boats were constructed

Northton machair, Harris

with Hazel or Willow frames, covered with tanned hides. Tarred woven cloth, perhaps using nettle fibres, may also have been used.

Similarly, apart from the stone lower courses, nothing remains to indicate what their houses looked like. Since Lewisian Gneiss is hard to quarry, it seems probable that the upper walls were built from turves. Roofs would then have been constructed from local wood, driftwood or whalebone, and thatched with heather, reeds or straw, depending on availability.

NMS

Replica Neolithic pots from Eilean an Taighe, North Uist

Carved stone object

Shulishader Neolithic polished stone axe and haft

NMS

NMS

STANDING STONES are a feature of the landscape in the Western Isles, ranging from individual monoliths and small stone circles to the large and dramatic stone setting at Callanish overlooking Loch Roag. The dates of erection are unknown as yet, but the majority are assumed to be Neolithic monuments dating from around 3000BC or later.

Callanish has a complex of standing stones. The main setting is a central ring of large monoliths with radiating stone rows which run roughly east, south and west. A double armed avenue projects slightly east of north. Unusually, there is a small chambered cairn in the centre of the ring which post-dates the largest monolith.

In addition to the main setting, there are five or more smaller stone circles near Callanish, as well as chambered cairns. Excavations here have revealed *Grooved Ware* similar to that found in Orkney and dating from about 3000BC, as well as sherds of *Beaker* pottery dating from perhaps 2000BC.

Various astronomical alignments have been suggested at Callanish. These include sunrise and sunset at the solstices and moonset at the major lunar standstill. This occurs every 18.6 years, when the Moon sets at its extreme northerly azimuth and the lunar eclipse cycle restarts.

Whether such solar and lunar events are really part of the design of Callanish or other stone settings is open to speculation. The Neolithic people would have been more aware of the seasons and the regular movements of the Sun, Moon, planets and stars than many people today.

Small stone circle at Callanish

Pobull Fhinn stone circle, Langass, North Uist

Callanish at midsummer dawn

The stone circle at Pobull Fhinn in North Uist is also very dramatic. It commands a panoramic view over Loch Eport, the North and South Lees and Eaval to the east, and the flat expanse of North Uist. There are obvious possible astronomical alignments. The site may be connected with nearby Bharpa Langass chambered cairn.

The majority of the other monoliths throughout the islands seem to be isolated but some, as at Gramisdale on Benbecula, are the remnants of circles, or are near to chambered cairns. Some may be seamarks or commemorate long forgotten events.

The original function of such large standing stones as Clach

an Truiseil on Lewis, the tallest in the Outer Hebrides, or Clach Mor a' Che on North Uist is not clear but there are legends relating to them. These include mythical tales about fairies and giants, memorials to Viking chieftains and celebrations of

clan battles. Such mysteries are all part of the pleasure of visiting these ancient sites. Evocative times to visit include dawn, dusk, when the moon is full, or when the mist rolls in from the sea.

Clach Mor a' Che, North Uist

Gramisdale, Benbecula

STANDING STONES TO VISIT		
Lewis	Callanish	84
	below Steinicleit	94
	Clach an Truiseil	94
	Achmore	82
Gt Bernera	above bridge	100
Harris	Traigh Iar	117
North Uist	Pobull Fhinn	140
	Sornach Coir' Fhinn	141
	Clach Mor a' Che	139
	Carinish	142
Benbecula	Gramisdale	144
South Uist	above Stoneybridge	156
	Pollochar	163
Barra	Borve machair	172

Standing stones above the bridge, Great Bernera

Adabrock Bronze Age hoard found at Ness, Lewis in 1910

BRONZE AGE The period between about 2000BC and 700BC is referred to as the Bronze Age. It is characterised by changes in burial practice, from communal chambered cairns to individual interments in stone lined cists. These were frequently covered by a barrow of earth or a stone cairn. Bodies were often cremated, the ashes usually being buried in a pottery container. Inhumation was also practised.

Beaker pottery also appears at this time. These fine containers are often found associated with burials from this period. They are finer than Neolithic pots and usually highly decorated, often with cord marks. They may have contained food or drink to accompany the deceased on their journey.

The ruins of small round houses which date from this period are quite common in the Western Isles. Middens and field walls may be apparent. Burnt mounds date from this time. These piles of fire blackened stones are usually situated next to a watercourse and are often accompanied by a trough. Stones were heated in a fire and used to boil water, either to cook meat, or as a sauna, or perhaps both.

Only limited evidence of metalworking has so far been discovered here. At Northton in Harris some splashes of bronze suggest that casting may have taken place. At Dalmore some metal frag-

Gold torc and rings dredged from near the Shiants

Bronze Age pot

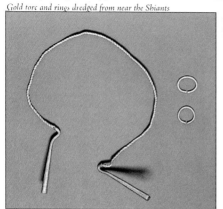

ments were found in a limited excavation on an eroding shoreline. Some evidence of bronze working has been found at Cnip in Lewis.

This period was marked by a deterioration in climate and the encroachment of blanket peat bogs over large areas. Windblown sand also covered areas which in Neolithic times were agricultural land. This lack of evidence may simply reflect the fact that most sites are covered by sand or peat.

Adabrock Hoard In May 1910 whilst cutting peats at Adabrock in Ness, Lewis, Donald Murray came across a hoard of bronze artefacts. These included parts of a large vessel with a decorated rim, socketed axes, a spearhead, a chisel, a hammer and razors as well as a gold bead and amber beads. Two whetstones complete this dramatic find.

Bronze swords have also turned up in peat banks. Those from South Dell on Lewis and Iochdar on South Uist are typical *Caledonian swords*. Along with a number of socketed axes, these have also been found on Skye. These stray finds from the late 19th century may have been deposited intentionally, and seem to date from the late

Bronze Age.

Arrowheads of quartz or flint also turn up in the Bronze Age. These tanged and barbed objects are usually beautifully made and probably unused. They may be stray finds, but are also commonly found with burials. For example, one was found in Bharpa Langass as a late deposition.

The evidence suggests that the Outer Hebrides were in close touch with the outside world in this period and many new fashions in technology, but that life was harder than in the Neolithic Age.

Dalmore, Lewis, site of Bronze Age domestic remains

Tanged and barbed arrowhead

Bronze Age house, Allt Chrisal, Barra

BRONZE AGE SITES TO VISIT		
Lewis		
	Callanish	84
	Adabrock, Ness	96
	Dalmore	90
	Cnip, Uig	103
Harris		
	Northton	118
North Uist		
	Bharpa Langass	140
South Uist		
Iochdar (sword)		154
	Cladh Hallan	162
Barra		
	Allt Chrisal	178

Replica Iron Age house at Camas Bosta, Great Berneray

IRON AGE The term *Atlantic Roundhouse* is often used for the domestic building styles common in western and northern Scotland from about 700BC to early medieval times. The shortage of timber meant that stone was used for the walls and internal divisions.

They were quite large and roomy inside with roofs built using large timbers, perhaps imported. Driftwood or whalebone was probably also used. They were lined with turves supported by straw or heather ropes (G *Sugan*, ON *Soo'an*, Straw Rope) and thatched with heather, straw or reeds as available.

Roundhouses were often built on small islands on lochs and reached by a causeway. Such dwellings are referred to as *crannogs*. They were also sited on small hills or on the machair, often just above the shore. It is thus likely that many have been lost due to erosion by the sea.

It now seems that roundhouses, duns and brochs are part of an evolution in building styles. All of the duns so far excavated have intramural cells, galleries or stairs resembling the larger brochs. Good examples are scattered throughout the islands from Loch an Duna in Lewis to Barra Head lighthouse.

Elsewhere in Britain massive roundhouses were constructed of wood. All that remains are post holes, visible in aerial photographs or by geophysical survey. The so-called

Replica Iron Age house at Camas Bosta, Great Berneray - interior

Crannog on Great Bernera - reached by a causeway

Riff Broch at Uig showing intramural gallery

Atlantic Roundhouses are now thought to be a local development of a widespread style of building.

Brochs and Duns in the Outer Hebrides seem to have been isolated structures, not usually surrounded by settlements. While those situated on islets in lochs would have had easy access to water, those on rocky knolls would not, since the local Lewisian Gneiss is not porous and wells are rare in such places.

Excavation has shown that these buildings were really farmhouses, often with long occupation histories, rather than strongholds, perhaps more a product of fashion rather than defence needs. Brochs had more than one internal wooden floor, accessed by internal stairways.

The smaller duns were on one level; indeed the blackhouses which persisted into the 20th century would not have been that much different inside. With their thick walls, massive roofs and central hearths these houses would have been

Excavated aisled wheelhouse at Kilphedar, South Uist

quite comfortable, though perhaps not to modern taste.

Another development was the wheelhouse, which was usually built on the machair. A large circular hole was dug in the sandy soil, which was lined with a drystone wall. Supports were then built radially to prevent the exterior walls from collapsing inwards and the structure was roofed over. Unfortunately the only well preserved examples are at Jarlshof in Shetland. A wheelhouse at Kilphedar on South Uist was excavated but is now partially collapsed .

There are a number of promontory forts in the Outer

Hebrides. The best examples are at Rubha na Beirgh near the Butt of Lewis, Caisteal Odair on the north-west point of North Uist, and near the lighthouse on Barra Head.

Iron Age Timeline	
BC	
c.700	Iron Age round houses
c.600	Oldest Broch deposits
c.200	Brochs at peak
c.100AD	Brochs abandoned

Iron Age Sites To Visit		
Lewis	Barvas	90
	Callanish	84
	Dun Carloway	88
	Loch an Duna	91
	Riff, Uig	103
Gt Bernera	Dun Bharabhat	100
	Houses, Bosta	100
Harris	Northton	118
North Uist	Clettraval	138
	Dun Torchuill	132
	Dun Sticir	132
Benbecula	Dun Buidhe	144
South Uist	Dun Altabrug	156
	Dun Mor	156
	Dun Uiselan	156
	Kilphedar Aisled House	162
	Dun Vulan	158
Barra	Allt Chrisal wheelhouse	178
	Dun Scurrival	175
	Dun Cuier	173
	Allasdale wheelhouse	173
	Dun Ban	172
Vatersay	Dun a' Chaolais	180
Pabbay	Dunan Ruadh	183
Barra Head	Sron an Duine	185

Wheelhouse at Allt Chrisal, overlooking Vatersay Sound, Barra

Dun Carloway intramural stairway

Dun Carloway The most prominent and best preserved broch is Dun Carloway, not far from Callanish. It is built on a rocky hillock, in common with many other similar monuments. As in all brochs, the walls are hollow. The inner and outer walls are bound together with large lintels. These form the floors of the intramural galleries, which are accessed by stairs. The walls are over 3m thick at the base, and the interior walls rise vertically from the scarcement at about 2m above the floor.

The exterior walls have a marked batter and slope inwards considerably. The maximum surviving portion is about 9m high, while the missing north side reveals the construction. No doubt many of the stones are in the ruined blackhouses below.

Brochs remain conspicuous in the landscape and there are many throughout the Outer Hebrides that are worth visiting. Most are now robbed out and reduced to piles of rubble. However, in many cases, intramural galleries and stairs can be discerned. Some remained in use for many centuries, even into medieval times.

A few of these sites have the remains of extensive outbuildings or settlements. Dun Vulan on South Uist as well as Dun Torchuill and Dun Sticir on North Uist also have outlying ruins.

Pictish comb

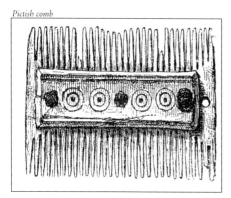

Penannular brooch

Pictish Period There is very little influence so far of direct Pictish influence in the Outer Hebrides beyond two symbol stones. Both are Class I stones with well known Pictish symbols. Neither have an archaeological context.

The Benbecula stone could be related to the monastery at Balivanich. It has a disc with three small discs inside, perhaps representing the Holy Trinity, and a decorated rectangular comb box. The Pabbay stone has a crescent and V-rod, or broken arrow, as well as a flower symbol. It also has a later crude and more deeply incised cross.

Excavations at Dun Cuier, Barra, Eilean Olabhat, North Uist and Loch na Berie, Lewis have revealed many Pictish-style artefacts, such as combs. Evidence of metalworking included moulds, ingots, metal fragments, pins and penannular brooches. Fine quality jewellery was obviously being made in the Outer Hebrides during Pictish times.

Although the evidence is

Dun Carloway survives to a height of 9m

sparse it is clear that cultural, and presumably trade, connections with the outside world were active in Pictish times. Clearly more awaits discovery.

Pabbay Pictish symbol stone

Pictish spindle whorl

Benbecula Pictish symbol stone

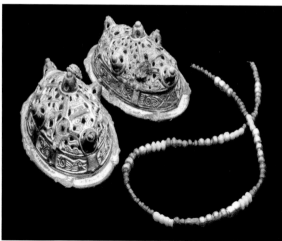

NMS

Viking gilt bronze brooches and necklace from Cnip, Lewis

Vikings The islands were perhaps Pictish at the time of the first Viking incursions. The existence of several islands named *Pabbay* implies that Celtic monks were present when the Norsemen arrived.

The Vikings were already settling in Orkney by the late 8th century, and first attacked Iona in 795AD. They must therefore already have been familiar with the Western Isles by that time. Norse domination of the western seaboard of Scotland was to continue for nearly 500 years. They were variously referred to as *Lochlannaich*, Fjordmen, *Finngaills*, White Foreigners, *Nordmanni*, Northmen, or simply *Vikinir*. During this time the Western Isles were often referred to as the *Innse Gall*, Islands of Foreigners, by the Scots and Irish, and as *Sudreyar*, Southern Isles, by the Vikings themselves.

Although few written records exist from this time apart from some saga mentions, there is much placename and linguistic evidence for the Norse settlement. This is very apparent in Lewis where a large proportion of townships and natural features have names of Norse derivation. Western Isles Gaelic also incorporates many Norse words.

Very few distinctively Norse artefacts have been found, apart from several pagan burials at Cnip on Lewis and on Hirta. Two Norse silver hoards have been discovered in the Western Isles, at Oronsay, North Uist (c.1780) and in the Castle Grounds, Stornoway, in 1988.

The *Orkneyinga Saga* tells us that the first immigrants to Iceland included people from the Hebrides, no doubt of Norse-Pictish descent, who left to avoid paying Norwegian taxes. It now seems that the Norse settlement may have been relatively peaceful, but the takeover total, unlike the violent Viking raids.

A most interesting inscribed stone was found at Cille Bharra, on Barra. This has Christian Celtic symbols and Norse runes which read, *After Torgeth, Steiner's daughter, this cross was raised*. The stone is a replica.

The island site now occupied by Kisimul Castle is said to have been the site of 11th century Viking fortifications. It seems likely that something similar may have existed at Stornoway with its excellent harbour and fertile surrounding land.

Several Norse domestic sites have been excavated, at Barvas in Lewis, at Udal in North Uist as well as at Bornish, Drimore and Kildonan in South Uist, but no Norse era building is on

Excavation of a Norse settlement at Bornish, South Uist

public view. No doubt many have been built over or reused by succeeding generations. Perhaps most were built using imported wood and local turf with stone footings.

During the early Norse period the Western Isles were used as Viking bases, and at various times came under the nominal control of the Earl of Orkney or the King of Man, themselves under the King of Norway. The Norse influence in the west stretched from Lewis to the Isle of Man and settlement towns in Ireland.

Viking grave at Traigh na Berie, Lewis

Silver hoards usually include amounts of hack silver which would have been weighted

Celtic/Norse stone at Cille Barra   *Viking grave at Traigh na Berie, Lewis*

VIKING & NORSE TIMELINE	
AD	
c.500	Irish papae arriving
795	Iona first attacked
995	Sigurd the Strong baptised by force
c.1000	Sigurd makes Earl Gilli Governor
1014	Battle of Clontarf Isles under King of Man
1066	Stamford Bridge
1098	King Magnus Barelegs' expedition to the West
1156	Southern Hebrides lost
1263	Battle of Largs
1266	Treaty of Perth

NORSE SITES TO VISIT

Lewis	Uig Sands	104
	Lews Castle grounds	74
	Cnip	103
	Stornoway	72
	St Olav's Church	80
North Uist	Udal	136
South Uist	Bornish	159
	Kildonan	158
	Calvay Island	160
	Kilphedar	162
Barra	Kisimul Castle	170
	Cille Bharra	174
St Kilda	Village Bay	188

King (one of 8)

Queen (one of 8)

The Lewis Chessmen are said to have been found in sand dunes on the east side of Uig Bay on Lewis in spring 1831. The British Museum purchased eighty two of the gaming pieces in early 1832 from an Edinburgh dealer called TA Forrest. The Scottish Antiquaries then acquired the remaining eleven in 1851.

Pawn (one of 19)

The pieces are carved from Walrus ivory and probably date from the second half of the 12th century. Nothing is known of their provenance but there are many colourful tales. Most likely they belonged to a prosperous person who hid the collection for safekeeping from marauders. Whether this was a merchant, cleric or wealthy Lewisman is open to imagination.

Speculation about the origins of the Lewis Chessmen has been rife since their mysterious appearance in 1831. It is generally agreed that they are in the tradition of art from Trondheim. There are strong similarities with other carving and artwork made in the late 12th century in this northern seat of the archbishop.

There are also suggestions that the objects may originate from Iceland. At this time skilled craftsmen and artists were employed by the church to produce fine works. Many of these were trained in Trondheim and Walrus ivory was readily available in Iceland.

Regardless of their place of origin the 93 pieces represent almost 4 complete chess sets of extraordinary craftsmanship. They are the earliest to look familiar to chess players today. The Bishops seem to be an Icelandic innovation, later taken up in Britain.

The so called Warders are in fact Berserkers, which in Icelandic refers to fighters wearing bearskins. They are

Knight (one of 15)

Bishop (one of 16)

mainly depicted biting the tops of their shields as they prepare to make a frenzied attack. Their function seems to have been similar to the castles pieces today, to make fast brutal attacks.

It has been suggested that some of the chessmen may have had a dual role in both chess and the Scandinavian game, Hnefatafl. In this board game the king is in the centre and is defended by his warriors.

There is no evidence of colouration on any of the pieces to differentiate the sides. This of course may have worn, or been washed off whilst deposited under the sand at Uig. Regardless of all the mysteries, the Lewis Chessmen merit a trip to the British Museum or the National Museum of Scotland to see the marvellous craftsmanship. Some are now exhibited at the new Museum nan Eilean in Lews castle, Stornoway.

Warders or Berserkers (three of 12)

Knights (two of 15)

Replica Birlinn "Aileach" which sailed from Ireland to the Faeroes

The Lords Of The Isles

During the 9th century, the kingdoms of Dalriada and Pictland were merged under Kenneth MacAlpin. The centre of power of the new Kingdom of Scotland moved east, while Norse power was increasing on the western seaboard. The title Lord of the Isles originates from the 10th century; Norse rulers depended on the sea to wield power, and were referred to in Gaelic as *Ri Innse Gall* (G King of the Isles of Foreigners).

Around 1100 the western mainland came under Scottish control, while the Isles remained under the Norwegian crown, controlled by Scottish-Norse families. In about 1156 the Norse-Scottish Somerled, married to the granddaughter of the first

Ri Innse Gall (Godfrey of the Isle of Man), took control of the Southern Hebrides.

Chieftains in the Hebrides always had divided loyalties until 1266 when the Treaty of Perth ceded the Hebrides to Scotland. The Annual of Norway was paid by the Scots until 1468, when Orkney was impignorated to Scotland.

Previously the Hebrides were controlled by a mix of the Norwegian Crown, the Kings of Man, the Earls of Orkney, and various Irish Kings. Norse power in the west was waning in the later 13th century while the Scots were becoming more interested in the islands. After the unsuccessful campaign of the Norse King Haakon Haakonson in 1263, power slipped to the Scottish Crown.

The principal families remained fiercely independent, taking sides in the Wars of Independence, where some gained much and others lost everything. In particular Angus Og MacDonald's support for Robert the Bruce gained him much power and influence, and enabled him to greatly increase his family's interests in the Hebrides.

In 1354 John of Islay, son of Angus Og, took on the title of Dominus Insularum, having supported David II and then Robert Stewart (later Robert II), and achieved more control of the Hebrides than anyone before him. When he died in 1387 he ruled the Hebrides from Islay to Lewis excluding Skye, as well as large areas of the Mainland.

This power was centred on Islay and depended on having control of the sea. His successors strove to expand their power until eventually John of Islay plotted with Edward IV of England against the Scottish Crown. This was a step too far and his title was forfeited in 1475, and finally again in 1493.

Birlinn carved on the tomb of Alasdair Crotach

A skoth, a Hebridean yole or skiff

Despite attempts to regain the title by the MacDonalds, the existence of such a centre of power was too big a threat to the Kingdom to be allowed to revive. Today the heir to the throne holds the honorary title of Lord of the Isles.

The West Highland Galley, (ON *Byrdingr*, cargo ship), or Birlinn, the basis of all power in the Hebrides and West Highlands, developed from the Viking longship. In the 12th century the starboard steering oars were replaced with stern hung rudders. These open boats were very well suited to the waters of the area whether for military, piracy, trade or fishing uses.

These fast and seaworthy vessels enabled the Lords of the Isles and their successors easy means of transport around the

Weaver's Castle off the south of Eriskay was a pirate's lair

Hebrides for lawful and less lawful activities. Similar craft remained in use until the end of the 19th century.

By the early 17th century the government had started to take strong measures against the owners of Birlinns, particularly after the Union of the Crowns in 1603, when transport of Hebridean mercenaries to Ireland came to an end. After this, large boats were superseded by smaller versions suited to inshore fishing

and communication between islands rather than carrying large crews of fighting men and their booty.

In 1991, a replica galley called *Aileach* sailed up the west coast and on to the Faeroes. This boat was built in the west of Ireland in a manner very similar to Viking ships. Many small fishing boats around the Hebrides are still clinker built, but sadly wood construction has almost universally given way to fibre glass.

Dun Sticir on North Uist is an Iron Age broch which was reused

Borve Castle on Benbecula was a Clanranald stronghold

LORDS OF THE ISLES TIMELINE

AD	
1098	King Magnus Barelegs' expedition to the West
1156	Somerled takes Southern Hebrides
1263	Battle of Largs
1266	Treaty of Perth
1354	John of Islay becomes Lord of the Isles
1493	Lordship of the Isles forfeit
1603	Union of the Crowns

SITES TO VISIT

Ronan's Chapel, Rona may date from the 7th century

EARLY CHURCHES There are many ancient chapel sites in the Western Isles. There is no evidence that Columba ever visited, but the influence of Irish seaborne monks was felt from the late 6th century. Placenames suggest that *Papar* (ON priests) were present at the time the Vikings arrived; there are several Pabbays (ON *Papa-oy*, Priest's Island). Incised stones with crosses have been found and there are dedications to Irish saints.

The two oldest extant chapels are on remote islands. On Rona (*Ronaidh*) the chapel may date from the late 7th or early 8th century. There is a small oratory or cell with a corbelled roof at its east end.

The chapel is surrounded by an oval enclosure with many cross-shaped grave markers, some of which may be 7th to 9th century and others 12th or 13th. The dedication could be to the real St Ronan, but the name Rona is Norse (ON *Hraun-oy*, rough island).

On Sula Sgeir there are several beehive cells with corbelled roofs. St Ronan's sister is said to have gone there where she was found dead with a Shag nesting in her chest cavity.

St Flann's Chapel on Eilean Mhor in the Flannan Isles is another small stonebuilt chapel of Irish type on a remote island. Its date is unknown, but it is clearly ancient.

Cille Bharra on Barra is dedicated to St Barr, or Finbar. There are three chapels on the site, which may date from Norse times or earlier. An interesting carved stone was found in 1865 with runes on one side and a Celtic cross on the other, which is from the 10th or 11th century. There are also three medieval tombstones which may be grave markers from MacNeill chiefs.

At Howmore on South Uist there are ruins of several medieval chapels. The largest, of which only the east gable remains, is Teampall Mor, which may date from the 13th century, while the other three chapels are smaller and newer. The site is the burial place of the chiefs of Clan Ranald.

Teampall na Trionaid at Carinish in North Uist is said to have been founded by Beahag, daughter of Somerled, in the 12th century. It was a school in the middle ages and is mentioned in 14th century records. Today the buildings are ruinous but, in the 19th century, the church had carved stone decorative work and a spire.

St Olav's Chapel, Gress, Lewis

Chapel ruins at Howmore, South Uist

Kilbar, Barra

Teampall Chaluim Cille, Balivanich, Benbecula

The old church dedicated to St Columba at Aignish in Lewis may be 14th century. There is a gravestone to Margaret, daughter of Ruairi, who was chief of the MacLeods of Lewis and died in 1503. The ancient cemetery is being eroded by the sea.

Teampall Mholuaidh at Ness in Lewis is dedicated to the Irish St Moluag. It may date from the 14th century or earlier and is the site of an ancient cult where the sea-god Shony was celebrated on All Saints Day. The church was renovated in the early 20th century.

On Benbecula there is an ancient chapel at Nunton which is dedicated to the Virgin Mary and associated with a nunnery, whose stones were used to build

Teampall na Trionaid, Carinish, North Uist

Clanranald's new house and steading in the 18th century. The convent may also have had connections with the Monach Islands.

Teampall Chaluim Cille (G Columba's Church) is now a ruin on a small mound near Balivanich. It gave the village its name, Baile na Mhanaich (G Township of the Monks) and is said to have been established by St Torranan from Ireland, who landed at Calligeo (G the Geo of the Monks). This monastery may have continued to function until the 17th century.

The church at Rodel in Harris is dedicated to St Clement and is the second largest medieval church in the Hebrides. It was built in the 1520s by Alasdair (*Crotach*) MacLeod

of Dunvegan, whose grandiose tomb occupies the south west wall of the choir. Alexander MacLeod's tomb dominates the east end of the church and there are several other interesting gravestones in the north transept. The tower has several carved stone ornaments including a Sheela na Gig.

OLD CHURCHES TIMELINE	
AD	
563	Columba on Iona
7ᵗʰ-8ᵗʰ c	St Ronan's Chapel
7ᵗʰ-13ᵗʰ c	Howmore Chapels
c.1300	Teampall na Trionaid
14ᵗʰ cent	St Columba, Aignish
	Teampall Mholuaidh
c.1520	Rodel Church
	Aignish Church

SITES TO VISIT

Flora MacDonald & Bonnie Prince Charlie

Flora MacDonald

FLORA MACDONALD was born in 1722 at Milton on South Uist. After the death of her father and the abduction of her mother to Skye she was taken into the care of MacDonald of Clanranald. She had some education in Edinburgh and was a practising Presbyterian.

Several unsuccessful attempts to overthrow James II were made before the Glorious Revolution of 1688 when William of Orange and Mary, sister of James, were appointed as monarchs. James fled to France. There were abortive rebellions between 1689 and 1715 in favour of James, the Old Pretender. Finally, in 1745, *Bonnie Prince Charlie*, or the Young Pretender, had a disastrous and flawed final attempt.

Flora MacDonald's birthplace at Milton, South Uist

Prince Charles Edward Stuart landed at the Prince's Strand on Eriskay on 23rd July 1745. He raised his standard at Glenfinnan on 19th August and marched south via Edinburgh to Derby before retreating north. The Jacobites occupied Inverness but were routed by the Duke of Cumberland's vastly superior Government forces at Culloden on 16th April 1746.

With a reward of £30,000, or over £1m today, for his capture, *Bonnie Prince Charlie* went on the run. He ended up in Benbecula on 27th April 1746 after a wild crossing of the Minch. The Prince and his companions were to spend the next few months as fugitives on South Uist, Lewis and Benbecula.

Despite the price on his head and local knowledge of his hiding places, he was not given up to the authorities, and finally escaped to Skye from Rossinish in Benbecula, with the help of Flora MacDonald. Lady Clanranald of Nunton House was a key player in organising this by obtaining passes for Flora, an Irish maid called Betty Burke and the boat crew to go over to Skye.

The Prince reached Portree and eventually left for France on 20th September 1746, never to return to Great Britain. Whether the Government really wanted to catch him, or merely ensure his departure from Britain is not clear. There are many stories about

Samuel Johnson and James Boswell visited Flora MacDonald at Kingsburgh

Bonnie Prince Charlie

his short time in the Western Isles as a fugitive.

The main effects of the rebellion were the demise of the traditional clan system and the rapid development of commercial landlordism. This lead to the clearances, emigration and the establishment of the crofting system.

One of the Prince's companions was Neil MacEachan who had fled to France with him. His son, James, was to rise to fame under Napoleon. He became a Marshall in the French army and visited his father's birthplace at Howmore in 1826.

Surprisingly, the Prince's less than illustrious life in exile, mostly chasing ladies it seems, appears to have done nothing to reduce the myth and romance of the '45, which in reality was brutal and ill planned. It certainly had very little to do with the welfare of the people of the Highlands.

Flora MacDonald was briefly held in the Tower of London.

She is said to have told the Duke of Cumberland, son of George II and Commander-in-Chief in Scotland, *"that she acted from charity and would have helped him also if he had been defeated and in distress."*

Her bravery and loyalty had gained her much sympathy, not least because of her good manners and gentle demeanour. Dr Johnson said of her that she was, *"a woman of soft features, gentle manners, kind soul and elegant presence."* This is quite a compliment from the famously grumpy and critical Johnson.

In 1750, she married Allan MacDonald of Kingsburgh on Skye, who was an army captain. They farmed at Flodigarry in Skye. During their famous tour in 1773 Samuel Johnson and James Boswell visited the MacDonalds at Kingsburgh.

In 1774 they emigrated to North Carolina. Her husband fought as a Colonel on the loyalist side in the American War of Independence. Flora

returned to South Uist in 1779. Allan was released in 1784 and they went back to Skye in 1787. She died at Kingsburgh in 1790. Apparently her shroud was a sheet once slept in by Bonnie Prince Charlie but this is probably as fanciful as many other stories about him.

Flora was buried at Kilmuir cemetery on Skye accompanied by a huge crowd of mourners. Dr Johnson's tribute is carved on her tomb, *A name that will be mentioned in history, and if courage and fidelity be virtues, mentioned with honour."*

Flora MacDonald's memorial

A c'rofting couple outside their blackhouse

CROFTING The present system of land tenure in the Western Isles is the result of local, national and international events over the last 300 years. Until the Jacobite rebellions of 1715 and 1745 and their violent aftermaths, the West Highlands and Islands were largely left to themselves by successive Scottish and then British governments. After the Battle of Culloden, the ancient clan system, which had survived in the area long after such systems had died out elsewhere, was brutally repressed. This resulted in centuries of hardship, destitution and emigration for the people as well as depredation of the landscape.

Until 1745, most of the property in the Highlands and Islands was held under a system whereby the clan controlled ownership. The chief did not personally own the land, although under the feudal system it was nevertheless theoretically held under the overlordship of the King.

In the wake of the civil war new laws bestowed the status of landowners on the clan chiefs. In modern language the land was nationalised at zero compensation and taken by the clan chiefs for nothing. These chiefs proceeded to live and act in the manner of landed gentry elsewhere, but had to find a means to generate the income to keep them in their new found position.

The system of land tenure was likely little changed since prehistoric times. It was a community based society of subsistence farming, augmented with a little fishing. It was based around the clan system whereby the chief could demand men to bear arms in times of emergency but otherwise the people were left to get on with life. Hebridean Galleys were a major source of power and influence in a time when inter-clan and inter-family conflict was common.

During the French Wars many products and raw materials were in short supply and either prices became elevated or alternatives were found. Small black cattle had long been a sought after product of the Highlands and Islands and their prices soared. At the same time abundant seaweed resources provided the ideal raw materi-

Children outside their blackhouse home at Stornoway

al to make kelp, a good source of potash, which is essential for glass making and munitions manufacture.

Kelp is made by burning dried seaweed in pits. The very labour intensive process depends on plenty of cheap labour, but it could be very lucrative for the land owner. The extensive beaches on the west coast of the Outer Hebrides are especially good for seaweed harvesting.

At the same time sheep farming was becoming very attractive with high prices both for mutton and wool due to the booming industrial revolution in the south. Small tenants were cleared off the land upon which they had lived for centuries and forcibly relocated in areas suitable for kelp-making on plots of land too small to be viable on their own.

Inevitably with the cessation of hostilities the kelp boom came to an end and suddenly the proprietors had no further need for the large population of small tenants. This was aggravated by famine in the late 1840s due to potato blight and bad harvests. Despite some famine relief effort the government and land owners invoked a major emigration programme to Canada and Australia which was to result in the loss of tens of thousands of people from the Highlands and Islands but was much to the ultimate benefit of their destination countries.

North Uist crofter's cottage

Lochmaddy eviction

Kelp burning was very dirty work

The Congested Districts Board provided shared bulls

Memorial to the Pairc Deer Raid, Lewis

LAND WARS During the late 18th and the 19th centuries the Established Church ministers usually tended to err on the side of landowners and sheep farmers and did not often support tenants or criticise evictions. There was a growth of religious revival and evangelism which was greatly aided by the publication of the Gaelic Bible and the introduction of Church schools. In 1843, the Disruption and establishment of the Free Church of Scotland was seen as a victory for smallholders but as a threat by the landowners, and was one of the seeds from which grew the surge of opposition to landlordism by the crofters and their supporters.

The history of land holding in the Western Isles is quite different to Orkney and Shetland, which remained under Norse rule until 1468, and where the land was held by Udal Law. Under this system much of the land was held under owner occupation, ever since the first Norse settlement in the 9th century, while the rest was held by the earl, church or king. Udalers owned their land absolutely and could not be cleared nearly so easily. Norse dominance in the north was complete, whereas this may not have been the case in the west.

The lack of security of tenure for crofters meant that there was no incentive to improve houses, buildings or agricultural practices and an indifference to stock breeding, resulting in poor quality animals and low cattle prices. During the 1880s wool prices crashed and

many sheep farms were turned over to deer forests. At the same time the crofters finally started to become proactive and from 1881 until the 1920s there were a series of rent strikes, land seizures, and refusals to obey courts and officials.

Throughout the Western Isles lazybeds or *feannagan* may be seen, often on the most inhospitable of places. These ridges were raised by people evicted from their homes and forced to glean a living elsewhere. They were created with great effort, by carting seaweed, animal manure and domestic midden to the area to augment the meagre turf which was present to grow potatoes and grain.

The Land Wars are commemorated by a series of cairns on Great Bernera, at Gress, Aignish and Pairc on Lewis. The actions of these crofters in the 1880s were to be the catalyst for change in the control of crofting lands, but the outcome did not immediately solve all of their problems.

Public opinion in the country was changing in favour of the crofters, due to very successful political campaigning. *The Napier*

Gress Land Raid cairn, Lewis

Aignish cairn, Lewis

Royal Commission Inquiry into the Condition of Crofters and Cottars in the Highlands and Islands was set up in 1883 and reported in 1884. The Crofters Act of 1886 finally gave crofters security of tenure and compensation for buildings and improvements as well as power to fix rents. The Act did not solve the other central problems for crofters and cottars, which included the issues of land ownership and availability.

In 1897 the Government finally started to purchase more land for crofters. It was after the WWI before the Board of Agriculture finally addressed the issue by eventually purchasing over 200,000 acres of land for crofts. The Stornoway Trust was for long unique. It was the only area to accept Lord Leverhulme's offer of ownership in 1923 and administers it on behalf of the people.

During the 20th century there have been many attempts to solve the so called *Highland Problem*; however the central issue of land ownership remains. The continued fossilization of traditional crofting, a creation of the early 19th century, has been ensured. Most people remain tenants who do not

The Aignish Riots took place in January 1888

own or control the land. The system of government grants, combined with a bureaucratic Crofters Commission, are probably the factors which most limit economic development in the islands.

Most young people do not return home to work after their education, and depopulation is a serious threat for many of the remoter areas. Only a fundamental reform of land tenure where local communities have much more influence on land usage can begin to allow the potential for social and economic progression and thus viable local populations.

The Land Reform Act (Scotland) 2003 has allowed several communities to buy up estates, which are now run for the benefit of the local economy. These include parts of Lewis, Harris and South Uist. The largest to date was the £4.5m buyout of South Uist, Eriskay and Benbecula by *Storas Uibhist* (G The Wealth of Uist). Covering 92,000 acres the estate covers nearly 25% of the Outer Hebrides.

"LAND WARS" TIMELINE	
c.1760	Sheep farming
c.1800	Crofting system introduced
1843	Disruption in the Kirk
1850s	Many evictions
1874	Bernera Riot
1884	Napier Commission
1886	Crofters Act
1888	Aignish Riot
1919	Coll and Gress raids
1923	Stornoway Trust

Great Bernera Riot cairn

Woman carting peats

Girl herding sheep, Ness, Lewis

CROFTING remains an important part of the social and economic life of the Western Isles. There are over 6,000 crofts, but few are large enough to provide a living. Crofters have the right to buy their land for the price of a few years' rent. Few have opted for this due to the way in which agricultural support grants apply to crofting.

There are also a few small farms, especially on the Uists. The main production is Blackface lambs for fattening on the Scottish Mainland. Cattle are also kept on the Uists and Barra, where grazing is better, and holdings bigger. Hay, silage and some oats are grown for winter fodder as well as potatoes for home use.

By its nature, crofting is a low intensity method of agriculture and as such is environmentally friendly. Most crofters have one or more additional jobs, or are retired. Traditionally, this work might have been weaving or fishing, but many are now just as likely to be in a City office, on an oil rig or oil related ship. At the same time, the land has helped to retain the scattered rural population structure.

Young people have always left the Western Isles for further education and work. In the past many men joined the Royal or Merchant Navy, or worked on fishing boats, while their wives and children looked after the croft. This is still the case today, as many emigrate to the mainland or abroad to find work, with the result that in several parts of the islands the population is in severe decline.

At present sheep and wool prices are improving, but low prices in the recent past and changes in subsidies have encouraged a reduction in numbers. Cattle prices are more buoyant, but the market today is for larger, fast-

There are lots of old grey Fergies, but this one is red!

Highland Cow on Harris

er growing breeds, which are inherently unsuited to the small scale environment of crofting. Some Highland Cattle, or Highland crosses, are kept, which are hardy enough to outwinter and meet a speciality beef market.

The crofting community has always believed that the land was theirs. Hopefully the 21st century will see the process of reform continued to the ultimate benefit of the local communities. However the process has taken nearly 300 years since the upheavals of the early 18th century.

Agricultural developments that have taken place in other island communities have, to a large extent, bypassed the Outer Hebrides. Active crofting is essential in maintaining the diversity of wildlife in the islands. In particular grazing and cropping of meadows is needed to stop the growth of rank vegetation.

Peat bank on North Uist

Sheep gathered in for shearing on South Uist

Potatoes grow very well on the light machair soil

Crofter with sheep, South Uist

Cultivating the machair, South Uist

Living room at No 42 Arnol, Lewis

BLACKHOUSES The preserved and reconstructed blackhouse at 42, Arnol in Lewis was inhabited until 1965, having been built in 1885. It is one of the last remaining examples of a long tradition of house building which goes back to Viking times or earlier where people and domestic animals shared the same subrectangular buildings. Blackhouses are so named because they had no chimneys, the smoke escaping through the thatched roof.

The name also had a derogatory connotation which implied that the inhabitants were not very civilised, an assumption which was based on no evidence. Conversely, many eminent master mariners, doctors, engineers and other educated people grew up in such places throughout the Highlands and Islands.

Such houses were usually built from stone and turf on a stone foundation and were lined with wood. Many ruins of these dwellings may be seen all over the Western Isles. The walls were double skinned with a filling of clay and small stones between the inner and outer faces and up to 2m thick, while the roofs were formed from driftwood or whalebone couples which rested on the inner wall.

The roof was then covered with slatted planks supported by purlins. A layer of heather turf was put in place and finally the roof was thatched with oat or bere straw, or Marram Grass, and tied down with heather ropes weighted with stones.

Drains were incorporated to remove rainwater and effluent from the byre end which was at the lower end of the house. Often a small barn was attached to one side. The ben end might be just one room, but in later houses, as at 42 Arnol, there was a living room/kitchen and a sleeping room with box beds. A cooking pot or kettle was suspended over an open peat fire in the middle of the floor. Many blackhouses were later modified to have chimneys and hearths and became whitehouses of which there are many examples in the Uists.

The peat reek (smoke) acted as a disinfectant and deodorant, and the sooty thatch made good manure. The proximity of people and cattle perhaps reduced tuberculosis to some extent as ammonia from the cattle urine can kill the bacillus. Exposure to cowpox also gave resistance to smallpox, which dairy maids rarely contracted.

Heather and choir ropes and homemade baskets

The byre at No 42 Arnol

Blackhouses may appear primitive and unhygienic by contemporary standards, but they were well-adapted to the climate and resources available to their inhabitants. The traditional breed of black cattle was small and easily handled and would have provided milk, cheese and butter. Some sheep, a pig and hens would have been kept while fish would have added to the staple diet of potatoes.

Thatched croft house at Howbeg with lazybeds

Fish and meat would have been smoked in the rafters, or salted down for winter. The houses would have been cosy in stormy weather, and could be built out of local materials by the community at almost no cost in terms of money. Their longevity is clear from the many roofless examples scattered throughout the isles.

Restored kiln and Norse type watermill at Shawbost, Lewis

Across the road from 42 Arnol, a mid 20th century house, 39 Arnol, has been preserved as an example of the type of dwelling which replaced blackhouses. It is a two up two down house built using concrete blocks. The dwelling is typical of many in rural Scotland and is furnished in the manner of the 1950s, with many interesting artefacts from the time.

Exterior of No 42 Arnol from the west

20th century kitchen with cast iron stove at 39 Arnol

Box bed and mid 20th century kitchen artefacts

Marion Campbell spinning wool by hand, Procropool, Harris

HARRIS TWEED The craft of weaving has been practised in the Hebrides for a long time. The Hebridean Sheep was bred for weaving rather than for knitting as in Shetland. The wool is strong and makes a tough thread ideal for the loom, and results in hard wearing cloth. By tradition it was the women who did the spinning, weaving and waulking and there are many customs and songs relating to the various processes.

Originally everything was done by hand which limited output and thus the quantity available for sale or barter. In the past the wool was dyed using various plants such as Crotal (lichen), browns, Lady's Bedstraw, reds, Alder, black, Heather, green and Birch, yellow. The wool was boiled up outside in a large iron pot until the required colour was developed. Urine was used both to wash the wool and as a mordant to fix the dyes.

Obtaining fast and beautiful colours from local plants was a major part of the skill involved in producing tweed. Once woven the cloth had to be laboriously waulked by hand. After soaking in urine the tweed was laid out on a table and thumped back and fore by a group of women, who sang special waulking songs during the process which shrank the cloth and gave it more body and strength, a process akin to felting.

Countess of Dunmore In 1842, the dowager Countess of Dunmore, who owned much of Harris, became interested and soon Harris Tweed was popular with sportsmen all over the country. By the late 19th century demand was greater than supply and gradually dyeing, carding, spinning and finishing became mechanised. All weaving is still done by hand at home. In 1909 a trade mark of the Harris Tweed Association was registered by the Harris Tweed Association (now Authority) which controls quality and production methods.

Hattersley Loom The introduction of the Hattersley loom in the 1920s, though still human powered, allowed much more efficient production and a greater range of designs and cloth weights.

Marion Campbell weaving on a traditional wooden loom, Procropool, Harris

Drying wool

Although the industry declined for a time, in recent years there has been a revival in demand. The clicking of looms in small sheds is a frequent sound in the Western Isles and it remains a substantial part of the local economy. The traditional width of the cloth is 30 inches, but many weavers are now using new double width looms.

Women rooing wool

Harris Tweed Act The 1993 Harris Tweed Act states that the tweed *"must be hand-woven by islanders at their homes in the Outer Hebrides and made from pure virgin wool dyed and spun in the Outer Hebrides"*. Marketing of the cloth is done by the HTA and by the main mills.

Lewis Loom Centre, Stornoway

Harris Tweed Exhibition

Harris Tweed is sold all around the world, but the vagaries of fashion and ups and downs of economies, mean that demand fluctuates. The orb trade mark symbol is the customer's guarantee of genuine quality in a product *"created for individuals by individuals."*

Samples of Harris Tweed

Harris Tweed Authority

Orb symbol Trade Mark

Harris Tweed Authority

Sheep shearing today

Dyeing wool in the traditional manner

Post Office sign on Barra

GAELIC No visitor to the Outer Hebrides can fail to notice that, for many of the inhabitants, the everyday language is Gaelic, not English. Despite several centuries of strenuous efforts by the Church and State to extirpate it, the language remains strong here and on nearby Skye.

Today most of the population of the Western Isles understands Gaelic. It is the language of everyday life for between 40% and 80% of the population, depending on the area and demographics. There are about 60,000 native speakers, mostly in the Outer Hebrides.

Arnol blackhouse signpost

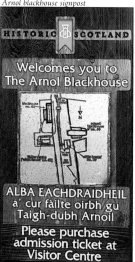

Various attempts were made in the past to eradicate it, including the Education Act of 1872, which forbade the use of Gaelic in schools. Although a lot of harm was done, all such measures failed to eliminate the language.

The political desire to destroy the clan system after 1745, plus increasing need to travel to find work, ensured that many Hebrideans had to learn English, just as did the many immigrants. It was to be the late 18th century before the combination of the Church and the Gaelic Bible taught many people to read and write their language. The introduction of school education for all was at first in English, although this was subsequently relaxed.

Today official attitudes to Gaelic are much more positive than in the past. The Gaelic Language Act of 2005 was passed by the Scottish Parliament to support the language, in direct contrast to the act of 133 years earlier. Gaelic culture in all its forms now receives a large amount of public support for radio, TV and publications, as well as music, other arts and edu-

cation. There are worries that young people do not use the language, but this is perhaps understandable when so many have to leave to find education and work.

"Celtic" Up until the late Iron Age "Celtic" was spoken across much of Europe. The term was invented by Edward Lhuyd, Keeper of the Ashmolean Museum, in 1707, as a result of his researches into the languages of Great Britain, Ireland and Brittany. He was one of the first to describe the similarities of Brythonic (Brittonic or P-Celtic) and Goidelic (Gaelic or Q-Celtic).

It is not clear what language the inhabitants spoke before the arrival of the Vikings. Presumably it was similar to that current in other parts of the north and west of Scotland. It may well have been a form of Brittonic, related to that spoken by the Picts.

Scottish Gaelic is closely related to Irish and to a large extent replaced Pictish over much of the Highlands and Islands. The succeeding influences of the Romans, Saxons, Angles, Norse, Danes, Normans and

French each left their linguistic marks.

Irish settlers to Argyll and the Inner Hebrides probably introduced Gaelic to Scotland around the 4th century. Modern Scottish Gaelic developed during the 12th century and later, as Norse power declined in the west of Scotland. Throughout this period, as the Kingdom of Scotland developed, Middle English was becoming the common language of the state.

Gaelic has an ancient and rich oral heritage, which was formerly preserved by the bards and passed from generation to generation. Although an Irish version of the Bible was published in the 16th century, it was not until the late 18th century that a Scottish Gaelic version was published and widely available. It is only during the last 300 years that extensive recording of this oral tradition has been made.

Old Norse Only a few Norse burials, silver hoards, domestic sites and chapels are so far known, despite nearly 500 years of dominance. In contrast they left a very strong impression in the form of placenames and language. A large proportion of the placenames in the Outer Hebrides are directly Old Norse (ON), while many more are Gaelic (G) translations from Old Norse.

Hebridean Gaelic has many loanwords from Old Norse, but what is perhaps surprising

19th century schoolroom, Hirta

Gaelic street sign, Stornoway

is the lack of influence over grammar despite Norse control lasting for so long. Latin, through the early church, and English through administration and trade have also had a major influence. Modern English also has many Gaelic words. In Lewis especially, the people speak with a distinct Norse tone in English.

For centuries, and especially after the failed Jacobite uprisings of the 18th early century, there have been official attempts to stamp out Gaelic. All have failed, despite the efforts of State and Church. In the last century there were concerted efforts to reverse this trend. It is only in the Outer Hebrides, Skye, Tiree

SOME POLITE PHRASES	
Gaelic	**English**
Fàilte	Welcome
Halò	Hello
Latha math	Good day
Ciamar a tha thu?	How are you?
Ciamar a tha sibh?	How are you? (plural)
Madainn mhath	Good morning
Feasgar math	Good afternoon
Oidhche mhath	Good night
Tapadh leat	Thank you (informal)
Tapadh leibh	Thank you (formal)
Dè an t-ainm a tha ort?	What is your name?
Dè an t-ainm a tha oirbh?	What is your name? (formal)
Is mise..., Mise...	I am...
Slàn	Goodbye (singular, informal)
Slàn leibh	Goodbye (plural, formal)
Dè a tha seo?	What is this?
Slàinte	Cheers, Good Health

Some Old Norse Placename Elements

Hebrides; Old Norse. English

a, o, or; *a*, burn
aith; *eið*, isthmus
os; *austr*, east
ayre; *eyrr*, gravel beach
bodha; *boði*, submerged reef
-back; *bakki*, banks
-bàgh, -way; *vagr*, bay
-bhat, water; *vatn*, water
big; *bygging*, building
-bost; *bolstaðr*, farm, dwelling
burg, borve, borgh; *borg*, fort
braca-, breck-; *brekka*, slope
broad, *breiðr*, wide, broad
brett-; *bratt*, steep
bro-; *bru*, bridge
-bol, -bost, -pol; *bolstaðr*, house
chule-; *sula*, gannet, solan goose
cleit; *klett*, low rock, stone house
cnoc, cnap; *knap*, hillock
-cro; *kro*, sheepfold
cumla-, -cuml; *kuml*, burial mound
dail, dal, -dale, -dall; *dalr*, valley
jub-; *djup*, deep
eilean, -ey, -ay, -a; *ey*, island
far-; *faer*, sheep
fiska; *fiskr*, fish
fladda; *flatr*, flat
-ford; *fjord*, wide bay
fors; *fors*, waterfall
foul; *fugl*, bird
garry, gearry; *garðr*, enclosure
geata; *gata*, gate
geodha; *gja*, chasm, geo
-gill; *gil*, narrow valley, ravine
gra; *gra*, grey
graenn; *graenn*, green
grut-; *gryot*, gravel
hack ; *hagi*, enclosed pasture
hall-; *ballr*, slope
ham, hamn-; *hafn*, harbour
-hellya; *hellir*, cave
-hellya; *hella*, flat rock
hellya; *helgr*, holy
hest; *hest*, horse
horn-; *erne*, White-tailed Sea Eagle
idri-; *ytri*, outer
-ist, -ista; *bolstaðr*, farm
tolm-; *holmr*, small island
òb, tòb; *hjop*, shallow bay
-house,-ass; *ass*, ridge
kirk; *kirkja*, church
langa-, -land; *langr*, long
lax; salmon
-lee; *hlið*, slope

Hebrides; Old Norse. English

ler-; *leir*, clay
ling; *ling*, heather
mel-; *mel*, sandbank, dunes
moll; *mol*, shingle beach
moul, mull; *muli*, muzzle, lip
mous-, muss-, -mo; *mor*, pl.mos, moor
muckle; *mykill*, large, great
myre; *myri*, wet meadow
-nis; *nes*, nose. point
nev; *nef*, small headland
noup; *gnup*, peak
pap-; *papa*, priest, monk
od-; *oddi*, sharp point
-ord, -ort, -ford; *fjord*, wide bay
òs, -ose; *oss*, burn mouth, estuary
qui-; *kvi*, cattle pen
ram-, ramas-; *hrafn*, raven
-ret; *reyy*, sheepfold
ron-; *braun*, rough, rocky
ruadh-; *raud*, red
russ-; *hross*, horse
saur; *sauðr*, sheep
scap-; *skalp*, ship
score; *skor*, ridge
-sta, -shader; *setr*, out-pasture
selli-; *sel*, setter hut
-shun; *tjorn*, small loch
-skaill; *skali*, hall, house
skel-; *skal*, soft rock
sgeir, skerry; *sker*, skerry
skalp-; *skip*, ship
slettr; smooth, sleek
so-; *sauðr*, sheep
stac, staca; *stakk*, pillar rock
staff-; *stafr*, staff, pillar, column
storr; *staurr*, stack, rock pillar
sten-, -stain; *steinn*, stone
-sta; *stadr*, homestead
suar-; *saur*, muddy, marshy
suar-; *svaðr*, sward, grassy
teangue; *tangi*, tongue
tote, -tobhta; *thopt*, site of dwelling, clearing
-ton, -town; *tun*, enclosure
-val, ven; *fjall*, hill
varka-; *virki*, castle, fort
vel-; *vollr*, valley
-vaig, way; *vagr*, bay
water; *vatn*, water
ùig; *vik*, bay

and Islay that the language remains strong. In much of the Outer Hebrides it is the language of the majority of the inhabitants.

Classical Gaelic was used in literature in Scotland and Ireland until the 18th century. The 1767 translation of the New Testament was the first major work to appear in Scottish Gaelic. It was to set a baseline for the modern written language due to its wide distribution and use.

Modern Scottish Gaelic uses only 18 letters, a, b, c, d, e, f, g, h, i, l, m, n, o, p, r, s, t and u. The letter 'h' is mostly used after consonants such as 'b' and 'g' for lentition. The grave accent is often used to indicate a long vowel. As a result modern Gaelic orthography is initially very confusing for native English speakers.

Placenames throughout the Outer Hebrides are heavily influenced by Old Norse. Many words have been incorporated into the language, especially regarding the sea, coastal features, boats, fishing and agriculture. Modern Gaelic also incorporates many loanwords from English and other languages.

Newcomers often translate existing placenames into their own language, so the present usage may often represent layers of ancient Brittonic, Norse, old Gaelic, English and modern Gaelic. Names of rivers, steams, estuaries and seaways seem to be especially persistent. In many cases they have been shown to date back well over 2,000 years, thus predating any of these languages.

Road signs throughout much of the Highlands and Islands are now bilingual. In some instances the old signs have been replaced by new ones in modern Gaelic only. As if to confuse the visitor, modern Gaelic orthography has been applied to many names perceived to be English, which are actually Norse. This is very sad as placenames are as much a part of history and culture as physical remains.

Signposts may have one or more versions of a name, while maps can have either, both or something different again. Ordnance Survey coordinates are included for most sites of interest mentioned in the text for this reason.

The visitor is strongly recommended to refer to the many sites on the Internet on Gaelic and the Outer Hebrides. Some explain spelling, meaning and pronunciation.

Cultural Events There are many Gaelic cultural events which take place during the year, including the Hebridean Celtic Festival in Lewis, Ceolas Music Summer School in South Uist, Harris Arts Festival and Barra Live. Several Mods, with traditional singing, piping, dancing, music, poetry, story telling and drama are also held.

SOME GAELIC PLACENAME ELEMENTS

Gaelic	English	Gaelic	English
abhainn	stream, river	fada	long
acarsaid	anchorage, harbour	faing	sheep fank
achadh	ach, field	feannag	lazy bed
aird	ord, headland	fionn	white, fair, blessed
aiseag	ferry	fuaran	spring, green area
allt	burn or stream	garbh	rough
àth	ford	geal	white
athair	father	gille	boy
beag	little	glas	grey darker, green
bealach	pass, gap, gorge	gleann	glen, valley
beul	mouth	gob	beak, point
bodach	old man	gobha	blacksmith
-an	diminutive (lochan)	gorm	blue, green of grass
aonach	ridge	greian	bright, sunny
baile	bal-, township or village	grian	sun
bàn	blonde, pale	iar	east
beag	small	inbhir	inver, river mouth
beinn	ben, mountain	innis	meadow
bharpa	heap of stones	iolaire	eagle
bidean	tip, point	kille	church
bogach	bog	làirig	pass.
braigh	brae, upland	leac	rock ledge, stone slab
breac	brown trout, speckled	leana	green meadow
bruach	bank	leth	half
buchaille	shepherd	liath	grey lighter
buidhe	yellow	linnhe	pool
cailleach	old woman	loch	lake, bay
caladh	harbour, bay	lochan	small loch, tarn
camas	bay	long	ship
càrn	cairn, heap of stones	lùib	bend
caisteal	castle, fort	mac	son
ceann	head, headland	machair	fertile coastal plain
caol	kyle, strait, narrows	maol	bare round hill
chaolais	narrows	meadan	middle
cill	church, chapel	moine	moorland
clach	stone	mol	shingly beach
clachan	village	mór	big
cladh	graveyard	muir	sea
claigeann	skull, head	poll	pool, pit
coille	woodland, forest	rath	fort
coire	corrie, cauldron, kettle	rathad	road
corran	point, sickle	ruadh	red, brown
crom	crooked	rubha	headland
cuidhe	enclosure, pen	scadan	herring
curach	bog, marsh	skòrr, skùrr	steep rocky hill
dail	riverside meadow	siar	west
darach	oak	sithean	fairy hillock
dearg	bright red	sneachd	snow
deas	south	sron	headland
donn	brown	teampall	church
druim	ridge	tigh, taigh	house
dubh	black	tioram	dry
dùn	broch, mound	tobar	well
eagach	notched	tràigh	beach
eaglais	church	tuath	north
ear	east	uaine	bright green
eas	waterfall	uaimh	cave

Uig Bay from Timsgarry

Crown Copyright

LEWIS forms the northern expanse of Lewis and Harris. It covers 683mi² (1,790km²) and holds about 75% of the population of the Outer Hebrides (c.18,500), two thirds of whom live in Stornoway and the surrounding area.

In modern Gaelic the island is called *Leodhas*, which in turn probably derives from the Old Norse *Ljodhus*, sounding house. This is an alternative name for the large halls where the Norse spent much time in winter telling stories, reciting poetry and drinking.

However the name is much more ancient and may be the island referred to as *Limnu* by Ptolemy around 150AD. Interestingly *limnou* means marshy in Ancient Greek. Since this word is at least 2,500 years old, the conclusion must be that the origin of the name *Lewis* is lost in the mist of time. But it probably is very apt since much of the island is indeed marshy.

Except in the south, most of the island is low lying. The interior is a vast peatbog, strewn with inn lochans. Society here differs from elsewhere in most of Scotland. The Church and Sunday observance remain strong and Gaelic is the first language of a high proportion of the people.

Traditional practices such as crofting, peat cutting and small scale fishing continue. Ceilidhs, traditional story telling, music and song events are held regularly. The Hebridean Celtic Festival held in Stornoway each July, is one of the high points of the local cultural year.

Lewis is a land of contrasts. Stornoway, with its busy harbour, Victorian buildings as well as its modern sprawl of housing and businesses is in contrast to the rest of the island. There is a diverse range of archaeological and historic sites to visit, many fine beaches and good opportunities to observe wildlife.

The Lewis Chessmen are perhaps the most iconic artefacts associated with the island

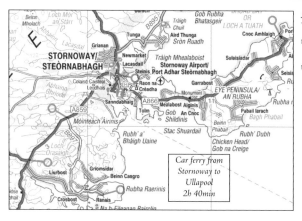

Crown Copyright

STORNOWAY, Steornabhagh (ON *Stjornavagr*, Steering or Anchorage Bay) is one of the best natural harbours in the Outer Hebrides and by far the largest settlement with a population of about 9,000. The original settlement was probably in the vicinity of Point Street, but no buildings remain which are older than the late 18th century.

Herring fishing drew the Dutch, English and Lowland Scots to the area in the 17th century and the town developed into a major fishing port during the 19th century. Most buildings date from this time or later; the oldest is said to be the late 18th century Fishermen's Coop building on North Beach.

The medieval Castle was the stronghold of the MacLeods who were said to be descended from the 12th century Norseman, Olav the Black, King of Man and the Isles. It is highly likely that there was a Viking stronghold on this site, and perhaps an Iron Age broch before that, although there is no evidence.

Clan MacLeod dominated the Isle of Lewis for about 400 years. The castle was the scene of dramatic events on several occasions. In 1506, Crown troops under the Earl of Huntly besieged it whilst searching for the forfeited Donald *Dubh* MacDonald, Lord of the Isles. The castle was finally destroyed in 1654 by Cromwell's soldiers after a battle with the MacLeods. The remains are under the old roro pier.

VisitHebrides

In 1598 James VI declared Lewis forfeit by the MacLeods and granted the island to the *Fife Adventurers* who were to civilise and colonise it. In October 1598 they arrived at Stornoway along with 600 soldiers. However they were chased off the island and their houses burned. The MacLeods were temporarily in control again, but in 1607 ownership again passed to the settlers.

By 1610 the MacKenzie Earl of Seaforth was in power and the family was to remain so until 1844. In 1628 Stornoway was erected to the status of a Royal Burgh,

Stornoway from Lews Castle grounds with the ferry MV "Isle of Lewis" arriving

but only briefly due to objections from other towns. The excellent harbour and rich fishing grounds of the Minch have ensured that fishing has always been important to the town. Today, whitefish and shellfish are the most important catches, while Herring and Mackerel are landed at Mainland ports such as Kinlochbervie.

In 1653 Cromwell's army built a fort on Goat Island, and a citadel where Point Street is now. By 1695 there were about 60 families in Stornoway with a church and a school, while by 1796 the population was 2,639. Herring was the main source of wealth to the town, which was a major fishing port for over 200 years.

Map of Stornoway in 1821

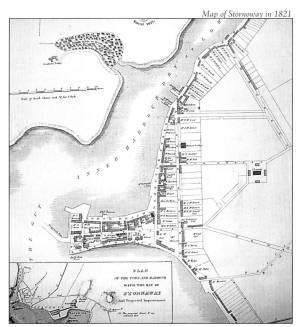

Stornoway Fishermen's Coop building may date from the 18ᵗʰ century

There is a panoramic view of Stornoway from the top of Gallows Hill. Vast amounts of soil were imported for the Mathiesons plantations. They are very attractive during spring and summer, with over 70 species of trees and shrubs, in strong contrast to the rest of the mostly treeless islands. Many wild flowers and woodland birds can also be seen here.

Woodland Centre An old sawmill near Lews Castle was renovated by the Stornoway Trust, creating the Woodland Centre. This has an excellent cafeteria, small shop and interpretative displays about the Castle grounds, which are being greatly improved. There are several interesting waymarked walks to follow.

Stornoway Golf Club was founded in 1890 on the site of Stornoway Airport. The original course was requisitioned by the Air Ministry in 1939. The present 18 hole course in the grounds of Lews Castle was opened in 1947.

Stornoway Trust Lord Leverhulme of Unilever bought the island in 1918. He had grandiose ideas about developing Stornoway as an industrial fishing port, but despite investing large sums he failed to get the support of the crofters of Lewis. He then offered ownership of all of Lewis to the people but only Stornoway accepted. Title to the town and parish of Stornoway was transferred to the Town Council in 1923. It is now administered by the Stornoway Trust, which until recently was unique as a form of community land ownership.

Lews Castle

Harbour The harbour is always interesting and is base to a large number of small fishing boats. Most fish for prawns, scallops or whitefish in the Minch. The harbour fills up with the colourful fleet on Saturday nights as crews spend Sunday ashore. Catches are landed at the fish market here, otherwise at Kinlochbervie, Ullapool or Mallaig.

An Lanntair Arts Centre is situated opposite the ferry terminal. There are regular exhibitions by local, national, and international artists.

Stornoway street furniture - reminders of the Herring fishing

Woodland Centre Lewis chessman

Stornoway Harbour sculpture

The latest films are shown in the cinema and many cultural events, including operas, plays and music are held. The coffee shop and restaurant has excellent views over the harbour. The shop stocks books, cards and crafts. The Public Library is situated in Cromwell Street. It has a good collection of local books for reference, as well as free Internet access and a large collection of books for loan.

Lewis Loom Centre in the Old Grainstore at 3 Bayhead should not be missed. The tour includes explanations of the structure of different wools, dyeing, spinning and weaving and there are some interesting things for sale.

LEWS CASTLE

After James Mathieson purchased Lewis in 1844, considerable development took place in the town. Lews Castle was financed from sale of opium in China. The Castle is owned by the Council, which has redeveloped it as a hotel and wedding venue. There is also the Outfitters Shop and the Storehouse Café. Behind is Lews College, a part of the University of the Highlands and Islands.

Museum nan Eilean is in an extension to Lews Castle and opened in 2016. The prize exhibit is some of the famous Lewis Chessmen. Visitors can *"discover how the distinctiveness of the Outer Hebrides is shaped by a unique combination of land, sea and people; hear about different people's lives; the diversity of experience, opinion and perception of living life on an Island; examine how people lived and worked from the earliest times to the present day, how their culture is expressed through the Gaelic language, religion and community life.*

An Lanntair Arts Centre

Stornoway in springtime

Stornoway by William Daniell, 1815

Isle of Lewis Sports Centre is a dual use Sports complex for schools and the public. Facilities include: fitness centre, pool, games hall, squash courts, health suite, climbing wall a large hall. Outside there is an Astro Turf pitch and running track.

Churches St Columba's Parish Kirk, one of the oldest buildings in the town, was built in 1794. St Peter's Episcopal Church has an eclectic selection of artefacts including a sandstone font from the Flannan Islands, a Dutch bell dating from 1631, a prayer book which belonged to the 19th century missionary David Livingstone and the 1608 *Breeches* bible.

Arnish Point The lighthouse here was first lit in 1852 and is unusual in that it was prefabricated on the Clyde rather than being built on site. The oil platform yard was built in the 1970s, but now lies idle, however if oil developments take place to the west it may see work again. Aerogenerators have also been fabricated here.

WWII Gun Batteries There are interesting gun emplacements on the seaward side of Arnish Point. The Royal Navy operated a coastal defence battery here during WWII. Two four inch gun houses, a Battery Observation Post and searchlight mountings remain.

Across the harbour there are two six inch guns in a setting at Battery Point next to the power station. They commemorate the many volunteers who trained here between 1876 and 1919 (NB433322). The old guns were found discarded on the shore.

A cairn above Arnish Point commemorates the visit by Bonnie Prince Charlie in May 1746 when he was attempting to escape to France. It is a monument to failure as nobody in Stornoway would assist him or find a ship. He was not allowed into the town, but neither was he betrayed.

The War Memorial on *Cnoc an Uan* (NB418343) was opened in 1924 to honour

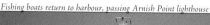

Fishing boats return to harbour, passing Arnish Point lighthouse

Stornoway War Memorial

the 1,151 Lewismen killed in WWI out of a total of about 6,700 serving in the forces. Unsurprisingly, returning servicemen were determined to have land to themselves. This site was chosen because all four Lewis parishes are visible from it. The Memorial also commemorates the 376 personnel killed in WWII.

Sir Alexander MacKenzie, a partner in the North West Company, was born in the town in 1764. He was the first European to travel across Canada overland, and the Mackenzie River is named after him. Another Mackenzie, born in 1752, became Surveyor General of India and was responsible for the first maps of parts of the subcontinent.

Stornoway Airport Captain Fresson first landed his Dragon Rapide on the then golf course in 1934, which was developed as an airfield in WWII for Coastal

Command. Anti-submarine, anti-shipping and convoy escort patrols took place from here and many American aircraft passed through on their way to Britain.

From 1986 to 1993 Stornoway was a Forward Operating Base for NATO and the runway was greatly extended. Although no longer a NATO base the airfield has benefited greatly from the military investment. A large new passenger terminal was opened here in 2001.

Stornoway The area has welcomed visitors since long before the first Viking entered Stornoway Harbour in the late 700s AD. Over the centuries fishermen and seamen from Holland, Scotland, Norway, the Baltic and further afield have used the port. *High heid yins* and ordinary folk have come and gone. Some have streets named after them, or commemorative plaques about them. It is a unique place, Gaelic yet British, Hebridean yet Scottish, laid back yet bustling. It makes a good base from which to explore Lewis and Harris.

Memorial to those lost on "HMS Iolaire"

HMS IOLAIRE TRAGEDY
The return of servicemen was made even more tragic by the loss of the Admiralty yacht, HMS *Iolaire* on 1st January 1919. She struck the Beasts of Holm, off Holm Point, only 2mi (3km) from Stornoway. 205 Lewismen were lost within sight of home. That 71 survived was due to a Nessman who managed to swim ashore with a line. There is a memorial at Holm Point (NB444305) which overlooks the seemingly innocuous rocks. A footpath now runs to this poignant site.

Tree stump in the Castle grounds

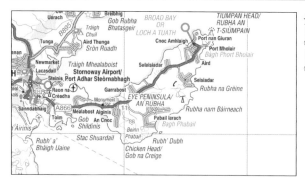

AIGNISH To the east of Stornoway lies the peninsula of Aignish or Eye (ON *Eggnes*, Ridge Ness), also known as Point, which is connected to the rest of Lewis by a sandy tombolo. *Braigh na-h-Aoidhe* (G ridge, ON *eid*, ayre or tombolo). The beach on the north side is one of the finest in Lewis. Both sides are good for walks and birdwatching.

Loch Branahuie at the east end of the Aignish tombolo is also very good for visiting and resident waterfowl. *The Braighe*, the bay to the south, holds large numbers of seaducks and divers in winter.

Eaglais na h-Aoidhe is a roofless 14th century church at Aignish, dedicated to St Columba. An earlier 6th century chapel may have been founded by St Catan.

There are two interesting grave slabs in the church, one to the 15th century Roderic II and the other to his daughter, Margaret, wife of the last Abbot of Iona.

Aignish Riot The nearby Crofters' Cairn commemorates the events of 1888. A meeting in the old churchyard on Christmas Day 1887 decided to give a Mr Newall, of Aignish Farm, two weeks to move out his stock. On 9th January 1888 a riot ensued after a large party of raiders tried to drive his animals to Stornoway.

They were stopped by a Sheriff Fraser with the help of a party of Royal Marines and a company of Royal Scots. Fraser read the *Riot Act*, and eventually the mob dispersed after the arrest of 11 men. Aignish Farm was finally broken up into crofts in 1905. Thus, ultimately, the landowner's plans were defeated.

The Eye Peninsula is densely populated with many crofts and two small harbours at Pabail and Port na Giuran. The seemingly oddly named Chicken Head (ON *Kirku Ness*, Church Ness) is called *Gob na Creige* on the map, but in Gaelic is *Ceann na Circ*. There is a ruined chapel on the cliff edge (NB508292) and a large Kittiwake colony below.

Tiumpan Head, the most easterly point on Lewis, has expansive views across the Minch on a clear day. The lighthouse was first lit in 1900 and automated in 1985. This and other nearby vantage points are good places to watch for Risso's and other Dolphins in late summer, as well as for migrant birds in season.

Prehistoric sites include Dun Bayble (NB516305) and Clach Stein (NB517318) both near Bayble and a chambered cairn (NB524331) near Garrabost. The famous Shulishader axe was found in peat near the township and dates from about 3150BC.

Braigh na-h-Aoidhe, usually called The Braigh, is a lovely stretch of reddish sand on the north side of the tombolo

15th century grave slab

Tiumpain Head lighthouse - good seawatching site

St Columba's Church or Eaglais na h-Aoidhe

Aignish Riot in 1888

Memorial to the Aignish Riot

Loch an Tiumpan is a good place to see waterfowl and waders

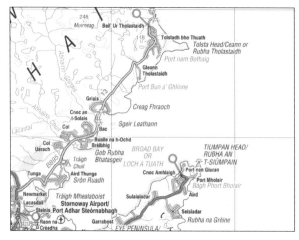

dunes. The pools below Col Uarach are good for waterfowl and waders. Coll and Back merge into a significant village with many crofts. Peat roads run far into the moorland.

Traigh Gress is another fine sandy beach. The remains of a wooden steamship emerge at low tide. Nearby there is a memorial to the Gress Land Raids after WWI in protest at Leverhulme's plans for economic development rather than crofting.

NORTHEAST of Stornoway lie the townships of Tunga (ON *Tunga* (ON spit of land), Coll *Kula*, low hill), Back (ON *Bakki*, ridge), and Gress. (ON *Gress*, grass) The fertile Torridonian sandstone makes good agricultural land backed by dunes and machair. This was the scene of much unrest in the Land Wars.

Most sandy beaches on Lewis are on the west side, but a fine series stretches around Broad Bay. They extend from Aignish all the way to Tolsta and are sheltered by headlands with low cliffs.

Tunga The Tunga saltflats can be accessed from Tunga (ON *Tunga*, Tongue). They are good for waterfowl and waders. The dunes and extensive sandy beach of *Traigh Mealabost* (ON *Meal Bolstadir*, Sandy Farm) can be accessed from Steinis (ON *Stein Nes*, Stony Point NB448339).

St Olav's Church (*Teampall Amblaigh* NB490416) is one of the few extant chapels dedicated to a Norse saint in the Western Isles. It may date from the 12th century. This is not surprising considering that the Vikings would have settled the best land first. The windows are interesting with very narrow outer slits.

Traigh Chuil is a 1.5mi (2km) stretch of sand backed by

Sheilavig Mor is a lovely little cove with a small sandy beach and low cliffs. Northeast of Gress and a short walk over the moorland, there is luxuriant grass and many lazybeds above the beach and interesting cliffs.

Carn a' Mharc (NB473438) is a large ruined chambered cairn inland from Gress. It is about 3km (2mi) inland on the northeast side of Abhainn Ghriais. A peat track leads most of the way.

Tolsta To the north, the road rises over moorland before descending into Tolsta (ON *Toli's Stadir*, Tolly's Farm). There are wonderful panoramic views from here on a clear day, especially from Tolsta Head.

St Olav's Church, (also called St Aula's or Teampull Amblaigh)

St Olav window showing narrow slit

Traigh Gheardha

The Bridge to Nowhere, north of Tolsta

Stacks on Traigh Gheardha

The beaches and low cliffs of Tolsta are among the most attractive in the Western Isles. *Traigh Mhor* (G Big Beach) is over 2km long, backed by dunes and machair. At its southeast end, Tolsta Head has small stacks and natural arches. Traigh Giordale and Port Beag are sheltered from all directions but the southeast.

Traigh Gheardha (ON *Gerd*, Farm) is at the end of the road. It has spectacular small stacks or castles set in a very attractive
Traigh Mhor

sandy bay. The greens and blues of the sea are more like the Caribbean than the Minch. These beaches are deservedly popular with local people.

Wreck on Traigh Gress

THE BRIDGE TO NOWHERE

North of Tolsta the road ends at the *Bridge to Nowhere*. During Leverhulme's time on Lewis there were plans to build a road from Tolsta to Ness. However, only the elegant concrete bridge over the River Garry was built. A track leads about a mile further before petering out.

From here is a fine but strenuous walk along the coast to Ness over rugged moorland. The many lochs are excellent for Red-throated Divers. Great and Arctic Skuas nest on the moors, Peregrines inhabit the remote cliffs and Gannets may be seen offshore, Golden and White-tailed Eagles are sometimes seen.

Little huts called *airighs* or shielings dot the landscape. In the past cattle were grazed on lush moorland grass in summer. They were accompanied by young women and girls who stayed in the huts, to tend and milk the cows. They spent the summer making butter and cheese which was used to pay rent in kind. Some was kept for winter use.

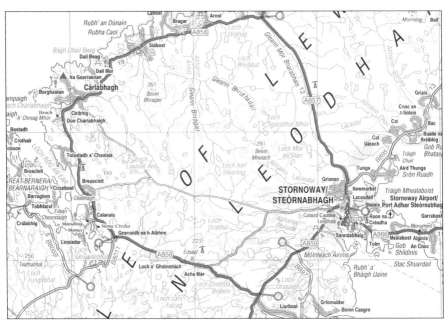

WESTSIDE There are several ways to get to the west side of Lewis from Stornoway. The interior of the island is a vast moorland, dominated by heather and dotted with countless small lochs. There are virtually no habitations inland, apart from Achmore.

Barvas Road (A857) The road to Barvas runs northwest across uninhabited moorland and through Gleann Mor Barvas before reaching the west side. Settlements are scattered along the coast all the way northeast to Ness and southwest to Garynahine.

Pentland Road The most scenic route follows the line of a railway proposed by Leverhulme in the 1920s. The plan was to land fish at Loch Carloway near the entrance to Loch Roag and transport it to Stornoway for processing and shipment. The scheme was abandoned due to local opposition. The concrete bridge at Carloway was part of this route.

Thanks to this project the present single track road runs across the moor from Marybank to Carloway. Just west of Stornoway it passes the municipal rubbish dump, a fine place to see gulls and buzzards. At Loch Vatandip the road branches right to Carloway, and left to Achmore. Later it branches right to Carloway and left to Breasclete. Red and Black-throated Divers breed on many of the lochs.

Garynahine Road The main road (A858) turns west at Tom Mhic Leoid and undulates across the moorland past Achmore, many lochs and conifer woods.

Eithshal (223m) overlooks the inland settlement of Achmore. A steep road leads to its summit, which is dominated by TV and mobile phone masts. There is a panoramic view over Lochs to the mountains of Uig and Harris

A typical peatbank on North Uist

View from Eithshal over many lochs to the mountains of southern Lewis and north Harris

from here. On a clear day the greens, blues and mauves of the landscape are quite spectacular.

Peatbanks are scattered along all of these roads. Many are still worked for fuel in spring. A special spade called a *tuskar* (ON Torf *Skera*, turf cutter, G *tairsgeir*) is used to cut and throw the turves onto the bank. When partially dry they are set up in threes, then carted home where peatstacks are built.

Tree stumps with roots are often dug up in peatbanks

Neat banks and stacks are a source of great pride, and communities have varied methods of cutting, setting up and stacking. Old grey Ferguson tractors (*Fergies*), with double back wheels are a common sight everywhere on Lewis. Many have been lovingly restored.

Achmore

Peat is still regularly cut for fuel

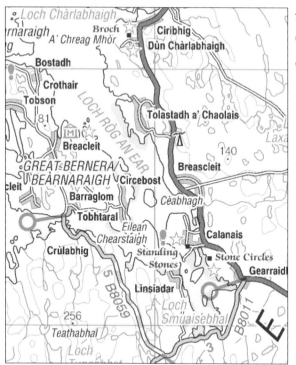

about 2900BC, while the chambered cairn and rows may be of later date. It seems likely that the monument may never have been completed and that avenues may have been planned for all four axes.

The 33 Lewisian Gneiss monoliths form rows, which radiate from a central circle and are arranged like a Celtic cross. The northern avenue is slightly east of north, while the southern arm is aligned due south. The eastern and western arms in turn face south of east and due west.

The stones were partially buried in peat which had accumulated since perhaps 1500BC, but were fully revealed when this was cleared in 1857. This action destroyed most of the archaeological evidence which may have been present. The surfaces have weathered into fantastic contours and the crystals in the rock give it a very beautiful texture, which varies with the light.

Obvious solar alignments are the equinoctial sunset, and local noon, but other alignments are quite possible. It has been suggested

CALLANISH (ON *Kjallar Ness*, Keel Point) The standing stones and chambered cairns of the Callanish (*Calanais*) area on the east side of Loch Roag form one of the most remarkable Neolithic sites in Britain. A good place to start a visit to the west of Lewis is the Callanish Visitor Centre which has an interpretation area, an interesting shop and a cafe. The main monument is situated just up the hill.

The inner stone ring of the main site here probably dates from

Midsummer sunrise at Callanish

Major lunar standstill

that the eastern row is aligned with the rising of the Pleiades around May Day, or Beltane. This would have been about the time when crops were planted.

Lunar Standstills The 13 monoliths in the ring may reflect the 13 months of the lunar year. During each month moonrise and moonset vary from north to south and back due to the relative movements of the Earth and the Moon. This is because the plane of the Moon's orbit is inclined by about 5° to that of the Earth's around the

Sun. The direction of this inclination varies over an 18.6 year cycle. As a result, at the major lunar standstill, the declination of the moon varies from a maximum of 28.5° to a minimum of -28.5° over 2 weeks. The apparent movement of the moon stops and reverses.

The term standstill was coined by Professor Thom and is analogous to solstice (L *solstitium*, sun stoppage) when the celestial body appears to stop and reverse direction. At the latitude of Callanish (58°N) the Moon just skims the horizon at its major standstill.

It appears to "dance" along the ridge to the south which is called *Cailleach na Mointich* (G Old Lady of the Moors). It sets behind the hill to the southwest, only to momentarily reappear, or flash, in a notch just to the west. This is very reminiscent of the sun's behaviour at Maeshowe and the nearby Watchstone before and after the winter solstice in Orkney.

In about 325BC, Pytheas the

Greek circumnavigated Britain and perhaps even visited Iceland. He is indirectly quoted by the 1st century BC historian, Diodorus Siculus as, "*Having seen a round temple on an island no smaller than Sicily while sailing around Britain*" and that, "*The path of the Moon seen from this island was very low in the sky. The god visited the island every 19 years*", the 18.6 year cycle.

The Moon was said "*to dance from the Spring equinox until the rising of the Pleiades*", or Beltane (May Day).

CALLANISH			
Sunrise and Sunset Times			
Midsummer	sunrise	04:21	BST
	sunset	22:36	BST
Equinoctial	sunset	18:44	BST
Midwinter	sunrise	09:12	GMT
	sunset	15:37	GMT
May Day	sunrise	05:32	BST
	sunset	21:16	BST

OTHER ALIGNMENTS

Small stone circles
Chambered cairns
Lunar major standstill
Lunar months
Lunar year
Local noon

Midsummer sunrise

It is impossible to confirm whether Pyrheas visited Lewis in the 4th century BC, but it is entirely possible. Using his solar observations, Hipparchus later made calculations, and one of the latitudes measured was the crucial 58°N at which the Moon skims along the horizon at its major standstill.

Whether or not the site was actually intended to have solar, stellar or lunar alignments will never be proven, but no one can visit Callanish without being overwhelmed by the confluence of sky, water, landscape and monoliths, whatever the season, weather or time of day.

Small circles Apart from the main stone setting (NB213330) there are several other smaller, but remarkable stone circles to visit in the area, including *Cnoc an Gharraidh* (NB223326) and *Cnoc Fillbhir Bheag* (NB226328) near the A858 just before the turn off to the Visitor Centre. *Cul a Cleit* (NB247303) is about 1km off the A858 and *Ceann Hulavig* (NB230304) off the B8011 on a small hillock overlooking Loch Roag. Each of these names is a mixture of Gaelic and Old Norse describing monuments built by people whose language and culture we do not know.

Chambered cairns An unusual feature of some of the stone circles in this area is the presence of a central cairn. Excavation of the cairn at the main site suggests that it may have been in use between 2500 and 1750BC. It is unique for the Outer Hebrides in resembling some cairns in Orkney. *Grooved Ware* and *Beaker* pottery sherds were found here.

The most spectacular views of the main Callanish setting are from Loch Roag and it has been suggested that the tallest mono-

The northern avenue with its impressive outermost monolith

The central circle and chambered cairn

lith may originally have been a sea marker. There are at least another twenty stone settings, standing stones and chambered cairns in this area, which was clearly of great symbolic importance in Neolithic times. Perhaps a geophysical survey will reveal structures to rival those on the Ness of Brodgar in Orkney.

Cnoc an Gharaidh to the east of the main setting

Cean Hulavig overlooks Loch Roag from a small hill on the B8011

Weathered Lewisian Gneiss
The stones have many fine lichens

Cnoc Filibhir Beag has 17 upright stones

Dun Carloway stands on a prominent hillock above the township

CARLOWAY (ON *Karlsvagr*, Karl's Bay) On the A858 north from Callanish, the township of Breascleit has a standing stone and a chambered cairn. The ex shore station for the Flannan Isles lighthouse, called *Taigh Mor* (G Big House) is situated nearby. Families of the light- keepers stayed here before automation in 1971.

The broch of Dun Carloway (G *Doune Carlabhagh*, NB190413) is the most complete and spectacular of any in the Western Isles and dates from perhaps the 1st century BC or earlier. In common with many other such brochs it is prominently situated on a small hillock overlooking the township. The walls still reach more than 9m in height.

The double walls are over 3m thick at the base and enclose galleries accessed by a stairway. The scarcement is 2.5m

Intramural staircase

Intramural lintels

above the floor, which is 7.6m in diameter, and this was probably the main habitation level. It would have been supported by wooden posts. Many of the original stones are no doubt in the walls of the ruined blackhouses below the broch.

A narrow doorway on the west side has a guard cell on the right and jambs for a wooden door. The interior walls are vertical, but the exterior is much thicker at the base, thinning towards the top with a pronounced batter. The drystone walls are very well constructed and no doubt will survive many more millennia. The building techniques used clearly show the considerable skill of the Iron Age masons who built these dry stone towers.

The main part of the broch was cleared out in the 1920s without proper archaeologic-

The former shore station of the Flannan Islands lighthouse

al study. The northeast cell was reinvestigated in 1972 and large numbers of pottery sherds were found, along with part of a quernstone and much evidence of fires. The suggestion is that the broch was still occupied as late as 700AD.

Clan Warfare In about 1500 a group of Morrisons were surprised here by a gang of MacCauleys, who climbed the walls and threw burning heather into the broch, thus asphyxiating their arch enemies. It seems that people

were still living here in the late 1800s. Dun Carloway was in use for well over 2000 years. It is one of the most evocative brochs in the Outer Hebrides.

The site has been in State guardianship since 1887. The nearby Doune Broch Centre helps visitors to better understand the monument and its history, as well as brochs in general. It has a small shop, interpretation displays and toilets. The path to the broch offers fine views over the township.

Dun Carloway in c1900

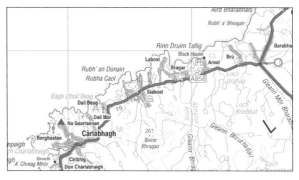

Carloway To Barvas

Here the coastline is low rocky cliffs with beautiful sandy bays such as at Dalmore, Dalbeg and Shawbost. There are many small lochs, behind shingle storm beaches, which are attractive to Otters. The townships of Shawbost, Bragar and Arnol are almost continuously settled, having ruined blackhouses intermingled with 20th century dwellings and croft buildings.

North of Carloway, the 19th century Gearrannan blackhouse village (NB194442) has a hostel, self-catering cottages, and a shop with museum and tearoom. The inhabitants were crofters and fishermen who pulled their boats up at nearby *Geodha Ruadh*.

Walk A coastal path runs from Gearrannan to Dalbeg. It passes two promontory forts, which might just as easily be monastic as physically defensive, then a ruinous Norse mill. Further on is the site of a Bronze Age settlement which was revealed after a storm in 1982. Large amounts of pottery and other artefacts were recovered.

Dalbeg The walk ends at the delightful little cove of Dalbeg. This beach is dangerous to swimmers, and surfers should take great care. Large seaworn stones are a feature here. A stream flows into the sea across the sand from Loch Dalbeg, a good site for Otters. The loch has beautiful Irises and Water Lilies in summer.

Shawbost Norse Mill Just before Shawbost there is a restored Norse mill and kiln (NB244464). The millstone is turned directly by a vertical axis waterwheel. There are many in the Western Isles, but this is the only one in working order. They were used until the 19th century.

The mill workings are visible below the millstone. Water from a burn is funnelled to the mill race by a stone lined lade. The millwheel turns the upper millstone; grain is fed into the centre by a mechanism which moves the hopper, hence the clicking sound and the name "click mills". Meal gathers in a groove below the lower stone.

Shawbost Museum is a small but interesting folk museum in the community centre. It has many artefacts relating to the history of the area.

Gearrannan, a restored blackhouse village near Carloway

Bragar broch

Restored Norse mill & kiln at Shawbost

Whalebone arch at Bragar

Shawbost Beach is at the head of a pretty north facing cove. This 200m expanse of sand is separated from Loch a' Bhaile by a shingle ayre. This little beach is one of the many lovely secrets of West Lewis. There is a fine short circular walk from the Community Centre around the township taking in *Siabost na Thuath*, the beach and *Siabost bho Dheas*.

Bragar Broch lies on a small island on *Loch an Duna* at Bragar connected to the shore by a causeway (NB286475). The broch is 16m in diameter outside and 9m inside. An internal scarcement can be made out at a height of about 3m. Although the broch is ruinous the site is very evocative, especially on a misty day when modern buildings are obscured.

WHALEBONE ARCH The lower jaw bones of an 85ft Blue Whale form an unusual gateway. The whale came ashore in 1920 with an explosive harpoon still embedded in its body. The crofter who removed it was lucky. It exploded in his shed, but he was not there at the time. The arch has been coated in fibre glass for protection from the elements.

Shawbost Norse Mill interior

Dalbeg is a delightful sandy cove

CARLOWAY TO BARVAS	
BEACHES	
Barvas	90
Dalmore	90
Dalbeg	90
Shawbost	90
BLACKHOUSES	
Arnol	92
Gearrannan	90
Shawbost Museum	91
NORSE MILL & KILN	
Shawbost	90
BROCHS	
Bragar	91
Carloway	88
WHALEBONE ARCH	
Bragar	91

Interior with central hearth, minimal furniture and box bed

ARNOL BLACKHOUSE (NB311493) is under the care of Historic Environment Scotland. A development of much more ancient houses, people and animals were all under one roof. Smoke escaped through the thatch from the peat fire in the centre of the living room floor. It was last occupied in 1965 having been built in about 1885.

The house closely resembles domestic buildings from Norse times or earlier. These were often built from turf, with a timber lining and stone foundations. Variations on the longhouse theme were lived in well into 20th century. Materials used depended on local availability of stone, timber and turf.

The walls are about 1.8m high. The gap between the inner and outer stone skins is filled with earth, peat and ashes. The timber in the roof is driftwood or from shipwreck; whalebone was also used. Slats or straw or heather ropes (*simmons*) were used to cover the purlins.

Grass or heather turves were laid face down on top. The turf absorbed soot from the fire and was later used as fertiliser. Finally the roof was thatched with heather, bracken, straw or reeds held down with ropes and stone weights. Frequently old Herring nets or wire netting was used to secure the thatch.

The byre was on the downhill end, with an *oddle* hole in the gable end. This drained into the midden. Dung and waste straw bedding would have been pushed out daily. Obviously the human inhabitants shared the byre with the cattle. The hens had free range and came in and out at will through an opening.

The dung which built up over the winter was cleared out after the cattle had been put outside. The gable end was often partly demolished to do this. Seaweed, dung and sooty turf from the roof were all used as manure.

The barn is directly opposite the main entrance. It was used to hand-thresh oats and bere, and to store straw, meal and tools. By leaving the

The byre

Stackyard and back of house showing barn and main part

doors open a through draft would help in winnowing.

Ventilation is important in houses without chimneys. Smoke escapes through the roof but fresh air was essential. The byre roof is lower than the domestic end, an oddle hole allows fresh air in. The smoke and ammonia in the roofspace repelled insects and also preserved meat or fish.

Blackhouse Museum, Arnol showing byre end, barn and peatstack

No 42 Arnol is a late survivor of a long tradition of such houses. The introduction of Government grants for crofters to build new houses and improve existing ones ended usage of this type of dwelling..

Heather rope baskets   *Kitchen cupboards from the 1950s*

39 Arnol across the road is furnished in the style of the 1950s. Typical of houses from the mid 20th century it was built of concrete blocks with asbestos slates on the roof. The kitchen has a cast iron stove and furniture of the time. Many such houses now lie abandoned.

1950s style kitchen with cast iron stove in 39 Arnol

Visitor Centre There is a small visitor centre with shop, interpretation panels and toilets nearby.

Bedroom with box beds

Loch na Muilne RSPB Reserve is a short distance across the moor to the east. The star attraction in spring and summer is breeding Red-necked Phalaropes. Dunlin, Snipe and Golden Plovers also nest here. Whooper Swan and Greylag Geese stop here on migration.

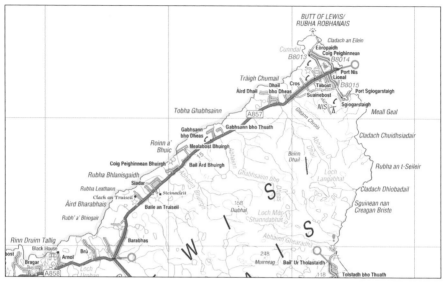

Clach an Truiseil is the tallest monolith in the Outer Hebrides, William Daniell 1815

Steinicleit near Shader, probably the remains of a chambered cairn

NESS (ON *Nes*, headland) is the most northerly part of Lewis. The road from Barvas to Ness runs through a series of crofting townships, making the area one of the most densely populated rural areas of Lewis. New houses, old houses, loom sheds, small shops and working crofts line much of the road, interspersed by areas of moorland.

Ancient Stones At 5.7m high, *Clach an Truiseil* (NB376538) is the tallest monolith in the Western Isles. It may be a prehistoric sea marker. A battle between the Morrisons of Ness and the Maccauleys of Uig is said to have taken place here.

Just to the north, in Shader (*Siader*), the enigmatic site of *Steinicleit* is probably a very ruined chambered cairn, perhaps overlain by a later domestic structure. The mound in the centre has a kerb of stone slabs around it, while the footings of walls lead off from the site, which may have been occupied from 3000BC.

Chapels There are many old chapel sites on the west of Lewis, most of which are close to the shore and ruinous. *Teampall Pheadar* (St Peter's, NB380550) is a grassy mound above *Mol Eire* beach at *Siader*. There is another larger *Teampall Pheadar* at Swainbost (NB508637). *Teampall nan Cro Naomh* (Holy Cross, NB433594) at Galson, now ruinous, was fairly complete in the 1820s.

Port Stoth *Teampall Ronain* (St Ronan, NB524654) above the cove of Stoth, a sheltered bay east of the Butt, is said to be the oldest chapel site in the Western Isles. *Port Stoth* was the main landing site for stores for the Butt of Lewis lighthouse, and for the Ness area before Port of Ness was built.

Interior of Teampall Mholuaidh (St Moluag's Church), Ness

Lochruban, a rock stack off *Roinn a' Roidh* (NB507661), near the Butt, has a small beehive shaped cell and legend has it that Pygmies lived here. It is probably a monastic cell. Ruins of similar structures exist nearby at *Cunndal*.

Teampall Mholuaidh The restored *Teampall Mholuaidh* (NB520652, St Moluag's Chapel) is said to have originally been built by the Vikings. The roof timbers were driftwood from Stoth. The present church may date from the 14th century or later. There was also once a Norse castle near this church called

Olvir's or Olaf's Castle. It is logical that the Vikings would settle and take control of Ness and perhaps Norse remains will be found in future surveys.

St Moluag's was associated with the healing of wounds

NORTH TO NESS	
ARCHAEOLOGY	
Adabrock	96
Clach An Truiseil	94
Dun Eistean	99
Steinicleit	94
CHAPELS	
Teampall Mholuaidh	95
Teampall nan Cro Naomh	95
Teampall Pheadar	95
Teampall Ronain	95
COASTAL	
Buail A Muigh	97
Butt of Lewis	98
Port of Ness	96
Port Stoth	95
Rionn a' roidh	95
Swainbost Sands	97
Traigh Dail	97
ATTRACTION	
Ness Heritage Centre	97
St Ronan's cross slab	96
Traigh Dhonnchaidh Centre	98

Teampall nan Cro Naomh at Galson by William Daniell 1815

Port of Ness Harbour

Richard Jones

and sores, however it was deemed too sacred for women to enter, particularly if pregnant. Meetings were held twice a year, at Candlemas and Halloween when eating, drinking, dancing and dalliance went on until dark. Afterwards, mass was held until morning.

Anyone suffering from mental illness could be cured by walking seven times sunwise around the church. After a drink of water from St Ronan's Well, at Port of Stoth, they had to sleep overnight in the building.

Another ancient custom in Ness was the annual sacrifice of ale to the sea-god, *Shony*. Every house contributed "*a peck of malt which was brewed into ale, and one person waded out to his waist with a cup of ale and cried, "Shony I give you this cup of ale, hoping that you will be so kind as to send us plenty of sea-ware for enriching the ground next year"*. (Seaweed was used to fertilise the land).

This was done at night and after the offering everyone went to the church which was lit by candlelight. They remained standing and quiet for a while before the candle was extinguished and then everyone went outside. Ale was consumed and the remainder of the night was spent singing and dancing.

The **Port of Ness** has a picturesque, but silted up, little harbour. It is very exposed to easterly gales and unsuitable for large vessels.

Adabrock Hoard In 1910 Donald Murray found a large cache of bronze objects in a peat bank at Adabrock, above Port of Ness. Apart from two bronze swords and some limited evidence of metal working, this is the only major such find in the Outer Hebrides.

Placenames Even more than in the rest of Lewis the placenames are mostly Norse, masked by the new Gaelic names on signposts. There is much attractive coastal scenery in Ness, including the lovely beach of Buail a Muigh at Port of Ness, the sheltered sandy cove of Port Stoth and the series of sandy beaches on the west side from Traigh Dell to Eoropie. The yellowish Swainbost Sands are particularly picturesque.

The sand dunes and machair are a riot of colour in summer with many wild flowers, while the cliff tops are covered in a carpet of Thrift. Although the cliffs are nowhere very high,

Ness yole

Cross-slab from Rona

Eoropie Beach

the ancient gneiss rocks are contorted and weathered into fantastic shapes, especially at the Butt of Lewis.

Vikings According to legend, the Vikings tried to tow the Western Isles back to Norway by attaching a rope to the natural arch at *Rionn a' Roidh*. They pulled so hard that the

land broke apart, leaving the trail of islands from Barra Head to the Butt of Lewis as they are now.

Ness Historical Society has its Heritage Centre in the Old Cross Primary School. A large variety of artefacts, photographs and other items illustrate the life of Ness:

domestic life, social life, fishing and the sea. The most interesting is the small cross-slab which is pierced with three holes and which has the figure of a man inscribed on it. This grave marker came from the cemetery on Rona, and some say that it marked the resting place of St Ronan himself.

Port of Ness Buail a Muigh

Swainbost Sands

THE MEN OF NESS

The Men of Ness have always been great seamen. It was said that *"no Nessman of working age ever died in his bed"*; they either lived to old age or drowned at sea.

They fished offshore using longlines and handlines from *sgoths*, descendants of boats used by the Norse, like the yoles used in Orkney and Caithness. There was a great tradition of boat building here, which has recently been revived.

Annually, in late summer, a party of Nessmen depart for Sula Sgeir, a small rocky island 65km (40mi) to the northeast. They harvest 2,000 young Gannets or *gugas* in a traditional hunt.

Geo at the Butt of Lewis with Thrift

Arts and Music Centre Nearby, *Taigh Dhonnchaidh* (Duncan's House), at 44 Habost, is an arts and music centre committed to the promotion and enhancement of Gaelic language, music and the arts. The house was left to the Ness Historical Society by the late Duncan Morrison, who was a well known music teacher.

Butt of Lewis This headland, the most northerly point in the Western Isles, is a good place for seawatching. Gannets may often be seen fishing. During migration times many species may be seen on passage. Cetaceans, such as Minke, Killer, or Pilot Whales, and Risso's Dolphins may sometimes be observed. At every season, time of day or weather, the Butt always has a fresh aspect.

The lighthouse was first lit in 1862 and automated in 1998. Its 37m high red brick tower is in contrast to the rather forbidding local rocks. The lens installed in 1905 is still in use, although the lamps are now electric and powered by solar cells. A DGPS station is based here providing ships with extremely accurate position information. *"Guinness Book of Records"* says it is the windiest place on the coast of the United Kingdom.

Midsummer sunset at the Butt of Lewis

Butt of Lewis lighthouse with summer colours, from the east

Dun Eistean (NB535651) is on a large rock stack off Knockaird, northwest of the Port of Ness and has for long been associated with the Morrisons of Ness. There are several ruins, a perimeter wall and a water reservoir. The mound on the seaward side was probably a small Norse castle, later rebuilt and eventually deliberately slighted.

The Clan Morrison is said to be of Norse origin and descended from Olaf the Black who became King of Man and the Isles in 1226. They held the hereditary title of *Breive* (G *Breitheamh*, interpreter of the law) for many generations. Although Ness may seem remote today, it was readily accessible by sea. The influence of these *Breives* may have extended as far as the Mull of Kintyre.

The site was occupied during the 15th to 17th centuries, when clan warfare was rife. It was used intermittently as a defensive refuge and eventually captured by the MacLeods, who sacked it.

A footbridge now provides easy access. Nearby, in Habost, there is a large red boulder called the blood stone. Here the Morrisons are said to have smashed the heads of the Macauleys.

Roinn a' Roidh, the headland southwest of the Butt. Lochruban is on the far right.

Richard Jones

GREAT BERNERA (ON *Bjornoy*, Bjorn's Island) was the first of the small islands in the Western Isles to have a fixed link. This is by a pre-stressed concrete bridge, built in 1953. Lobster, crayfish and crab fishing as well as fish farming are the two main economic activities. Though small, the island has much to interest the visitor.

Just over the bridge and overlooking Sruth Earshader there are some monoliths standing sentinel over this narrow stretch of water. Two large stones and several smaller ones may have originally been part of a circle. There are lovely views over Loch Roag from here.

Standing stones overlooking Great Bernera bridge

Dun Baravat (NB156356) is a galleried dun dramatically situated on a small island on Loch Baravat and is signposted (about 1 mile north of the bridge). It is joined to the shore by a causeway about 30m long. Part is over 3m high and the remains of a scarcement still exists although the interior is confused by later buildings.

Breacleit The Local History Society has an exhibition and information about the island and its past in the Village Hall, which also has a cafe. The nearby island shop is also well worth a visit.

Bernera Riot In 1874 there was a riot on Bernera. When the sheriff-officer, Donald Munro, who was also the factor, attempted to serve writs of eviction on 56 households, he was pelted with sods and stones. Three crofters were arrested but found not guilty when tried. Munro was convicted of assaulting one of them whilst handcuffed and sacked from his several public offices. A memorial to these events stands north of Breacleit (NB153378).

Camas Bosta, (G, bay, ON *bolstadir*, farm) at the north end, is a beautiful sandy beach overlooking Little Bernera. Winter storms in 1992 exposed a number of structures which on excavation proved to date from the Iron Age to Norse times. Three of the houses date from the 6th to 8th centuries AD, and have the figure of eight layout typical of Pictish dwellings.

The dwellings had a large main room about 6m in diameter, a smaller one on the north side and the entrance to the south. They were built into the sand with double-skinned drystone walls. The circular shape would have resisted the pressure of the sand and also resulted in the very good structural preservation.

The houses were backfilled after excavation in 1996. The outline of three can be seen in the sand on the top of the beach. A replica has been built nearby which is based on one of the excavated structures. While it is not known what the actual roof would have looked like, the reconstruction gives a vivid impression of the amount of space available in such a dwelling. Overall the construction is not very different to later blackhouses, such as the one at Arnol.

A restored Norse type mill, resembles the one at Shawbost, lies near the coast east of Breacleit, (NB168372). Slightly further on is an interesting lobster pond on

Camas Bosta showing outlines of houses

Dun Baravat on Loch Baravat - typical galleried dun

a small inlet off Loch Risay (NB173373). This was built by local people in the mid-1800s to keep their catches alive. The lobsters could then be sold at the best time of year for prices and survival in transit. Then as now, demand was high in the festive season.

Kirkibost Pier is the fishing harbour. Great Bernera is not a very good island for agriculture, being quite rocky, but it has been well known for its lobster fishery since at least the 16th century. The waters of Loch Roag are shallow and sheltered, with many skerries, making ideal crustacean habitat. The harbour may not be the prettiest, but the lobsters are excellent.

Camas Bosta is the only sandy beach on Great Bernera

Interior of replica Iron Age house

Kirkibost Harbour

BOSTA WALK

This area is excellent for walking. A circular walk via Siaram Bosta, south along the coast, then back past Loch a' Sgail and the Shelaval (87m NB143391) offers lovely views. Although the terrain is rocky the walking is easy. Lichens and wild flowers abound.

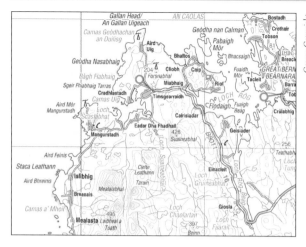

Crown Copyright

UIG (ON *Vik*, Bay) The B8011 to Uig crosses the *Abhainn Grimersta* where it enters Loch Roag. This river rises in Loch Langavat and is rated as one of the best Salmon rivers in Scotland. The road passes many small lochans which are covered with Water Lilies in summer.

Gisla has a small hydro electric power station which was operational in 1960. It generates 720kW and was for many years the only such plant in the Outer Hebrides. There are wild and spectacular views over Little Loch Roag and Loch Roag all along the B8011.

This is an area of great natural beauty with dramatic coastal scenery and a backdrop of mountains. The ever changing light, clean Atlantic air and proximity of the ocean all combine to impress the visitor, no matter what the season or weather.

Beaches The sandy beaches are especially varied and impressive. *Traigh na Berie* on the Valtos Peninsula is a long sweep of sand protected by the islands of Pabay Mor and Vacsay, while the beaches at Cliff and Mangersta are much more exposed to the Atlantic swell and can be very dramatic in stormy weather.

Broch Although Uig may seem isolated today, there is plenty of evidence for past occupation. The Iron Age broch at *Loch na Berie* (NB104352) may have been of similar proportions to Dun Carloway. It was preserved under windblown sand and accumulated peat. The first floor gallery is complete and clearly shows the characteristic building techniques used.

The waterlogged site resulted in good preservation of artefacts, but also means that it is hard to view the structure. It seems that the site may have been occupied up until the 9th century AD.

Traigh na Berie

Broch at Loch na Bertie

Uig Bay from Timsgarry with the mountains of Harris in the background

Dun Bharabhat (NB099354) is on a small loch nearby. It is built like a small broch, with galleried walls and internal stairs, but with a diameter of only 11m it was probably never very high. There are a series of Norse type mills on the burn leading down towards *Traigh na Berie*, and lovely panoramic views from the top of the hill.

Wheelhouses Several wheelhouses have been excavated in the Cnip area. These were built into the sand dunes and had radial "aisles" to support walls against the pressure of the sand. Though nothing is visible here to the visitor,

Glen Valtos is a glacial valley

there is a dilapidated example at Kilphedar on South Uist.

Vikings Several Viking Age burials have been found in the sand dunes above *Traigh na Berie* which are in close proximity to earlier Bronze Age graves. One female, who was in her late 30s, was buried in the 10th century. She was accompanied by a distinctive pair of oval brooches, a necklace of glass beads, a comb and iron tools including a small sickle. Another such burial was found in the early 20th century near *Bhaltos* school with a mixture of Celtic and Norse artefacts.

Glen Bhaltos runs from *Miavaig* to Timsgarry and was formed as a result of glacial meltwater scouring a path to the sea. The large deposits of sand and gravel at Carnish are also glacial. *Miavaig* (ON *Mjo Vik*, Narrow Bay), once the steamer harbour, is now home to a variety of small boats as well as the shore base for fish farms.

Carved wooden Lewis Chessman

has remotely controlled communications masts. The former administration block is now a small hotel, while many of the other buildings have been converted into houses.

Chapel On *An Bheannaich* (NB038379), a headland about 1km west of Aird Uig village, is a small ruined chapel called *Taigh a' Bheannaich* (G the Blessing Place). A track leads most of the way to this early Christian site.

Unusual croft sign

Aird Uig On the road towards *Aird Uig*, there is a panoramic view from *Fornaval*, which is accessible by road (205m, NB061359). On a clear day the Flannan Islands and even St Kilda may be visible from here. Gallan Head is the site of an old NATO radar station, built in 1954 and abandoned in 1963. The site still

Uig Sands The view over the wide expanse of the Uig Sands changes constantly as the tide ebbs and flows. Perhaps the best viewpoints are from Timsgarry and Crowlista (NB040336), from where the yellowish sands combined with the mountains in the background complement each

other to make a most satisfying scenic experience.

Dun There is a ruin, Dun Borranish, on a small rocky knoll at the northeast end of the bay (NB050333) which is cut off at high tide. The sands ebb dry but are covered at high water. The river from Loch *Suainaval* (ON Sweyn's Hill) winds around the northeast of the Bay.

Baile na Cille At *Baile na Cille* there is an ancient ruined chapel in the old graveyard (NB048339). The walls of an 18th century church make a sheltered garden for the adjacent, and welcoming, Baile na Cille Guest House.

ROTOR radar at Aird Uig in the 1950s

The Brahan Seer was born at Baile na Cille

Dun Borranish is at the northeast side of Uig Sands

Uig Bay from Timsgarry at low tide

The Brahan Seer Kenneth MacKenzie was born at Baile na Cille around 1600. Late one evening his mother was herding cattle near the old cemetery, when suddenly all the graves opened up. Spirits roamed about, but soon only one remained abroad.

Mrs MacKenzie bravely walked up to the grave and jammed it open with her distaff. Soon the last spirit returned. She was a princess from Norway who had been lost at sea and was so impressed by the woman's bravery that she told her to seek a particular blue stone from a nearby loch for her youngest son, Kenneth.

This gained MacKenzie the *second sight*; he could predict the future. He worked for the Seaforths at Brahan Estate in Easter Ross. Unfortunately Lady Seaforth took a great dislike to his predictions and had him burnt in a tar barrel at Chanonry Point. The blue stone he cast away, never to be found by mortal man again.

Uig Sands

Midsummer sunset over Uig Bay

THE LEWIS CHESSMEN In 1831 a large collection of exquisitely carved ivory chessmen was discovered buried in a small stone cist in the dunes on the south side of Uig Bay. The pieces date from the mid 12th century (Late Norse Period) and are carved from Walrus ivory.

They may have been carved in Norway and have belonged to a merchant. As with Norse silver hoards, their origin is enigmatic. Most are held by the British Museum and the National Museum in Edinburgh; some are on display in the Museum nan Eilean at Lews Castle in Stornoway.

Mangersta Beach faces the Atlantic and always has breakers even in calm weather

Ardroil is on the south side of Uig Sands. Here massive sand dunes are backed by a large area of machair. There is a nicely situated camping site. This is perhaps the best place from which to explore Uig Sands on foot.

Carnish has more spectacular beaches and saw some of the most ruthless clearances of the 19th century. The Seaforth MacKenzies and then James Matheson cleared large numbers of people from the land to create huge sheep farms. Most of the former inhabitants were shipped to Canada, where their descendants continue to thrive to this day.

Mangersta Sands are open to the Atlantic Ocean which never sleeps. Even on a calm day there are still breakers. The ancient dark rocks of the cliffs contrast with the greens and blues of the sea to create a beautiful but wild scene. *Aird Mor Mangersta* is an excellent viewpoint over this wild and dramatic coastline. The cove of Sheilavig is especially romantic.

The St Kilda Centre is planned for Geodha Sgoilt, above Mangersta Beach, with panoramic views to the Flannans and, on a clear day, St Kilda. "*It will be an outward-looking centre of worldwide significance, offering some-*

thing completely unique. It will be an iconic building in a spectacular landscape with state-of-the-art technology to bring the experience of St Kilda closer."

Brenish The townships of *Islivig* and *Brenish* are among the most remote on Lewis, but were never cleared. The highest hill on the island, *Mealsival* (574m) which can be climbed from Islivig. The line of tops to the south dominate the scene here. Golden Eagles nest in these hills.

At Brenish the remains of another Norse type mill are in the burn on the left, while there are ruins of a fishing station at *Camas a' Mhoil*. There

Sheilevig is an attractive cove south of Mangersta

Luckenbooth design at Mangersta

Mol Forsgeo at Mealista is exposed to the Atlantic Ocean - sometimes it is sandy and sometimes all pebbles

are also buildings and mast mountings from a major military presence here in WWII. A Chain Home radar station was installed here in 1942. The remnants include the power station, hut bases and concrete anchors for the mast support cables.

Mealista is at the end of the road south from Uig. *Mol Forsgeo* is a lovely sandy beach with rounded boulders, backed by machair. *Taigh nan Cailleachan Dubha* overlooks *Mol Forsgeo*. There was a medieval nunnery here as well as another ancient chapel and graveyard (NB990243).

Further to the south, there are more little beaches as well as a slip for launching boats.

Abhainn Dearg Distillery

Whisky production started at Carinish in 2008 in an old Salmon hatchery. None had been made on Lewis since the demolition of the Shoeburn Distillery in 1844. Although James Mathieson made his fortune selling opium he was a teetotal.

The distillery has small stills, each with a capacity of c.2,000l. Both single malt and newly distilled whisky are available to purchase. Maturation is in Bourbon American Oak casks.

Abhainn Dearg Distillery is based at Carinish

Abhainn Dearg Distillery

Abhainn Dearg Distillery

Abhainn Dearg Distillery

Mangersta viewpoint

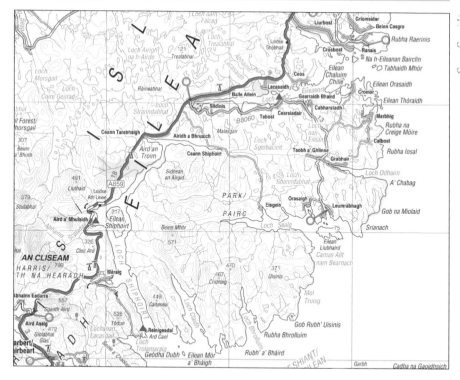

Loch Erisort

Loch Erisort The road south from Stornoway crosses the peat-covered Arnish Moor before reaching Loch Erisort. This long sea loch is only separated from Loch Seaforth by about 2 miles. There are strings of settlements along both shores, the biggest of which is Balallan

with its attractive white painted little Post Office and working crofts.

Pairc is a peninsula with only two miles of land separating Loch Erisort and Loch Seaforth. The old name for this area was *Durna* (ON *Deer Ness*, Deer Point). The B8060 meanders across the moor to Loch Sealg. The dramatic and remote scenery is well worth a visit, while scattered crofting communities provide a contrast to the otherwise rather barren landscape.

Eilean Chaluim Cille is a tidal island at the south entrance to Loch Erisort. It is also known as Oronsay (ON *Orfjara*, island joined to land at low water), and has an ancient chapel dedicated to St Columba (NB385210), *Eaglais Chaluim Chille*.

Dun Cromor is a ruined Iron Age galleried dun on an islet connected to the shore of Loch Cromor by a causeway (NB402207). The gallery is

Balallan Post Office

Dun Cromor is accessed from a submerged causeway

Deer Park Raid Memorial

clearly visible and the north part of the islet is enclosed by a wall. It can only be reached if the water level of the loch is low or by boat.

Loch Erisort from Balallan

Park Deer Raid A large cairn commemorating the Land Wars is situated south of Balallan. In late 1887 the Deer Park Raid was organised with much publicity by crofters and cottars from Lochs. A large number of deer were shot over two days.

The purpose was to draw attention to the plight of people being cleared from the land, in this case for the benefit of sport shooting. The military were called in and six of the men were tried in Edinburgh. They were acquitted, largely as a result of

their strong arguments for a better deal for crofters. The raid was a big success in terms of publicising the clearances and the situation of the people in the islands.

Wildlife The remote and isolated area of *Pairc*, particularly the large unpopulated area west and south of Eisgein is particularly noted for its

birds. Red-throated and Black-throated Diver, White-tailed Sea Eagle, Golden Eagle, Merlin, Golden Plover, Greenshank and Dunlin all breed here. The only access is by foot, but a visit here is well worth the effort and planning needed. The eagles and divers which are likely to be seen make this an essential birdwatching hike.

Loch Seaforth

Seilebost is perhaps the most beautiful of the many beaches

Isle of Harris · Na Hearadh

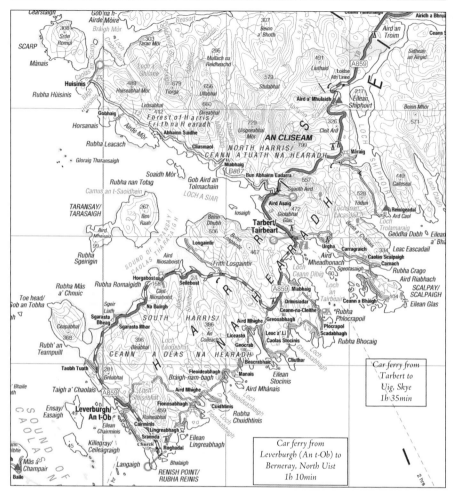

Harris (G *Na Hearadh*, from ON *Herad*, Parish) is divided from Lewis by Loch Resort on the west and Loch Seaforth on the east, with Loch Langavat in the middle.

Allt Thomnaval with Clisham in the background

The Harris Mountains complete the barrier between the two parts of the island. The split is said to date back to Norse times, but is probably much earlier. The topography of the north of Harris is mostly remote, wild and mountainous, ideal for hillwalkers, eagles and, at times, mist.

Loch Seaforth Approaching from Lewis, Loch Seaforth divides Lewis from Harris. As the road climbs the steep hill after Ardvourlie a fine panoramic view unfolds.

Clisham (ON *Klif Hamar*, Cliff Hill, 799m) and its sisters dominate the landscape. Often covered by mist, the mountains are both mysterious and majestic.

Rhenigidale (NB229018) is a remote township, accessible by road since 1989. Prior to then it was one of the most isolated settlements in the Western Isles, requiring a 3 mile walk over the moors from Urgha or Maraig to reach it. An excursion into this beautiful and untamed countryside is well worthwhile, as is a brisk stroll to the top of *Toddun* (528m NB210030) for spectacular views.

Bunavoneader Before Tarbert the B887 turns west, passing the whaling station at Bunavoneader, set up by a Norwegian company in the 1890s, to manufacture fertiliser. Leverhulme bought the facility in 1922 to make sausages for sale in Africa, however the enterprise was a failure and shut down after his death in 1925.

Bunavoneader and Abhainn Eadarra

The Harris mountains and West Loch Tarbert from Ardhasaig

Hydro-Electric power is now generated in a small scheme at Bunavoneader pioneered by the North Harris Trust and partners. A 100kW Francis turbine will produce c.371,000kWh annually.

West Loch Tarbert A narrow winding road continues westwards from Bunavoneader through wild and beautiful scenery with many spectacular views.

NORTH HARRIS EAGLE OBSERVATORY Take the track north from *Meavaig* (NB101063) for about 2km. About 20 pairs of Golden Eagles are resident on Harris. The track continues to Loch Vishimid through a remote and dramatic landscape. Further on, another track leads inland to a hydro power station and finally to the remote and deserted village of Kinlochresort.

Hushinish, West Loch Tarbert

NORTH HARRIS	
Amhuinnsuidhe	114
Bunavoneader	113
Clisham (799m)	113
Eilean Glas	115
Hushinish	114
Loch Seaforth	113
Rhenigidale	113
Scalpay	115
Scarp	114
Tarbert	114
Toddun (528m)	113
West Loch Tarbert	114

"MV Hebrides" at Tarbert

Amhuinnsuidhe Castle was built in 1868 by the Earl of Dunmore. Next to it is a dramatic waterfall up which Salmon leap as they return to spawn. The castle along with the 55,000 acre Amhuinnsuidhe Estate was bought for £4.5m by the North Harris Trust in 2003.

Hushinish, at the end of the road, has a fine sandy beach. Scarp (ON *Skarpr-oy*, Cliffy Isle) lies just offshore to the west. A track leads north from here to Cravadale (ON *Grafir*, ravine) where there is an old fishing lodge. The golden sands of Traigh Mheilen (ON *Miel*, Sand) face Scarp over the shallow and often turquoise Kyle of Scarp.

Rocket Post In July 1934 a German engineer, Gerhard

Zucher, tried to show that rockets might be used to deliver mail and other light supplies to isolated places. The missile exploded on landing near Hushinish and scattered its cargo widely. The unique *Western Isles Rocket Post* covers are much sought after by philatelists.

Tarbert (G *An Tairbeart*, isthmus) The main road continues through the mountains before descending to West Loch Tarbert and finally reaches the village of Tarbert which is the main ferry port. With its range of accommodation and services this makes a convenient base. Nestling in its sheltered position at the head of East Loch Tarbert, the village is the main settlement on Harris.

The characteristic bare rock glints in the sunshine, especially after rain. The steep streets and interesting shops are well worth exploring. The ferry *MV Hebrides* crosses to Uig on Skye and Lochmaddy on North Uist. She is 99m long, does 16.5kt, is 5,506GRT and carries 600 passengers and 90 cars.

Scalpay (ON *Skalpr-oy*, Ship Isle) has thrived in a way unusual in the Western Isles. In the 1840s about 40 families cleared from Harris and Pabbay settled here. Most of the *Scalpachs* are either fishermen or merchant seamen, but some of the crofts are still worked. The western bays are excellent harbours and neat houses cluster around the shores. Catches are mainly crustacea and scallops.

Tarbert Stores - a unique emporium

Caolas an Scarp from Hushinish slipway

West Loch Tarbert sunset from Ardhasaig

ISLE OF HARRIS DISTILLERY

"The concept for the distillery grew out of a realisation that the island's natural assets could best be harnessed to address its acute economic problems through a project that brings this special place and its qualities to the attention of a wider audience. "

Eilean Glas (G White Isle), on the east side of Scalpay, is the site of the oldest lighthouse in the Western Isles, first lit in 1789. The present one was built in 1824, and automated in 1978. There is a fine walk over the moor to it from Kennavay (NG230950) and panoramic views from Ben Scoravick (104m, NG237958).

Scalpay was connected to Harris in 1997 by a rather elegant steel bridge, which makes access much easier than in the past. The population of over 400 is proof that vigorous communities can survive in such apparently challenging environments. It bears comparison with Whalsay in Shetland.

Situated at the head of East Loch Tarbert in the centre of the village, the distillery opened in September 2015. It plans to produce 300,000 bottles of *The Hearach* malt whisky annually. A unique gin, flavoured with sugar kelp and other botanicals, is also being made using a small copper still, *The Dottach*.

The company raised £8.3m in equity from around the world and £3.1m in grants to fund the business. The first batch of *Na Hearach* is planned to be released in 2019, limited to 1916, the number of inhabitants of Harris. Their gin is already on sale.

"We want to make a 'Social Distillery', with the future of Harris at its heart, not only to enrich the island, creating an enterprise that will thrive for decades and even centuries to come, but to send the magical, elusive spirit of the island out into the world."

Malt whisky stills

The Dottach gin still

Scalpay bridge

Eilean Glas lighthouse, Scalpay

Crown Copyright

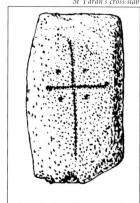

WEST HARRIS In contrast to the east coast, the west side of Harris has a fringe of beautiful golden sandy beaches interspersed by headlands. The road passes though a lunar like landscape before the large sandy expanse of Luskentyre opens up.

A series of stunning beaches, each seemingly more dramatic than the previous unfolds as the road winds around the coast. All are backed by dunes, machair and rocky hills. The names are as lovely as the beaches, Seilebost, Traigh Iar, Horgabost, Borve, Traigh Steinige and Scarista. The Harris beaches are spec-

tacular in all weathers and in all seasons. On a fine summer's day they are ideal for a family outing or a pleasant stroll. On a rough winter's day with large waves crashing in and clouds scudding they present an altogether different, yet equally satisfying aspect.

Broch The township of *Na Bhuirgh* (Borve) takes its name from Dun Bhuirgh (NG033940) overlooking the Sound of Taransay. This is a very good example of a placename transition from Old Norse through English to modern Gaelic orthography.

Taransay The attractive island of Taransay lies off the west side of Harris. Day trips run from Horgabost beach during the summer. The BBC series *Castaway 2000* was made on the island.

Taran may have been St Ternan, a 5th century Pict from Angus who was converted by St Ninian during his mission among the Picts. Ternan founded a Christian establishment or *banchor* at present day Banchory. He is often referred to as the *Bishop of the Picts*.

St Taran's Cross, now in the National Museum of

Traigh Seilebost faces the Sound of Taransay and Luskentyre

St Taran's cross slab

Traigh Iar, Horgabost

Scotland, was found at Paible. There are two ancient chapels near the landing (NG030992). One is dedicated to St Taran (where women were buried) and the other to St Keith, (where men were buried). The name *Clach na Teampall* (NG013008) suggests another chapel site but there are no ruins.

There are three duns, one near Paible on the coast (NG036996), another at *Corran Raah* (NB041005) and one on *Loch an Dun* (NB022013). The south-facing sands on *Loch na-h Uidhe* form one of the finest of all the Harris beaches.

Golf Course The 9 hole Isle of Harris Golf Club on the links at Scarista is in a dramatic and scenic location. It was established in 1939 and has been described as *"one of* the world's top hidden sporting gems"*. Visitors are welcome, but the course is closed on Sundays. It claims *"to be one of the world's finest settings for a game of golf."*

Traigh Steinige is small but perfect

Luskentyre has an immense area of beautiful beach backed by the Harris Mountains

WEST HARRIS	
Borve	116
Ceapabhal (365m)	118
Dun Borve	116
Leverburgh	119
Luskentyre	117
Northton	118
Rodel Church	122
Roineabhal (460m)	120
Scarista	119
Seilebost	116
Taransay	116
Traigh Iar	117
Traigh Steinige	117

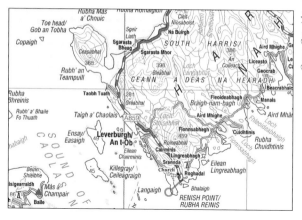

Northton At Northton (*Taobh Tuath*) there is a large area of tidal salt flats, sheltered from the west by Chapaval (365m) and Toe Head. This is one of the best places in the Western Isles to see waders, which breed on the machair and feed on the marsh. The road runs close to the sea at high tide.

Excavations in the machair on Toe Head have shown a sequence of occupation from Neolithic to Iron Age times. A wide range of artefacts including *Hebridean* and *Unstan Ware* pottery, *Beaker Ware* and Iron Age burials were found. Occupation periods range from before 3000BC to after 2000BC. In

particular, a large quantity of Bronze Age Beaker pottery was found during detailed excavations in the 1960s.

There is a ruined chapel at *Rubh' an Teampuill* (NF970913) which is said to have been built by Alasdair Crotach, who built Rodel Church, in the 16th century. It is worth continuing on to the top of Chapaval (365m) from where a panoramic view extends from St Kilda in the west (65km, 40mi) then over the Sound of Harris and on to North Uist and finally to Skye in the east (75km, 50mi).

Croft 36 is a highly innovative business based at Croft 36 in Northton. It is an outside catering and pie/bakery business. They specialise in local produce including Seafood, Rabbit, Mutton and Venison.

"We deliver ready to eat meals (pre-booked) to holiday homes, campervans and tents. Meals may also be collected from our shack, along with Patisserie style baking which includes Bread, Tarts, Quiche and Cakes, with some gluten-free or vegetarian. Hot Pies, Pastries and Soup available all day."

SEALLAM! VISITOR CENTRE has exhibitions on the history and natural environment of the Outer Hebrides. Co Leis Thu?, is a major genealogical resource based on the work of Bill and Chris Lawson. Anyone researching their Hebridean family tree should start here.

Northton (Taobh Tuath) saltmarsh

Traigh Scarista from Northton

Scarista House, *"We have stayed at Scarista House for the past 10 years and love it. Where do I start. The rooms are individual, with well chosen furniture,comfortable beds and lots of great books. This is a TV free zone and with the huge library and drawing room there is a chance to really escape. The food is always excellent. I have never had anything but the most elegantly presented large portions. The sea food is especially good. The owners are what makes this place special. They are accommodating and helpful with real attention to detail."*

Traigh Scarista extends for over 2km. The pristine sands are backed by dunes, machair and marshland. In summer breeding birds, wild flowers and bumblebees make this a fine location for naturalists. This is a place where variations in the landscape due to weather, time and season are truly apparent.

An t-Ob (Leverburgh) South of Northton the single track A869 follows Glen Coishletter, a narrow, rocky valley, to Leverburgh. The village of *An t-Ob* (ON *Hjop*, bay) was a tiny harbour until Leverhulme decided to develop a major fishing port here. Having abandoned the excellent harbour of Stornoway, work started in 1920 to develop a new pier and facilities to handle landings from up to 50 trawlers.

The plan was to supply the national chain of 400 *Mac Fisheries* fish shops and by 1924 the project was ready to start processing catches. However Leverhulme died of pneumonia in 1925 and the project was cancelled with losses of at least £0.5million. The Board of Lever Brothers decided that the project was no longer viable due to the postwar economic recession. Work stopped immediately and the South Harris Estate was sold for only £900.

William Hesketh Lever was Liberal MP for Wirral. In 1907 he promoted a private member's bill to increase income tax to provide a state pension for the elderly. The

Leverburgh RNLI Lifeboat

Car ferry and boats at An t-Ob or Leverburgh

Traigh Scarista with Ceapabhal (365m)

Old Age Pension Act was passed in 1908. Mac Fisheries was sold in the late 1970s, and had proved a sound investment for Lever Brothers.

Today *An t-Ob* is again a thriving village. The start of a car ferry service from here to North Uist in 1996 was the catalyst for much new development. Several creel boats operate out of here catching prawns, crabs and lobsters.

Viewpoint A side road turns inland near the school. It crosses wild and rocky terrain, passing several lochs on the way, as it winds around the north flanks of Roineabhal (ON *Hraun fjall*, Rough Hill) to Ardvey. The summit (460m, NG403861) offers a superb panoramic view after a hard slog over rough ground from Lingerabay. A track leads part of the way to a quarry.

Rodel (ON *Raudha Dalr*, Red Dale) with its impressive church and tidal harbour lies at the southern tip of Harris. Once the main port on the

Traigh Iar

Isle of Harris Golf Club

Traigh Iar light on water

Ant-Ob (Leverburgh)

island, the inner part is tidal, but visiting yachts often moor in the outer basin. There is a ledge at the entrance so access is dependent on tide.

Rodel House was built in 1781 for Alexander MacLeod who had recently bought Harris. He had made a fortune as the captain of an East Indiaman. His plan was to develop fishing on the island, but this was to fail on his death in 1790.

In the early 1800s there were about 150 habitations in Rodel but MacLeod's son had them cleared to make a farm for himself. Eventually the house became a shooting and fishing hotel, which is now refurbished. Small fishing boats still work from the harbour.

A walk to Renish Point gives a similar view to that enjoyed by the artist William Daniell nearly 100 years ago. Rodel is a beautiful place where there is a sense that time has stopped. There are beautiful panoramic views of the Sound of Harris from Renish Point.

Rodel from Renish Point in 1815 by William Daniell

St Clement's Church, Rodel

ST CLEMENT'S CHURCH

at Rodel (NG467832) is a splendid 16th century church which stands out as it is the only medieval building of any size to survive intact in the Western Isles. It was built on a rocky knoll overlooking Loch Rodel by Alasdair *Crotach* (humpback) MacLeod, of Harris and Dunvegan, who died about 1547.

The church was established in the 1520s and was probably complete by the 1540s. It is about 25m long with a 30m tower at the west end and

is built of local gneiss. The sandstone detailing is said to come from Carsaig on Mull. The tower is decorated with a corbelled string course half way up with sculpted panels on each wall face.

On the north is a bull's head, the centrepiece of the Clan MacLeod crest. On the west side there is a figure, who may represent St Clement, with a bull's head at his feet, and on the east a woman who is exposing her genitals and holding a child. This type of decoration is called *Sheela na*

gig and was common on early Irish churches. It may be that the charms of the *Sheela na gigs* were intended to distract the evil so that the faithful could carry on with their devotions free from Earthly temptation. The west wall panel depicts two males, one in a kilt, and the other in jerkin and hose in a suggestive pose.

Restored in 1784, and again in 1787, after being damaged by fire, the church was last renovated by the Dunmores in 1873. It is now maintained by Historic Scotland. The building is approximately 20m by 5m inside with arched entrances to the transepts, the north being decorated with schist, the south with sandstone. On the south wall of the nave is the tomb of William MacLeod, son of Alasdair *Crotach*, who died in 1551. This tomb was badly damaged by a fire in 1786, but the date 1539 can still be seen.

The tomb of Alasdair *Crotach* is said to be one of the best such sculptured tombs to sur-

Interior with Alasdair Crotach MacLeod's tomb on left

Detail with bishops and hunting scene

vive in Scotland. Nine carved panels are arranged between an upper moulding and the recessed arch which encloses the tomb. The centre panel represents Christ on a cross, while the other panels depict the apostles.

The recess under the arch has three rows of panels of which the top three are angels. The centre five have the Virgin and Child in the centre with panels showing bishops on either side. To the left is a castle and to the right a galley under sail. The bottom panel is a hunting scene where Satan and Michael weigh the souls of the departed. The inscription reads *"This tomb was prepared by Lord Alexander, son of William MacLeod, Lord of Dunvegan in the year of our Lord 1528".*

The north transept has a selection of graveslabs which used to cover burials in the floor. They date from the 16th and 17th centuries. A stairway leads from the nave into the tower, the top of which can then be reached by another stair and ladders. A window looks west across the Sound of Harris.

Interior from north transept

16th and 17th century graveslabs to various MacLeods

Man in jerkin and hose

Man in kilt

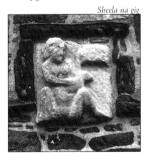
Sheela na gig

EAST HARRIS South from Tarbert the east coast road, or *Golden Road* passes through The Bays, a wild and inhospitable coast where the ancient rocks are mostly bare. This area only became inhabited when the fertile west side of Harris was cleared for sheep farming in the 1800s.

The townships have interesting names, being derived from Norse and Gaelic. They include Lickisto (*Liceasto*), Geocrab (*Geòcrab*), Flodabay (*Fleòideabhagh*), Ardvay (*Àird Mhighe*), Manish (*Mànais*), Finsbay (*Fionnsbhagh*) and Lingarabay (*Lingreabhagh*). Formerly, they were only accessible by sea or by tracks.

Golden Road In 1897 a road was built to join all these settlements up with Rodel, which was dubbed the *Golden Road* on account of its cost. It winds tortuously along the coast through wild rocky country. There are fine views across the Minch to Skye and beyond.

The Golden Road makes a most picturesque drive. It can be approached from the north by turning left off the A859 about 3km south of Tarbert, or from the south from Rodel. In either case leave plenty of time to admire the views along this slow, narrow road.

Feannagan The people had to scratch a living from potatoes and oats that they grew on lazybeds or *feannagan* which can be seen everywhere along this coast. These are long narrow beds of soil which have been laboriously built up using manure, domestic compost and seaweed as well as what turf is available. They are remarkably fertile, but very labour-intensive.

Geology Although mostly composed of gneiss, dykes of softer volcanic rock run across Harris which date from the same time as much of Skye. Further south the landscape becomes even more bare, with exposures of red Feldspar, particularly so at Lingerabay. Gleaming white Anorthosite is exposed on the upper flanks of Roineabhal (460m), the large hill which dominates the south end of Harris.

Cottage at Manish

Sheep at Manish - dawn in midsummer

Harris Tweed Museum

Harris Tweed Museum

Marion Campbell spinning

Harris Tweed Company

Marion Campbell at her loom

Weaver at work on his loom

HARRIS TWEED is still produced in the traditional way by a small company at Procropool. The weaver can be seen at work on his hand loom. The Harris Tweed and Knitwear Shop stocks tweed and knitwear.

Harris Tweed Exhibition Centre in the old Drinishader Primary School, behind the shop, *"has a unique display of old and new pictures, artefacts and present day designer productions, whilst mannequins display designer tweed outfits that graced the catwalks of the world. You can also see a demonstration of weaving and view a small exhibition of Marion Campbell's tweed and weaving items."*

Marion Campbell BEM (1909-1996) was an icon of Harris Tweed. Her own sheep provided the wool, which she dyed and spun herself. She used an old fashioned loom which yielded a uniquely high quality tweed. She worked as a weaver for over 70 years and became a legend. Hundreds of people used to visit her shed every year to see her at work, the author included.

GOLDEN ROAD SOME GOOD VIEWPOINTS	
Flodabay	124
Lickisto	124
Lingarabay	124
Loch Geocrab	124
Loch Grosbay	124
Loch Stockinish	124
Manish	124
Procropool	124
Roineabhal (460m)	120

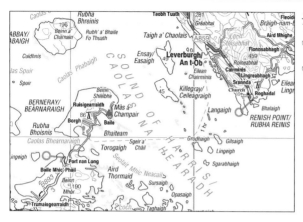

THE SOUND OF HARRIS lies between the south of Harris and North Uist. This stretch of water is strewn with rocks, skerries and sandbanks. The roro ferry was introduced in 1996 and has been a great success. It takes a tortuous, yet fascinating, route from Leverburgh (*An t-Ob*) to the north end of the Berneray causeway. *MV Loch Portain* uses a jet drive system to allow

it to navigate the very shallow passage.

It follows a complex buoyed course between the skerries and affords one of the best birdwatching trips in the Western Isles. Good views may be had of many species all year round. In spring and summer numerous seabirds breed here. Gannets often follow the boat and can be

seen plunge diving. Terns, Cormorants and Eider Ducks often pass close by. Flights of auks and Manx Shearwaters commute on the way from here to there. Grey and Common Seals haul out on the skerries, and Bottlenose Dolphins are sometimes also seen.

Birdwatching is equally good in the winter months. Long-tailed Ducks, Great Northern Divers, Velvet Scoters and the occasional Iceland or Glaucous Gull all may be seen.

Tidal streams in the Sound of Harris are complex, and vary between springs and neaps, day and night, and summer and winter. Together with all the other hazards, this makes the Sound quite a challenge for the yachtsman. The main channels are clearly marked

Gannet

Eider Duck

Arctic Terns

Sound of Harris from the east with Rodel and Roineabhal on the right

Sound of Harris from Beinn an Toib, Carinish

with buoys, beacons and posts, but great care must be taken.

There are magnificent views across the Sound of Harris from Beinn an Toib (103m), the hill southeast of the Harris ferry terminal. From Berneray the best panoramic viewpoint is from Beinn Shleibhe (93m) at the north end of the island.

MV "Loch Portain" leaving An t-Ob (Leverburgh)

Great Northern Diver

Long-tailed Ducks

Berneray from the ferry

SOUND OF HARRIS

BIRDS TO SEE, SUMMER

Arctic Tern
Cormorant
Eider Duck
Gannet
Guillemot
Manx Shearwater
Razorbill
Red-Breasted Merganser

BIRDS TO SEE, WINTER

Great Northern Diver
Long-Tailed Duck
Velvet Scoter

MAMMALS TO SEE

Common Seal
Grey Seal
Otter
Dolphins

Pobull Fhinn stone circle, with Loch Langass and Eaval in the background

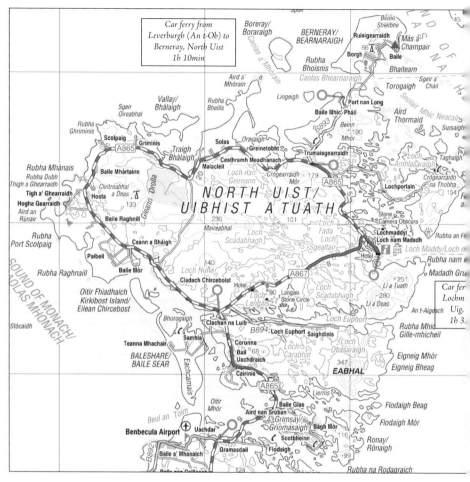

UIST, the *Vist* or *Ivist* of the Norse Sagas, may seem to derive from ON *Vestr*, west, but the name is probably much more ancient. Originally, the term applied to North Uist, Benbecula and South Uist together.

NORTH UIST is an island of contrasts. The east is dominated by the three hills of North Lee (ON *Hlith*, slope 250m), South Lee (281m) and Eaval (ON *Oy Fjall*, Island Hill, 347m), whose distinctive conical shape features in so many views. It is also a maze of lochs and inlets from the sea, of which there are at least 120. Some are fresh water and some are brackish. Lochs cover about a third of the island. Trout and Salmon fishing is excellent here.

The north and west coasts are fringed by magnificent sandy beaches backed by extensive machair, apart from the low cliffs at Griminish in the northwest. The centre of the island is mostly peatbog and lochs.

The island is separated from Benbecula by *Oitir Mhor* (G Big Sandbank), the North Ford, over which a causeway was built in 1960. The main car ferry arrives at Lochmaddy from Uig in Skye, but there is also a ferry from Leverburgh on Harris which arrives at the north end of the causeway to Berneray.

Lochmaddy from North Lee

Lochmaddy The village of Lochmaddy (G *Loch nam Madach*, Loch of the Dogs) takes its name from the two small islands at the entrance to the sea loch, *Madadh Beag* and *Madadh Mor* (G the Little Dog and the Big Dog). In former times it was known as *Chearsabhagh* or Kersivag (ON *Keris Vagr*, Keri's Bay).

Lochmaddy is situated in an excellent natural harbour which was used by fishermen and pirates long before the fine, but slightly incongruous, buildings of the 19th century were built. During the Herring Boom it was one of the main ports, along with Stornoway and Castlebay, for the landing and processing of catches in the Outer Hebrides.

North & South Lee The bay is peppered with small islands and skerries, and is said to have a coastline of about 70km (43mi). The view from the top of the North Lee is magnificent. From South Lee the view encompasses Loch Eport and Eaval. The walk in over the moor between all the lochs is quite arduous but worth the effort. The two hills can be more easily reached by small boat from Lochmaddy.

Madadh Beag, north side of entrance

Madadh Mor, south side of entrance

Lochmaddy old harbour, with North and South Lee in the background

NORTH UIST	
Baleshare	142
Balranald RSPB Reserve	138
Berneray	134
Bharpa Carinish	142
Bharpa Langass	140
Carinish	142
Clach Mor a' Che	138
Cleitreabhal (133m)	137
Committee Road	139
Cronaval	141
Dun Sticir	133
Dun Torchuill	133
Eaval (347m)	130
Greinetobht	136
Grimsay	143
Lochmaddy	131
North & South Lee	131
North Ford	130
Oitir Mhor	130
Pobull Fhinn	140
Sollas	136
Taigh Chearsabhagh	132
Teampull na Trionaid	142
Udal	136
Unival (140m)	139
Vallay	136

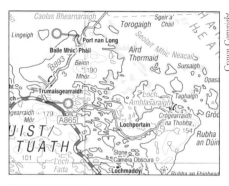

Crown Copyright

Dun Torchuill on Loch an Duin

Taigh Chearsabhagh

The oldest building in the village, *Taigh Chearsabhagh* (G House, ON *Keris Vagr*, Keri's Bay), was built in 1741 as an inn and was one of the first buildings on the island with a slated roof. It is now an inspiring local history museum and arts centre, with a cafe, a shop selling local books and crafts as well as the Post Office. *"Inspired by the unique island location there is a vibrant and stimulating exhibition and outreach programme going on throughout the year at Taigh Chearsabhagh."* Regular exhibitions are held in the gallery by local and other artists. Works by visitors include a number of sculpture installations in the vicinity.

On 15 September 1943 a USAAF B24 Liberator crashed on the North Lee with the loss of all 8 crew. A memorial and some debris are all that remains to remind us of this sad incident, one of many such wartime crashes.

There is an interesting waymarked walk around Lochmaddy village area which circumnavigates Loch Houram and also takes in sev-eral impressive 19th century buildings on the way, including the Old Court House (1827), New Court House (1875) , Bank House (1877) and other historical sites.

Otters The many small islands, lagoons and inlets here are an ideal habitat for Otters. They are often seen early and late in the day hunting for fish and eels in the ebb. The vicinity of the pier is a

Dun Torchuill on Loch an Duin

Dun Sticir, Port nan Long

Dun Sticir, Port nan Long

Loch Blashaval, west of Lochmaddy, with North Lee and South Lee in the background

good place to start looking for these elusive creatures.

North Route The A865 runs northwest from Lochmaddy, passing through a striking landscape which is dotted with countless lochs as well as by many sites of interest.

Archaeology North Uist has many archaeological sites, ranging from the Neolithic Age to Medieval times. Few are signposted, and many of the most interesting were back-filled after excavation. Luckily there are several monuments which are easily accessible and visually impressive. The Ordnance Survey map shows many duns, standing stones souterrains and chambered cairns. The challenge in finding these piles of stones is at least half the fun.

Dun Torchuill Near the turn off for *Bagh a Chaise*, *Dun Torchuill* (NF8897398) is perhaps the best preserved broch on the island. It is typical of the many such structures sited on small islands on lochs and accessible by man made causeways. Although most of these sites date from the Iron Age and some were occupied until Medieval times, others date from the Neolithic period.

Dun Sticir The B893 leads to Port na Long (Newtonferry) and the Berneray causeway. *Dun Sticir* (NF897777) is an example of a broch which was in use until Medieval times. It is built on a prominent islet on *Loch an Sticir*. The impressive causeway is about 3m wide, while the broch is 18m in diameter. There is a later rectangular building within the structure, possibly 16th century.

Taigh Chearsabhagh installation

IN MEMORY OF

THE DECEASED AIRMEN WITH THE
U.S. ARMY 8th AIR FORCE WHOSE
B-24 LIBERATOR CRASHED HERE
15 SEPTEMBER 1943

RALPH J. FISCHER   CLARENCE L. BALZER
EDWIN N. BUSCH   JACK E. WALLACE
MARTIN E. SALWAY, JR.   ELLSWORTH F. COLBURN
PRICE H. LAMBERT   WALTER A. MOORE
FREDERICK G. ZIEGENBUSCH CLYDE W. PLOG

AND THOSE PEOPLE OF LOCHMADDY
WHO GAVE KIND AND CARING ASSISITANCE

... thy rod and thy staff,
they comfort me... Psalms 23

WWII Liberator memorial

Sheep on saltmarsh, Port nan Long

Loch an Sticir, Port nan Long

Traigh Iar (West Beach) on the west coast of Berneray is over 4km long

Berneray (ON *Bjornaroy*, Bjorn's Island) lies to the north of North Uist in the Sound of Harris. It was traditionally called *Beàrnaraigh na Hearadh*, as it was part of Harris rather than North Uist. Now joined by a causeway opened by the Prince of Wales in 1999, it has a mostly rocky east side. In contrast, the west coast is a sandy beach over 4km long, backed by a wide expanse of dunes and machair. This can be reached along a road through Borve to a carpark on the machair.

There are several interesting monuments including the isolated standing stone, *A' Clach Mhor* (NF913807), with the remains of a ruined chapel nearby. Remains of blackhouses are prominent near the cemetery at the south end. The Gunnery is a 16th century fortified building and the birthplace of Sir Norman MacLeod, a noted scholar. The roofless Telford church at the north end dates from 1827. It has two doors, one for the Berneray folk and the other for the Pabbay worshippers.

Machair Berneray has a large area of machair which covers the whole of the west side of the island from the dunes to the low hills of the east. It is a riot of colour in summer, with

Loch Bhrusda from Ruisgearraidh

Harris from the north of Berneray

The Gunnery, Baile

Sandy beach, dunes and machair at the northeast corner of the island with Mas a' Champair in the background

a profusion of wild flowers. Many species of waders breed here as well as the occasional elusive Corncrake.

Mute Swans and Greylag Geese are present all year, while Barnacle and Brent Geese overwinter. Loch Bhuirgh is near the north end of the causeway. It is tidal and is a good place to observe waders, especially during the spring and autumn migration times. A track which goes from Borve to the graveyard passes close to the shore.

There are expansive views across the Sound of Harris from the north end. Loch Bhrusda is good for wildfowl and waders. Divers and sea-

Berneray Harbour is always full of small fishing boats

duck as well as Otters and seals may be seen from the causeway or around the rocky east bays.

Crofting and fishing are the main activities here, and the little harbour has a colourful array of boats. Berneray is famous for its fine pota-

toes and in former times large quantities were exported to Harris. The harbour was built in 1988 to shelter the fishing fleet, which catches mostly shellfish. The main settlement is around Loch a Bhaigh and at Borve, where there is a shop and tearoom.

Ferry MV "Loch Portain" at Berneray ferry terminal

A' Clach Mhor, Borve

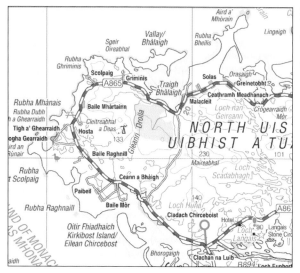

with fertile machair, plentiful seaweed, sea for fishing and transport all make it attractive.

Sollas suffered some of the most ruthless clearances of the 19th century due to the actions of MacDonald of Sleat in Skye. In 1849, 603 people were forced off the land. During this clearance a riot ensued during which Glasgow policemen were pelted with stones by the women. The brave yet shameless constables then set upon the women with their truncheons.

West Route The coast of North Uist from *Greinetobht* (G *Grein*, sunny, ON *Tofta*, homestead) to Clachan is a long series of sandy bays backed by dunes and machair. Only the northwest corner around Scolpaig has a rocky coast. Even here there are several sheltered sandy coves.

The machair and beaches at *Greinetobht* (NF825751) are especially beautiful, and it is worthwhile to take the walk out to *Aird a' Mhorain* (NF832792) where there is

an ancient cemetery. There are lovely views towards Boreray and Berneray from the long sand spit of *Corran Aird a' Mhorain*.

The Udal is on the west side of the headland (NF822781). This area has been extensively excavated as the headland was occupied from Neolithic to post Norse times. Although there is little to see above ground, it is easy to see why the site was so favourable for settlement. The sheltered situation behind the dunes,

Sollas Golf Course is a 9 hole links course on the North West of North Uist over-looking the Atlantic. *"It was built and maintained by local volunteers in the summer of 2001. The course is on the machair used by the local crofters who have given permission to use the land to play golf. In the winter, cows and sheep graze here so it is not unusual to have to play around them, and other obstacles they leave behind."*

Vallay This tidal island (ON *Vadill*, ford) was home

Renovated blackhouse at Sollas overlooking Traigh Bhalaigh

Corran Aird a' Mhorain looking towards Boreray

to the antiquarian, Erskine Beveridge, who lived in Vallay House in the early 20th century. The house is now derelict and the island uninhabited. Beveridge did much archaeological work in the area. The island is well worth a visit, but it is essential to check the tide times.

Traigh Udal. Aid a' Mhorain, looking southwest

Neolithic Sites Excavations at *Eilean Domhnuill* (G Donald's Isle) on Loch Olavat (NF746754) showed that the site was of Neolithic Age, and rebuilt on several occasions. The houses were rectangular with central hearths. A huge amount of pottery sherds were found, including plain bowls, *Hebridean Ware* and *Unstan Ware*. The former tend to be tall bowls or jars, while the latter are shallow, round, open bowls. Both have characteristic patterns of decoration.

Eilean an Tighe (G Isle of the House) on *Loch nan Geireann* is not connected by a stone causeway but excav-

ation revealed a very similar sequence to that at *Eilean Domhnuill*. The site has been interpreted as a Neolithic pottery workshop due to the quantity and quality of the ceramics found there.

There is a 19th century folly on Loch Scolpaig (NF731750), a tower built on top of a dun. Nearby, an ancient cross from *Cille Pheadar* grave yard has been somewhat incongruously used atop a Victorian memorial (NF726744) which overlooks *Baile Mhartainn*.

Cleitreabhal (ON *Klettr Fjall*, Rocky Hill, 133m,

NF749717) offers panoramic views and the summit can be reached by a road which starts near Tigharry. Nearby there is a chambered long cairn with an Iron Age wheelhouse built into its west end. Originally

Norse era cross at Cille Pheadar

19th century folly on Loch Scolpaig

Corncrake

BALRANALD RSPB RESERVE covers 640ha and includes beaches, dunes, machair, marsh and lochs as well as a visitor centre (NF718698). Many birds, especially waders and waterfowl, breed in or visit this area on migration due to varied habitat and suitable feeding grounds. In 2010 there were 40 pairs of Corncrakes here. This is also one of the best places to see and hear the Corn Bunting. The 3 mile walk around the Reserve takes at least 2 hours, but in practice can take much longer when detained by birds, flora and insects. In summer the machair is a sea of colourful wildflowers which attract many butterflies and bumblebees.

RSPB

the cairn was about 30m long with an imposing facade at the east end. Just down the slope is a standing stone and another ruinous chambered cairn.

On a clear day there are very fine views from this hill, sometimes extending as far as St Kilda nearly 70km (41mi)

distant. The whole west side of the Uists can be seen from this fine viewpoint.

Aird an Runair (NF688705) lies just north of the RSPB Reserve, and is a prime sea-watching site in spring and summer when the wind is onshore. Many birds on passage north or south use this headland as a waypoint on their flyways. The nearby beaches of Traigh Iar and Traigh nam Faoghailean are attractive to waders and often good places to observe migrants.

Clach Mor a' Che North of *Claddach Kirkibost*, at *Claddach a Chaolais* overlooking Kirkibost Island, the 2.6m high monolith of

Iron Age roundhouse within a Neolithic chambered cairn on Cleitreabhal

Neolithic chambered cairn on Cleitreabhal

Clach Mor a' Che (G Great Stone of the World) stands by the shore. Nearby there is a large but ruinous chambered cairn, *Dun Na Carnaich* (NF768663), with several orthostats still upstanding.

Claddach Kirkibost Centre
The Centre is in a renovated school and has a cafe which serves delicious food, with lovely views to the west. A small shop sells homemade jams, chutneys and oatcakes. It holds regular demonstrations of traditional activities as well as various cultural events. Childcare facilities and wifi internet access are also available.

Unival (ON *Hakonar Fjall*, Hakon's Hill, 140m, NF802673) offers panoramic views over the flat vista of sea, sand and shore to the west and south with lochs and hills to the east, all dominated by the sky. On the south-west side there is a chambered cairn, *Leatach an Tigh Chloiche* (NF800669). Several of the kerb stones remain standing, but most of the cairn has been robbed out. There is a dun on nearby Loch Huna.

Dun na Carnaich at Claddach a' Chaolais is a Neolithic chambered cairn

Committee Road This road leads across the moors from north of Claddach Kirkibost to Malacleit. It was built to provide work during the potato blight famine of the 1840s. There are several cairns and standing stones on the slopes above the road, while *Maireabhal* (ON *Mara Fjall*, Mare's Hill, NF808700, 230m) is another excellent vantage point. There are also good views over North Uist from the road itself.

Hebridean Smokehouse
"Peat Smoked Salmon stands out as the real thing, beautiful quality smoked salmon that tastes as good as it looks. All of their seafood is sourced from the pristine waters of the Outer Hebrides, with the salmon and sea trout uniquely of local origin.

Everything is prepared by hand before smoking with locally cut island peat to impart an unforgettably aromatic flavour. The fish is then hand sliced. Hebridean Smokehouse is a small family run company with a history of fish smoking on North Uist going back over 30 years, and we aspire to make the best smoked products available anywhere."

Clach Mor a' Che

Blackface lambs posing beside drying peats

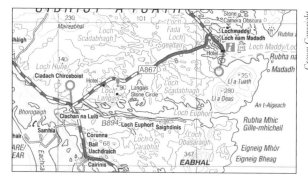

much to interest the angler, birdwatcher or archaeologist. All of the moorland birds of the Uists may be seen here. Divers breed on the lochs, while the Langass plantation (NF845655) is good for passerines and migrants. Raptors such as the Golden Eagle, Peregrine and Short-eared Owl quarter the moors, while Greenshank and other waders haunt the shorelines.

Cronaval Two chambered cairns also lie on the near-

BHARPA LANGASS (G Heap of Stones; ON *Langa Ass*, Long Rocky Ridge) is the best preserved Neolithic chambered cairn in the Outer Hebrides. It lies on the western slope of *Beinn Langass* (90m, NF838658), near a signposted carpark. Built of Lewisian Gneiss, it is 24m in diameter by 4.5m high. Some kerb stones remain on the north side.

This impressive cairn encloses a chamber which is intact and may be entered with care. The passage is nearly 4m long and slopes downwards into the oval chamber which is about 3m by 2m wide and 2m high. The chamber is constructed with massive monoliths, each of which must weigh several tonnes, with drystone walling filling in the spaces.

Beaker pottery sherds, a flint arrowhead and some cremated bones were found here in 1911. These probably are a Bronze Age deposition. There is a wonderful panoramic view across the moors and lochs to the hills in the west.

East Route The A867 road south from Lochmaddy to Clachan crosses an area of moorland and lochs with

Bharpa Langass Neolithic chambered cairn

Bharpa Langass Neolithic chambered cairn - chamber

Bharpa Langass Neolithic chambered cairn - passage

by slopes of Cronaval. One may be a Clyde type cairn (NF833627). A number of uprights remain among the heather, but no entrance passage seems to exist. Cronaval North (NF832630) is a ruined round cairn. Nearby there is another big robbed out cairn with a large chamber, close to *Loch Glen na Feannag*.

The area around Loch Langass and Loch Euport is dotted with signs of prehistor-

Pobull Fhinn stone circle, Loch Langass and Eaval

ic habitation. There is another more dilapidated stone circle 500m south of the B894 (NF829630).

Pobull Fhinn stone circle, Loch Langass and Eaval

View west from Bharpa Langass

North and South Lee from Beinn Langass

POBULL FHINN, (G *Fionn Gall*), Fingals People, meaning Norsemen or fair outsiders) stone setting (NF843650) is well preserved. It is situated near Langass Lodge on the south side of Ben Langass, about 1km east of Bharpa Langass.

The setting is oval, about 37m by 30m, and built on a levelled platform. It may originally have comprised 24 stones, the tallest being about 2.5m high. There are several fallen monoliths and one stands inside the main group. The site has a dramatic outlook over the watery landscape of Loch Langass and Loch Euphort with North Lee, South Lee and Eaval behind.

Fionn mac Cumhaill was a mythical Gaelic hero also known as Fingal or Finn. There is another stone circle to the south of the loch, *Sornach Coir' Fhinn* (G Fireplace of Finn's Cauldron, NF828630) off the B894, overlooking *Loch a Phobaill*. According to legend it was here that he and his band cooked the deer that they had hunted.

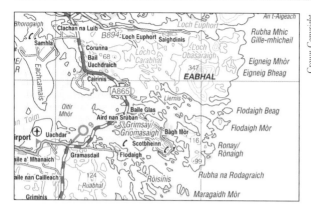

In a good example of 20th century progress, road widening virtually destroyed the once fine stone circle south-east of Carinish (NF833603). In 1915 there were 15 upright stones, but now there are just a few scattered remnants in the heather.

Bharpa Carinish The nearby Neolithic chambered cairn of *Bharpa Carinish* (NF837603) to an extent compensates for this official vandalism. At 50m long, 21m wide and 2m high and enclosing a chamber at least 6m long the cairn must have been very imposing.

Eaval There is a fine walk over the moors from the end of the *Claddach Chairinis* road to the summit of Eaval (ON *Ey Fjall*, Island Hill, 347m NF899606). The route passes inlets, lochs shielings and

Baleshare (G *Baile Sear*, East Township) is so called because *Baile Iar*, to the west, was lost to the sea in a great storm in the 17th century. A causeway built in 1962 joins the island to North Uist. This area of dunes backed by machair is another good place for birdwatching. The tidal pools and mudflats of *Traigh Eachcamais* are especially good for waders and waterfowl.

Teampall na Trionaid (G Temple of the Trinity, NF813607) at Carinish is said to have been founded by Somerled's daughter about 1200AD, and rebuilt by Amie MacRuari, whose son Ranald was the progenitor of Clan Ranald, about 1350. It was an important seat of learning in medieval times. The 13th century scholar, *Duns Scotus*, may have been educated here.

BATTLE OF CARINISH

In 1601 the Battle of Carinish took place here, and is still commemorated by the Ditch of Blood (G *Feith na Fala*). About 40 MacLeods from Skye had come to lay waste to North Uist and steal cattle.

They were taking breakfast in the precincts of the *Teampall*, when a much smaller group of MacDonalds attacked with swords, bows and arrows. After a fierce fight, the MacLeods were subdued. Only two escaped alive to their boats which had been left at Loch Euphort.

Teampall na Trionaid, Carinish

Bharpa Carinish chambered cairn with Eaval in the background

The North Ford from Benbecula looking towards Grimsay and North Uist, with Eaval in the background

the small *Dun an t' Siamain* (NF886595) before ascending to the summit cairn with its very impressive views. For a shorter route to the summit take a boat to Bagh Moraig.

Grimsay (ON *Grims-oy*, Grim's Isle) is joined to North Uist and Benbecula by the North Ford causeway which was opened in 1960 by the Queen Mother. Before this time the crossing could be hazardous due to quicksands, or by getting caught out by a rapidly rising tide. This picturesque small island has a circular road with many nice vistas across the fords.

Bagh Mor is particularly attractive, with views to Eaval and Ronay. The modern harbour at Kallin is the base for the many small fishing boats which operate in the area, which catch mostly lobster, crab, prawns and scallops. The Grimsay Boatshed Trust is a traditional boat building and repair business. It teaches and encourages boat building skills, for which Grimsay was once famous.

Archaeology At the eastern end of Grimsay the ruined *Teampall Naomh Mhichel* (G St Michael's Chapel, NF882548) is where the bodies of seamen carried ashore by the tide were traditionally buried. There is a partially rebuilt Iron Age wheelhouse on the northeast side between Loch Hornary and Bagh nam Feadag (NF864577).

Oitir Mhor and Benbecula from Grimsay

Thatched cottage at Claddach Chairinis

Fishermen cleaning their boat on Grimsay

BENBECULA (G *Beinn na Faoghla*, the Hill of the Fords) lies between the two Uists and is largely flat but dominated by the low hill of Rueval (124m) from which there is an excellent view of the island and the Fords.

The island is studded with many lochs. The west side has extensive sandy beaches with a wide machair plain, while the east coast is mostly rugged and backed by moorland. In WWII an airfield was established at Balivanich (G *Baile a Mhanaich*, Monkstown) which continues to be used

by the military as part of their Missile Testing Range, as well as by civilian traffic. Construction of a single track concrete bridge to South Uist was started in 1938 and completed in 1942, to facilitate the import of supplies during WWII. It was upgraded to the present causeway in 1983.

Archaeology There is much of archaeological interest on the island. At Gramisdale, near the North Ford, there are several standing stones (NF825562 and NF825553). The northern site has one upright and nine fallen

monoliths, while there is one upright and two fallen stones at the southern one. The remains of two chambered cairns lie north of *Loch nan Clachan* (NF813527).

Of several duns, *Dun Buidhe* (NF793547) near Balivanich is the most impressive. It is joined via *Eilean Dubh* to the shore by substantial causeways. The site was reoccupied in late medieval times.

A Pictish symbol stone, now in the National Museum, was found around 1869 on the shore at low tide near some ruins at *Strome Shunnamual*. This granite slab is incised with two symbols, a comb box, decorated with spirals and a disc with three smaller discs within, perhaps representing the Holy Trinity. The only other such stone so far found in the Western Isles was on Pabbay, south of Barra.

The only wheelhouse so far known on Benbecula is now

Gramisdale standing stones with Eaval in the background

Beach below Balivanich Airport

under one of the runways of the airport, and to date no Pictish or Norse domestic site has come to light, making the carved stone even more enigmatic.

Chapels Little remains of the monastery at Balivanich. The lichen-covered remains of an ancient chapel, *Teampall Chaluim Cille*, dedicated to St Columba (NF783549), and its associated well, *Tobar Chaluim Cille*, lie on the south east side of the village.

The old chapel at Nunton (NF768538) may date from

Ancient chapel at Nunton

Teampall Chaluim Cille, Balivanich

The west coast of Benbecula has lovely sandy beaches, South Uist is in the background

the 14th century. There was a nunnery in this area, *Baile nan Cailleach* (G Nun's Town), but this declined after the Reformation. The stones were said to be used for Clanranald's new house and farm buildings in the 1700s. Nunton Steadings has been renovated.

Borve Castle (NF773506) is said to have been built by Amie MacRuari in the 14th century and it was the Clanranald base for many years until Ormiclate Castle was built on South Uist. Little now remains of this once imposing building or of the nearby *Teampall Bhuirgh*. The name *Borve* suggests that

there may have been a ruined broch here in Norse times.

Nature For birdwatchers the west coast beaches, machair and lochs are good places to view waders, wildfowl, and gulls. Culla Bay and *Poll na Crann* or Stinky Bay, so called because of the smell of rotting seaweed which often pervades the beach, are especially attractive to waders in migration times. The drain from *Oban Liniclate* (NF785498) and the lochs nearby are particularly good for migrants.

The machair behind the dunes on the west side of Benbecula has an abundance of wild flowers in summer. This is partly due to low intensity grazing by cattle in winter. Several rare species of bumblebees thrive here.

Rossinish The east side of the island is rugged and remote. The track which leads to Rueval from the Market Stance (NF806537) goes on to the remote but beautiful Rossinish peninsula. The sandy beaches backed

Borve Castle was built by Amie MacRuari in the 1300s

Peter's Port was built in the 1890s but did not prove to be a good harbour

by machair and dunes on the north side of this headland (NF873538) are unusual for their east coast situation. Otters frequent these beautiful and unspoilt shorelines which, although only a few miles from habitations, give a feeling of isolation. Bonnie Prince Charlie was hidden for some time here in 1746.

Peter's Port The lack of a deep water harbour on Benbecula meant that goods were landed at Loch Skipport in South Uist and transshipped by small boat. In the 1890s the Congested District Board built a pier at Peter's Port on the south east extremity of the island. This typical example of official folly initially had no road to it. The approach is hazardous for large vessels and thus. Today small creel boats and recreational craft still utilise it.

In the 20th century the presence of the military has done much to boost the economy of the island. Today Benbecula is the centre of administration for the Uists and Barra. There is a large Community School at Liniclate. This incorporates a theatre, swimming pool, library, running track, fitness suite and a cafeteria.

MacGillivrays in Balivanich is particularly to be noted for its superlative selection of books on Hebridean and Scottish subjects. They also stock Harris Tweed, knitwear and many other interesting things.

Cattle grazing on machair fields at Borve

Benbecula farm on the west side

Benbecula Golf Course *"is naturally flat, which is popular with visiting golfers seeking a game in slightly different surroundings. It is maintained by the members and has a short back and sides more regularly than any other course! There are a number of testing holes to discover that will require great judgement and club selection and some natural hazards such as rabbit scrapes to add to the* fun of the game! Although only a 9 hole course, there are 18 tees in operation, so rounds are anything but repetitive.

Situated beside Benbecula Airport, the golf course is minutes away from Balivanich, the social and administrative centre for the Uists. Visitors can experience incredible views of the Monach Isles and Atlantic Ocean."

Wild flowers on the machair near Nunton

Boeing B17 Flying Fortress off South Uist

WORLD WAR II After all the social changes and upheavals of the previous 200 years, the mid 20th century saw much development, due to wartime necessity. During the 1930s Balivanich was one of the grass strips used by the De Havilland *Rapides* of Scottish Airways for the first regular air services to the islands. With war looming it was clear that air bases would be needed as far west as possible for anti-submarine and convoy protection work.

The runways were built by laying bitumen directly over sand which had been compacted. The resulting slightly flexible surface was not ideal, but was usable by the aircraft of the era due to their relatively low ground pressure.

Work on the South Ford road link actually began in 1938, while construction of the airfield started in 1940, and it became operational in August 1941. Although there was some local concern about the possible loss of traditional Gaelic culture due to the influx, the RAF personnel were made very welcome.

In late June 1942, 206 Squadron became operational on anti-submarine duties, with *Hudsons* which were soon replaced with B17 *Flying Fortresses*. These heavily armed long range aircraft achieved considerable success, sinking at least 12 U-boats. More importantly they forced the submarines to remain submerged in the area to avoid detection, thus denying them some freedom of action.

220 Squadron, with *B17s*, arrived in March 1943, both were reassigned to the Azores

Boeing B17 over Benbecula

Imperial War Museum

RAF Benbecula in 1941

South Ford causeway looking south from the Benbecula end

that October. *Swordfish* of 838 and 842 Fleet Air Arm Squadrons were deployed on short range patrols in August 1944. In September 1944 *Wellingtons* of 179 and 304 (Polish) Squadrons arrived but despite intensive patrols they failed to find a single submarine. Finally, 36 Squadron, also of *Wellingtons*, was based here until June 1945.

Today Balivanich remains a military airfield but is shared by civilian airlines. These provide daily flights to Glasgow, Stornoway and Barra. The airfield also serves the Missile Testing Range on South Uist. The continued presence of associated personnel and their dependents provides work and is a boost to the local economy.

Until the building of the causeways, Benbecula was isolated at high tide and during storm surges. The crossings could be dangerous on a rising tide, in the fog, or in the dark, and were never suitable for road vehicles. In fact the first outside direct links were by air, due to the lack of a suitable harbour.

The Fords are excellent places to see waterfowl and waders. In particular the south side of the South Ford is a favourite roost for waders at high tide. The road along the north west shore of South Uist at Iochdar and the eastern shore of Gualan tend to be particularly good. Care should be taken not to obstruct traffic on the causeways themselves.

There are spectacular views over the Fords from many locations. Perhaps the best are from the north end of Benbecula (NF825565)

Otters crossing sign at South Ford

and from the layby south of Creagorry (NF803479). Depending on the location, season, weather and time of day there are almost limitless combinations of land, water, sand and sky for the artist or photographer to interpret. The Fords can be dangerous on foot , so take care!

South Ford and causeway with the hills of South Uist in the background

Our Lady of the Isles on Rueval, South Uist

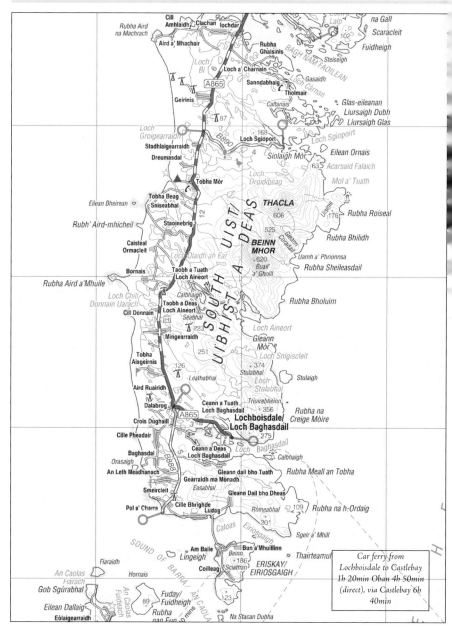

SOUTH UIST (*Uibhist a Deas*), the largest of the Uists, is another island of contrasts. The east side is mountainous with a rocky coast which is indented by several large sea lochs and faces the deep waters of the Minch. The Atlantic side has an almost continuous sandy beach with dunes and machair land behind, giving way in turn to peaty moorland. The whole west side of the island is dotted with innumerable lochs and lochans, many of which drain to the east.

Archaeology There are many sites of archaeological and historical interest on South Uist. These include Neolithic tombs and settlement sites as well as Bronze Age houses and graves. There are Iron Age duns and wheelhouses, Viking houses, Medieval chapels as well as ruined castles and big houses. While some are signposted, most are not and many are in a state of disrepair or neglect.

Drimore from Our Lady of The Isles on Rueval

Loch Bee, looking southeast towards Hecla and Ben Mhor

The east coast of South Uist from the sea, with Ushenish, Ben Mhor and Hecla

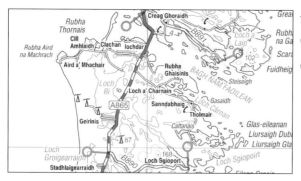

North End The north end is dominated by Loch Bee, a large, shallow loch which is open to the sea at high tide, and thus slightly brackish. There is a large resident population of Mute Swans, many of which are non breeding. The outlet to the sea at Clachan (NF770465) is a particularly good place for waders and wildfowl.

Our Lady of the Isles on Rueval

North Bay (NF748459), Ardivachar Point and nearby *Loch an t-Saile* are all good places to look for migrants. Greenland White-fronted Geese sometimes winter here. The nearby shop and workshop of Hebridean Jewellery at Iochar is well worth a visit.

Along the Iochar road a number of traditional thatched houses lie in various stages of decay. Some are now being renovated, but most are steadily reverting to nature. This whole area is low lying and prone to inundation during storm surges.

Loch Carnan is the first of several long indentations in the east coast of South Uist. A diesel power station is now

only used as a standby in case of problems with the undersea cable which supplies electricity from the Scottish mainland.

Our Lady of the Isles, by Huw Lorimer (NF777408), was erected in 1957 to guard the island against any ill effects from the nearby Royal Artillery base. There is a marvellous view from here across the machair plain to the west coast and to the Atlantic Ocean beyond.

South Uist Missile Range was set up in 1957 to test tactical nuclear missiles as well as air to air and ground to air weapons. More recently pilotless drones have been operated from here, including the first to cross the Atlantic.

The Range is operated by Qinetiq on behalf of the MoD and clients such as BAe Systems. It is based at RAF Benbecula with radars on Rueval and St Kilda. Entry to the launching area is prohibited when red flags are flying. The long term future of the Range remains in doubt.

Summer sunset from Loch Carnan

Sheep at Iochdar

Mute Swans at Iochdar

Loch Skipport has a dilapidated pier from the Herring boom times. This is a good point from which to explore part of the remote and wild east coast. The summit of Hecla (606m) is a hard 8km (5mi) return tramp. The imposing northern cliffs can be avoided by skirting to the east then southwest.

The isolated headland of Ushenish, is nearly 8km (5mi). The lighthouse here was first lit in 1857, and was automated in 1970. There is a track from the landing place at Mol a' Tuath. The complete circuit is over 32km (20mi), much of it hard going over boggy ground.

LOCH DRUIDIBEG

This National Nature Reserve encompasses most of the habitats of South Uist, stretching from the Atlantic coast almost to Loch Skipport in the east. During the breeding season part of the reserve is closed, but otherwise visitors have free access. There is a self-guided walk through part of the area. The Reserve is an important breeding site for Greylag Geese, which are resident here. There is a good example of a dun on the south side of the loch (NF778371).

COIRE HELLISDALE

The beautiful glacial valleys of Glen Ushenish, Glen Corrodale and Glen Hellisdale are well worth the effort of the long walk in. In particular the 260m high sheer craigs of Coire Hellisdale (ON *Hellis Dale*, Cave Valley) on the north-east face of *Beinn Mhor* (620m) are spectacular, especially early on a summer's morning.

Bonnie Prince Charlie spent some weeks in 1746 hidden near Glen Corrodale. *Uamh a Prionnsa* (Prince's Cave) is reputed to be one of his hiding places. Regardless of such stories this part of South Uist has a feeling of grandeur and remoteness which will more than repay the effort of reaching it.

Loch Druidibeg

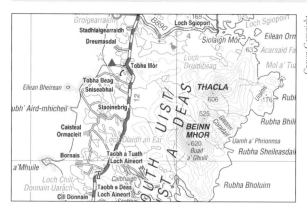

tower and the site may have been in use by Clanranald until the 17th century.

Flora MacDonald, who helped with the escape of Bonnie Prince Charlie from the Western Isles, was born at Milton in 1722, the daughter of the local tacksman. There is a commemorative cairn on the site of the house at Milton which is said to be her birthplace (NF742269).

Ormiclate Castle (NF740318) was built for Ailean, chief of Clanranald in 1701. It was burnt down in 1715, due to a kitchen fire, the day after its owner was killed at the abortive battle of Sherriffmuir. The gaunt ruin was never rebuilt, but its still standing gables attest to the quality of its construction, if not the success of its occupant.

Loch Einort almost splits South Uist in two, and indeed many of the machair lochs drain eastwards into it. At *Airidh nam Ban* (G Shieling of Women), there was once a nunnery, and later there was an inn here. This is a good departure point for exploring the surrounding hills.

Allt Bhogalair (NF800290) is a small river running off Beinn Mhor, in whose lower valley a small but very impressive native woodland persists. The steep sided ravine protects the rich flora from being grazed. Although mostly composed of Birch and Hazel, there is

Stoneybridge There is a tall standing stone (NF770321) nearly 3m high above Stoneybridge, which can be reached by road leading to a water pumping station, from where there is a panoramic view of the west side of the island. This is a good starting point to start for climbing Beinn Mhor, Beinn Corradail and Hecla.

Duns Nearby, Dun Altabrug (NF769344) is quite well preserved and may be reached by its causeway from the loch shore. Other dun sites include *Dun Uiselan* (NF777454), at the north end, and *Dun Mor* (NF776415), north of Rueval. *Caisteal Bheagram* (NF761371) on Loch an Eilean, near Howmore is a small dilapidated tower with several small windows which may be 14th century. There are ruined longhouses around the

Staneybridge standing stone

Dun Altabrug is on an islet in a loch which is joined to the shore by a causeway

an amazing diversity of plants here.

This interesting site can be reached from the end of the road which runs along the north side of Loch Eynort. A path runs across the moor for most of the way. The best times to visit this spectacular and remote haven are from May to August.

Caisteal Beagram on Loch an Eilean

Clanranald stone, Howmore

Howmore Church was built in 1858 and has a central communion table

One of the chapels at Howmore

Memorial to Flora MacDonald at her possible birthplace near Milton

HOWMORE CHAPELS

There are ruins of two chapels and two churches, at Howmore. The oldest may be 13th century, although there may have been a much earlier Christian settlement here. *Teampall Mor* (St Mary's) is 20m by 8m. The east gable with two windows survives. The smaller one is dedicated to St Columba.

The chapels are much smaller, with inwardly inclined door jambs and steep gables reminiscent of early Irish practice. A third was destroyed about 1866. An Clanranald armorial stone from here is now in the Kildonan Museum. It disappeared in 1990, but was found in London in 1995.

Rubha Ardvule is the most westerly point in the Outer Hebrides, and is an excellent place from which to watch birds on passage during migration times. The headland is rocky with shingle beaches. Long sandy beaches, backed by machair stretch for miles north and south.

Dun Vulan (NF714297) is on the south side of the peninsula leading to Rubha Ardvule and was partially excavated during the 1990s as it was being steadily eroded by the sea. A sea wall has been built to protect the site.

The original broch was built directly on sand and partially collapsed soon after construction. The bottom 4m of the tower has been preserved under the shingle of a storm beach. Excavation revealed the first floor, the lintelled entry passage, collapsed stairs and internal wall galleries.

Detailed studies of the extensive midden have produced much interesting information about the life style of the people who lived here in the first centuries AD. To the south two rectangular structures and a roundhouse were found under the midden.

Around 400AD, a Pictish house with three cellular rooms was built within the broch. Evidence for late Bronze Age occupation was also found, suggesting that the site was occupied for a very long time.

There is much evidence of ancient habitations on the machair in this area. It seems to have been the main centre of population until late Norse times, when the people moved inland to the blacklands, the fertile area between the machair and the peatbogs.

Norse Church On the west side of Upper Loch Kildonan (NF732283) there is a series of interesting ruins. These comprise of a large and impressive 12th century Norse church with a semi-circular apse at its east end and associated domestic buildings. There are also remains of several rectangular buildings on the nearby Eilean Mor, which is connected to the shore by a now submerged causeway.

There are strong similarities between this site and

12th century Norse church at Upper Loch Kildonan

Iron Age broch and outbuildings at Dun Vulan, Ruadh Ardvule

Finlaggan on Islay, the base of the Lord of the Isles in the 12th century. Kildonan may have been an important Viking settlement and Eilean Mor could be the *Tingwall* or Norse parliament of the Uists. The church also resembles the design of St Peters Church on the Brough of Birsay in Orkney, which may be contemporary.

Norse settlement Although a Viking Age settlement was found at Udal on North Uist, and a single house at Drimore on South Uist, typically Norse-style rectangular houses have until recently been notably absent from Western Isles discoveries. Recently, nine Viking houses have been excavated near *Trollaskeir* (ON *Trollr sker*, Troll's Skerry NF724275),

Looking south from Rubha Ardvule towards Barra

which date from the 11th century or earlier.

Neolithic Age Of the several Neolithic chambered cairns on South Uist, the most spectacular is on the north side of Reineval (NF755259). This well preserved tomb overlooks the fertile coastal plain and lochs of Milton and Frobost. It is about 21m in diameter and 4m high with large kerbstones still in place. Entrance orthostats remain on the south-east side and the chamber may still be intact.

KILDONAN CENTRE This heritage and cultural facility includes a museum, craft shop, cafe and an archaeology room. There is also a *Feis* room for musical events. T*aigh Tasgaidh Chill Donnain* was originally an old school which has been renovated and extended.

Margaret Fay Shaw The museum has a room dedicated to Margaret Fay Shaw (1903-2004), an American of Scottish descent, who spent her life collecting folksongs, folklore and Gaelic heritage on Barra and South Uist.

In 1935 she married John Lorne Campbell. They bought Canna in 1938 and went on to develop the foremost Gaelic library in Scotland in Canna House. She was buried in Hallan cemetery in December 2004. Her famous work *"Folksongs and Folklore of South Uist"* was first published in 1955 and is still in print.

Norse houses at Trollaskeir, Bornish

Reineval, a Neolithic chambered cairn overlooking Daliburgh

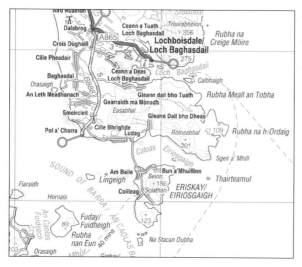

The road to Lochboisdale was built in the 1840s during the potato famine, just in time to assist in the forced emigration of over 1,000 people to Canada. During the Herring Boom of the late 1800s and early 1900s the port's convenient location and sheltered harbour made it important for the landing and processing of the Silver Darlings.

Several small fishing boats still work from here today, landing large quantities of shellfish, including crabs, lobsters, prawns and scallops. Roro services started here with the arrival of *MV Iona* in 1974. Nowadays the large Calmac ferry *MV Clansman* runs a triangular route from here to Castlebay on Barra and Oban.

Lochboisdale (*Loch Baghasdail*, ON *Kastel Vagr*, Bay of the Castle) takes its name from a ruined castle on Calvay, the small island which guards the entrance to Loch Boisdale. The castle may date from late Norse times. Its substantial walls are nearly 2m thick. The ruins include a small tower, with foundations, all of which are reminiscent of similar structures in Caithness and Orkney.

Viewpoints Departing from outside the school, the 8km return walk to the top of *Triuirebheinn* (357m), the hill to the northeast of the village, is well worthwhile for the panoramic view. A shorter but steep climb leads to the summit of *Beinn Ruigh Choinnich* (280m), the hill which dominates the village. There are wonderful views over Lochboisdale from here.

Sunset over Lochboisdale from the ferry

White Water Lilies grow on many of the lochs here

Lochboisdale from North Glendale

Lochboisdale from the south with Beinn Ruigh Choinnich (280m) in the background

Another easily reached viewpoint is the summit of *Aisgerbheinn* (NF755237, 126m), which can be accessed via a track opposite the road to the golf course. There is a dramatic view over the loch-strewn area of Daliburgh and the machair plain from here.

Chambered cairn The cairn at *Loch a Bharp* (NF777215), off the road to Lochboisdale is well preserved, no doubt because of its remote position. Situated at the northwest end of the loch, this site is well worth a visit, but beware the bog, burns and lochs on the way. It is about 26m in diameter and 6m high. Most of the kerb stones are still in place, and the corbelled roof of the chamber is undamaged.

Lochboisdale in the 1880s during the Herring fishing boom

Askernish Golf Course This 18 hole golf course on the machair was first opened in 1891. Although on flat machair, it has been described as *"second to none in the various elements which go to make up a really good course"*, having laid out originally by Old Tom Morris. In 1922 Askernish Farm was given over to croft-ing and the course was par-tially abandoned.

It has now been fully restored to its original state using trad-itional design. Environmental experts have already hailed the Askernish as *"the most natural links course in the world: the dunes' natural contours form the fairways, no artificial chem-icals are used in maintenance, and during winter months sheep and cattle graze the course!"*

Lochboisdale Harbour

Lobster boats hauled out at Lochboisdale

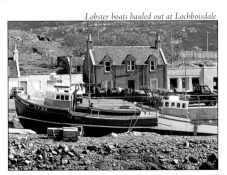

South Uist and Eriskay from the ferry to Castlebay on Barra

Kilphedar Near Kilphedar (G Peter's Chapel, NF733203) an aisled wheelhouse was excavated in the 1950s on the machair. Built into the sand, its circular stone wall is nearly 9m in diameter, with 11 drystone radial piers each with a space or aisle separating it from the outer wall. The central hearth can still be discerned, while the entrance passage runs in from the east.

An enamelled bronze brooch dating from about 150AD was found here, which may be of Roman origin. This is the only such excavated wheelhouse in the Western Isles which has not been backfilled, but it is in a sad state of neglect. The house was in excellent condition when cleared out, but without a roof is rapidly deteriorating.

Norse Settlement A large Norse settlement was partially excavated near *Sithean Biorach* (G Fairy Hillock, NF730199). Five longhouses, with outbuildings and middens were investigated. The site dates from the late 10th to the mid 13th century and revealed a wealth of artefacts. These include bone and copper pins, silver coins and broken Steatite pots. Burnt grain, animal bones and other detritus from the middens and house floors has revealed much about life at the time.

Chapels Two chapel names, *Cille Pheadar* (St Peter), which is said to be between the shore and *Loch Liana Moire*, and *Cille Bhrighde* (Kilbride) in the old burial ground at the south end, recall early Christian activity.

Cladh Hallan, the cemetery near Loch Hallan

Weaver's Castle, a pirate's haunt on Eilean Leathan, off the south end of Eriskay
Remains of an excavated Iron Age aisled house at Kilphedar

(NF734219), has a 16th century carved grave slab, perhaps originally from Howmore, or more likely associated with the ruined church on this site. It is typical of many such monuments in the Hebrides and may well have been carved by monks on Mull. The coastal location of the cemetery is common in the isles.

Pollochar overlooks the Sound of Barra, and an isolated monolith, which may have been moved, stands sentinel here on the shore (NF745144). This was perhaps a seamark to the western approaches to the Sound of Barra, which needs careful navigation to avoid its many skerries and sandbanks. The picturesque southern shore road leads to Ludag,

The beach at Kilphedar with mist rolling in from the sea

and then *Bagh Mor* with its expansive sandy beach and dunes. The public road ends at South Glendale, but a track leads across the moor to North Glendale and the south side of Lochboisdale.

The extensive lochs, streams and sea inlets of most of South Uist remain unpollut-

ed. Activities such as fish farming and agriculture are limited in scope and intensity. This means that angling for Salmon, Brown and Sea Trout remains excellent on the island. The same conditions are of course also beneficial to wildlife in general.

16th century grave slab at Hallan

Pollochar beach facing west towards the Atlantic

Standing stone at Pollochar, with Barra in the background

ERISKAY (ON *Eriks-oy*, Eric's Island) is a delightful small island on the north side of the Sound of Barra, and now joined to South Uist, near Ludag, by a causeway. Fishing is the main occupation here and boats are moored at *Haun* (ON *Havn*, Haven) and *Acairseid Mhor* (G Big Harbour).

Bonnie Prince Charlie made landfall here in summer 1745 from the French ship *Le Dutillet*, on the beach on the west side which is still called *Coilleag a' Prionnsa* (G The Prince's Cocklestrand). He then proceeded to Arisaig on the Mainland after evading an HM frigate.

The island is colourful with wild flowers in summer, especially where the sheep cannot reach. Eriskay ponies also graze some of the land and this helps enrich the flora. These ponies are said to descend from the native Scottish ponies and may be similar to those used by the Picts and Scots in battles.

Haun The church at Haun was built by Father Allan MacDonald, in the late 19th century. He was also a noted Gaelic poet and scholar. The altar is formed from part of a lifeboat lost off *HMS Hermes* in WWII and washed ashore. The bell is off the WWI German battlecruiser, *SMS Derfflinger*, scuttled in Scapa Flow in 1919.

There are pleasing views over the Sound of Eriskay and South Uist from *Beinn Scrien* (185m) and over the Sound of Barra from *Beinn Stac* (122m). Most of the houses are near the harbour at Haun, as is the pub *Am Politician*, which is easily recognised by its Harrison Line flag.

The famous "Eriskay Love Lilt" and other traditional songs and folklore were recorded in the early 20th century by Marjory Kennedy-Fraser and others. These promoted the island and helped preserve much oral memory in print.

The roro ferry terminal at *Coilleag a' Prionnsa* provides a car ferry connection with Barra. It operates every day including Sunday.

The causeway from Eriskay to Ludag was opened in 2001

Ciolleag a' Prionnsa and the ferry terminal to Barra

Memorial to Bonnie Prince Charlie

WHISKY GALORE On 5th February 1941 the 8,000GRT Harrison Line ship *SS Politician* accidentally hit a submerged rock off the east side of Eriskay. She was carrying general cargo to the USA including about 21,000 cases of malt whisky. Given wartime shortages and the slow response of the authorities, this was like *"Manna from Heaven"* to the islanders.

The "SS Politician", which went aground off Eriskay in 1941

"NEVER IN THE HISTORY OF HUMAN DRINKING WAS SO MUCH DRUNK SO FREELY, BY SO FEW"

With apologies to Winston Churchill

The ship was beached in shallow water and much of the cargo salvaged. The islanders "liberated" a large proportion of the whisky, hiding it in all manner of places on Barra, Eriskay and South Uist. Fishing boats from he east coast were also said "to have replenished their stores".

The Customs & Excise men did finally arrive. Several people were arrested and convicted, though without the co-operation of the local police. The film *Whisky Galore*, based on the book by Compton MacKenzie, then living on Barra, was released by Ealing Studios in 1949. It used Barra for much of the location work, and remains

a favourite comedy over 50 years later. It was directed by Alexander MacKendrick, and was Ealing's most profitable film.

The remains of the wreck can still be made out at low tide on a sandbank near Calvay Island. Several bottles were recovered during the laying of the electric cable from South

Uist by divers. Samples of *"Polly bottles"* as they are referred to can be seen at the pub along with newspaper articles and other memorabilia. Genuine articles have *"No Resale Without Federal Approval "moulded into the bottle. It is rumoured that samples still come to light even today during house renovations or clearances.

"Whisky Galore" poster

An Am Politician "Polly bottle"

SMS Derfflinger bell

Altar in St Michael's of the Sea from WWII aircraft carrier"HMS Hermes"

Kisimul Castle, Castlebay, Barra

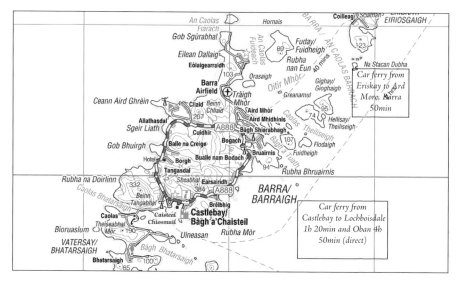

Barra (G *Barraigh*, possibly from ON *Barr-oy*, Broch Island, but more likely after the 6th century Irish follower of Columba, Finbar, St Barr). This beautiful little island encompasses the best of the Outer Hebrides, and is often referred to as the *Hebrides in Miniature*. There is a wealth of archaeology, history and wildlife, as well as a thriving Gaelic culture.

Castlebay (G *Bagh a' Chaisteil*) The harbour at Castlebay, the main settlement, is one of the best in the Outer Hebrides,

and is unique in retaining its castle. It was used as a base by Vikings and their descendants for many years. Trading, fishing, piracy and interclan warfare were all activities carried out from here.

The harbour was very busy during the Herring Boom of the late 19th and early 20th centuries. In 1869 James Methuen, an east coast fish merchant, started using the harbour as a landing and processing station for Herring.

Up to 400 boats fished out

of Castlebay during the short season, and over 2,000 people arrived to cope with the gutting, salting and packing into barrels. Fishing is still a major part of the Barra economy, and several boats work out of Castlebay. The larger vessels are based at Northbay, where the Barratlantic fish processing factory is situated. Most landings are exported fresh in large chiller trucks direct to the markets.

Today Castlebay is a lively little village, with a comprehensive range of facilities

Castlebay with "MV Clansman" at the pier

Our Lady of the Sea with Castlebay and the Bishop's Isles from Heaval

and services, including a community school complete with swimming pool. The *Feis Bharraigh* takes place for a week each summer, during which visitors and *Bharrachs* participate in the many musical and cultural events which are held.

Dualchas, (G Heritage) Barra Heritage and Cultural Centre, is next to the school. It has interesting displays, old photographs and genealogical information as well as a shop and cafe. It is *"a fascinating insight into the island's past."*

The Street, Castlebay

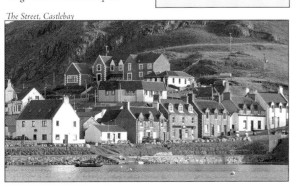

HEAVAL (ON *Hvit Fjall*, White Hill; part could also be ON Haff, Ocean, 383m), is the highest hill on Barra and dominates Castlebay. The Virgin and Child, sculpted from Carrara marble, *Our Lady of the Sea*, was erected in 1954. The ascent is a stiff, but rewarding, climb from an old quarry about 1mi northeast of the village. On a clear day all of the Bishop's Isles are spread out to the south and mainland Scotland stretches along the eastern horizon.

Kisimul Castle from the pier on a calm midsummer evening

Kisimul Castle (ON *Kastali Holmr*, Castle Holm) probably dates back to Norse times, but the existing structure is no earlier than 15th century. The first mention of Barra in the sagas is when Onund Tree-foot is said to have arrived with five ships in around 871AD and driven away the local chief, Kiarval. He then used Barra, no doubt Castlebay, as his winter base.

A few years later, Onund lost a leg at the sea battle of Hafsfjordr in c.874 whilst fighting on the losing side against King Harald Fairhair. In summer he and his men went on Viking cruises and overwintered on Barra. By the 890s, or before, he had settled in Iceland with other people from Barra and the Hebrides, including his neighbour, Aud the Deepminded.

Being on a small island, but with a very convenient fresh water spring, the site is ideal for defence, and was probably fortified long before the Vikings arrived. It may very well have been the site of a large Iron Age broch. It is claimed that Kisimul was the stronghold of the MacNeils since about 1040.

The original Norse structure here was probably a 3 storey tower, perhaps similar to the Castle of Oldwick in Caithness. In the 15th century the tower and curtain wall were rebuilt and internal buildings were also repaired or renewed. Later the curtain wall was heightened. The Castle was abandoned in the late 18th century, having been severely damaged by fire in 1795.

Castlebay, Kisimul Castle and Heaval from the ferry

MacNeil Coat of Arms

Boats transporting salt for fish curing used its stones as ballast and some are said to have been discharged in Glasgow, where they were reused for street paving. Herring boats also used it in a similar fashion whilst heading for the fishing grounds.

In 1937 Robert Lister MacNeil, the 45th Chief of the Clan, bought much of Barra, including the castle. He carried out a major restoration programme largely using stones from the many jetties around the bay, themselves built using bits of the castle.

Archaeological investigations in the courtyard found animal bones and shells in large quantities. Pottery sherds dating from Neolithic to late Medieval times indicate that the island has been inhabited for a long time.

Kisimul Castle is now in the charge of Historic Scotland, who leased it for 1,000 years. The rental is £1 and a bottle of whisky per year. It can be visited daily by a small ferry from April until September.

Castlebay from the ramparts

Kisimul Castle, Interior of the Hall

Kisimul Castle Courtyard

MV "Lord of the Isles" passing Kisimul Castle

Tangusdale and Dun Mhic Leoid with Ben Tangaval in the background

Dun Mhic Leoid (wrongly called Sinclair Castle in the 19th century, NL648996) is on a small island on Loch Tangusdale. This tower was originally three stories high and measures about 3m by 2.5m inside, with walls about 1.5m thick. St Columba's Well lies near the loch, marked by some white stones. Otters frequent the lochs and burns here.

Doirlinn Head There is a fine walk south to Doirlinn Head, and to the top of Ben Tangaval (333m, NL638991) from Halaman Bay. *Dun Ban* (G White Fort, NF631003) is a broch, in a dramatic cliff-top location. There is a fine view from the top of the hill.

Borve is named from the ruined broch, *Dun na Cille* (NF647016), at the head of a small geo, *Port na Cille*. In the

adjacent graveyard there are scant ruins of a little chapel, *Cille Bhrianain* (dedicated to St Brendan). A short standing stone is prominent near the gate onto the machair, which in summer is a sea of wild flowers. Many waders breed here and Oystercatchers are particularly common.

West Beaches The beaches of Allasdale, *Traigh Hamara*, *Traigh Tuath* and Halaman Bay all have their own character. Whether on a calm summer's evening, or during an equinoctial storm, the scene is constantly changing, dynamic, yet peaceful. The beach at Allasdale, or Seal Bay, is an especially popular place for selkies to haul out, and thus also for viewing them.

Chambered Cairn Further up the hill to the north, the large and apparently undisturbed mound of *Dun Bharpa* Neolithic chambered cairn (NF672019) is prominent. Several kerbstones are still standing and the entrance passage can be seen, facing down the valley. There is another chambered cairn (NF677012) further up towards the saddle of the valley below Grianan.

Wheelhouse There is an aisled wheelhouse, dating from the early centuries AD, inland near Allasdale (NF677022) which has outbuildings and an associated souterrain. This house is unusual in that most such dwellings in the Western Isles have been found in machair

Rough seas breaking at Halaman Bay

Allasdale from Beinn Mhartainn

From Greian Head looking south over Traigh Eais and Allasdale to Ben Tangaval

areas. This house sits at the top of a very attractive valley, well above the machair.

Broch *Dun Cuier* (NF664034), overlooks Allasdale beach. It was excavated in the 1950s and has now been shown to have been reused over a long period.

Barra Golf Course is nearby on *Aird Greian*. This unusual 9 hole course has fen-ces around the greens to keep the sheep out! There are also great views to admire when you are looking for your lost golf balls.

Greian Head The west coast of Barra is a series of curvaceous sandy beaches, backed by dunes and machair, interspersed by rugged headlands. From Greian Head (NF658047), above the Golf Course, with its abandoned WWII radio post, there is a particularly fine view southwards. A rough track leads to the top of the hill.

WALKS There are several pleasant walks in the area, which include a coastal route along the cliffs from Cleit to Suideachan along an old path which affords especially good views over the west of the island, and towards South Uist. *Beinn Mhartainn* (244m, NF664021), overlooks the attractive township of Borve, and offers outstanding views. Above Craigston, *Dubhairidh*, an old thatched cottage (G The Dark Shieling) has been renovated (NF673014) and is open to visitors in the summer.

Dun Bharpa chambered cairn

Dun na Cille, Borve

Port na Cille, Borve with Tangaval in the background

Traigh Mhor or Cocklestrand is also Barra Airport

BARRA AIRPORT The north of the island is quite different to the south, with expansive sandy beaches, backed by sand dunes and machair. Barra Airport is unique in that it uses the large flat expanse of *Traigh Mhor*, or the Cocklestrand, as its runways. Recently it has been voted as having the 10th most spectacular approach in the world.

Operations are dependent on the tide, but the Canadian Twin Otter aircraft used are eminently suitable for the job. There are daily flights to Glasgow and Benbecula at variable times. The beach is also the source of the wonderful cockles which may be found on local menus.

Cille Bharra (NF704074) overlooks Eoligarry and is said to be dedicated to St Barr or Finbar, of Cork, whose feast day is 27th September. The church may also have connections to St Brendan. None of the three buildings visible appear earlier than 12th century, but it is likely that the original foundation was much earlier, perhaps 7th century.

An unusual grave slab is now in the National Museum in Edinburgh. The stone has a Celtic cross on one side and a runic inscription on the other to *Thorgerth, Steiner's daughter*. A replica of this 10th or 11th century stone is in the North Chapel along with three 16th century carved tombstones, probably commemorating the MacNeils.

The door on the north wall of the church has inward-sloping door jambs and windows similar to early Irish churches, strengthening its founder's probable Irish provenance. In early summer the precincts are enlivened by swathes of Primroses.

The graveyard is still in use and has an interesting range of memorials, from very ancient to modern. The author Compton MacKenzie, of *Whisky Galore* fame, who lived on Barra during 1935-1945, is buried here.

Eoligarry East of the church, *Traigh Cille Bharra* is another vast expanse of sand at low tide, stretching to the tidal island of Orosay. It is backed by the fertile machair plain of

Twin Otter at Barra Airport

Thrift on the shore at Eoligarry

Eoligarry, which was cleared in the 1840s to make one large farm. It was eventually divided up into crofts again, many of which are still worked. The beaches here are vast areas of white sand. On a fine day the sea is a colour of turquoise giving a Caribbean ambience to the place. This is one of the best places to seek Corncrakes on Barra.

Traigh Eais and the west coast of Barra from Dun Scurrival

Dun Scurrival (NF695081) is dramatically situated on a rugged 50m hillock with stunning views over the west coast, *Traigh Scurrival* and the Sound of Barra. Parts of the walls and of the intramural galleries are visible. This Iron Age broch is one of several similar structures on Barra and the Bishop's Isles. Sites of such buildings are often indicated by the place name Borve from ON *Borg*, castle.

Swathes of Primroses in early summer

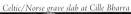

Celtic/Norse grave slab at Cille Bharra

The beach at Eoligarry jetty

Cille Bharra has ancient chapels, gravestones from many ages and wild flowers

Otter and Salmon sculpture at the ferry terminal, Ard Mhor

East Coast The east coast of Barra is rugged with rocky bays and low cliffs. The sheltered inlet at Northbay has some of Barra's few trees, excellent places to find migrant birds in spring and autumn. Several passerine species breed here. There is a statue of St Barr on an islet on the loch and modern collage of the saint made with sea shells on the nearby St Barr's Church. In spring Gorse and Broom enliven the scene with their yellow flowers.

Ard Mhor There is a roro car ferry which runs between Ard Mhor and Eriskay. Outside the terminal there is a fine sculpture of two Otters chasing a Salmon. This is a good place to look for these elusive creatures, which are usually seen in the gloaming.

Northbay has for long been Barra's second harbour. The Old Harbour is very sheltered and still used by small fishing boats. Aird Mhidhinis is the main base of the fishing industry on the island. It has a deep water pier and the Barratlantic fish factory. Prawns, Whitefish and Scallops landed here are trucked daily to the mainland. Fresh fish can be bought here.

Balnabodach is today a string of houses along the roadside above Loch Ob just south of Northbay. Near the shore the remains of earlier houses dot the landscape. Loch Ob itself is very sheltered and accessible from the sea by a narrow channel nearly 400m long.

During excavations, a Bronze Age arrowhead and large quantities of Iron Age pottery were found here. Flint scrapers and knives as well as pumice tools were also present. The dun on *Loch nic Ruadhe* just up the burn may have been contemporary with this occupation.

Later, blackhouses were built here, perhaps beginning

Northbay has a very sheltered inner basin

about 1750. Pottery, a clay pipe, broken tools and a copper thimble were among the artefacts discovered. In 1851 potato blight caused famine on Barra. Four hundred and fifty people were shipped out to Canada that year, including those from Balnabodach. In turn, they were soon replaced by families who were evicted from Borve.

Earsary The road winds through a series of townships with wonderful names, including Earsary (*Earsairidh*), Skallary (*Sgalllairidh*) and Brevig (*Breibhig*). Apart from the modern houses there are many ruined blackhouses, most of which date from the 19th century clearances.

There are fine views of the east coast of Barra, the Minch and Skye from the hill to the south of Brevig on the northeast flank of Heaval. The east side of the island is quite different from the west, with its rocky inlets and lack of sandy bays. It is worthwhile to walk or cycle rather than drive and not to be in a hurry.

Scots Pines and Gorse at Northbay

Cottage at Ardveenish, Northbay

Small boats at high tide, Earsary

Mosaic on Northbay Church

Earsary with Muldonaich in the background

Sound of Vatersay and the causeway from below the War Memorial

Barra War Memorial was dedicated in 1993, to commemorate those from the island who gave their lives in WWI (71) and WWII (44). Most were in the Merchant or Royal Navy, although some were in the Army. It is situated on the road to Vatersay overlooking Castlebay and the Sound of Vatersay.

Allt Chrisal During the building of the new road a detailed archaeological survey of the route and its environs was undertaken. A surprising range of sites were discovered ranging from the Neolithic to the 18ᵗʰ century. Most are in the small valley of *Allt Chrisal* (NL643977), a burn which runs off Ben Tangaval into the Sound of Vatersay near the northern end of the causeway.

From about 3400 to 1800BC there was a settlement on two levelled areas just above the road. Hearths, pottery, flint tools and a saddle quern were found, as were several stone burial cists. The pottery was *Grooved Ware* type, similar to that found in Orkney and Wiltshire. A rectangular oven in the floor may have been a kiln to fire the pottery.

About 400m east, a small heel shaped chambered cairn could have been the communal burial tomb for the settlement. This type of cairn is unusual in the Outer Hebrides, but common elsewhere.

Bronze age curved wall and hearth

Neolithic fireplace

Neolithic heel shaped cairn

Higher up there is a small circular stone hut, which is probably from the Beaker period. Nearby, a small cist contained a nearly intact beaker which may well have been used to drink ale made from barley.

The most dramatic building is an Iron Age wheelhouse, which lies up the slope to the west of the stream. The walls, piers and central fireplace can all be made out. It is unusual as, apart from the one at Allasdale, most such houses so far found in the Western Isles are built into sand dunes and not free standing as here.

The most recent occupation was in the 18th century, when a blackhouse with outbuildings, including a byre and kiln, were built near the Neolithic house. There are also remains of lazybeds nearby. This site was only occupied for perhaps 40 years. It is said that a plague of rats from a nearby wrecked ship drove the people out. Indeed, there was evidence of rats' nests in the foundations of the house.

Barra War Memorial was dedicated in 1993

Castlebay from the War Memorial

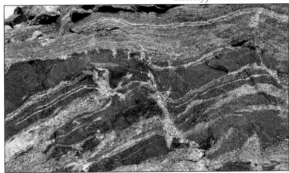

Lewisian Gneiss rocks exposed in road cutting at the War Memorial

Iron Age wheelhouse, uphill from the Neolithic site

Bronze Age house

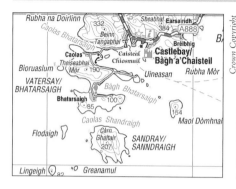

Sunset from Bagh Siar

Vatersay (ON *Vatrs-oy,* Wet or Watery Island) was joined to Barra by a causeway in 1990. Prior to this a small ferry ran across the Sound of Vatersay. Cattle were swum across behind boats. The island was bought in 1910 by the Congested District Board after a series of land raids in 1906 by crofters desperate for land. The island was then divided into crofts.

Vatersay Bay The road leads eastwards to sheltered Vatersay Bay with its lovely sands. The community hall is at the north end of the beach, which is one of the finest of many lovely such stretches of sand in the Outer Hebrides.

On the south side of Vatersay, *Bagh a' Deas* (G South Bay) faces south over Sandray. There is a particularly fine view from *Heillanish* (NL633935), the low headland to the west of the beach.

Archaeology On the north side of Vatersay, *Dun a' Chaolais* is a large ruined broch which commanded the Sound

Collapsed broch entrance

of Vatersay. The entrance and intramural spaces can still be made out.

Dun Vatersay (NL626947) is another ruinous broch on a knoll to the west of the village. It commands fine views over Bagh Siar, Vatersay Bay and the north part of the island.

Chapel On the east side, on the small island of Uineasain (NL665957), the ruined chapel of *Cille Bhrainain* is on a hummock above a lovely sandy beach facing Castlebay. There is a another fine beach at *Caragrich* on the way to this chapel site. A side road leads to Uidh for part of the way to this idyllic corner of Vatersay.

Dun a' Chaolais Broch, overlooking the Sound of Vatersay

Catalina memorial

IN MEMORY OF THE MEN
WHO DIED AND SURVIVED
WHEN THEIR CATALINA PLANE
CRASHED ON VATERSAY ON
12th MAY 1944
DIED IN CRASH ·

Flt Sgt	D. Clyne	Captain ·
Sgt	E. Kilsaw	2nd Pilot
Sgt	P. Lee	Navigator
Sgt	G. Calder	Wireless Op Mechanic - AG
Sgt	R. Beavis	Engineer
Sgt	R. Anstey	Wireless OP-AG
Sgt	R. Basset	Wireless OP-AG ·
Sgt	R. Whiting	Flight Mechanic
Sgt	P. Hines	Rigger-AG ·

Catalina crash site On 18th May 1944, an RAF Catalina on a training flight from Oban crashed into Heishival Beag above the east side of Vatersay Bay. Three of the crew were killed but the other six survived. There is a memorial at the roadside along with some remaining pieces of the aircraft.

Vatersay Bay faces east

Vatersay from Dun Vatersay

Annie Jane memorial, Bagh Siar

Bagh a' Deas from the west end
Bagh Siar on a misty day

ANNIE JANE of Liverpool was a brig wrecked on 29th September 1853 at *Bagh Siar* (G West Bay). Bound for Quebec with 450 passengers and 45 crew, she was hit by a severe Atlantic storm. The crew were unable to make her manageable and she grounded on rocks in Bagh Siar.

In one of the worst maritime disasters of the 19th century, 393 people were lost. Of these, 248 were buried at the top of the beach. There were 102 survivors, including the captain, because when the ship broke up the foredeck and poopdeck acted like liferafts. There is a poignant memorial to the disaster above the beach.

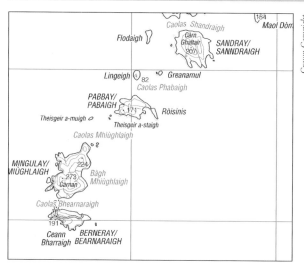

Sandray (ON *Sandr-oy*, Sandy Island) is named for its huge sand dunes on the east coast below Carnach. There is a galleried dun unusually situated at about 100m (NL637913) on the south east ridge of *Cairn Galtar* (207m), and a chapel, *Cille Bhrighde* (NL652919) next to the old settlement site, which is now buried in extensive sand dunes.

THE BISHOP'S ISLES The string of islands to the south of Barra was known as the *Bishop's Isles* because during Norse times they were part of the Bishopric Estate. Each has its own character, although all have been uninhabited since the early 20th century.

Pabbay (ON *Papa-oy*, Monk's or Culdee's Island) has a beautiful white sandy beach on the east side, at *Bagh Ban*. (G White Beach). The settlement was inland from this, and extensive ruins remain. A steep mound nearby has many grave markers, but may originally have been a domestic midden.

Pabbay Pictish symbol stone, has a flower and V-rod, or broken arrow, with crescent symbols, and has been

Sandy beach and dunes on the east side of Sandray

Sandray and the Sound of Sandray from Vatersay

Pabbay Stone from an old print

Bagh Ban, Pabbay

reerected. The stone has a later primitive cross at the top. Another simple cross slab is face down in the grass. The remains of a chapel lie about halfway towards the shore, mostly buried in sand.

Galleried Dun Up the slope, an Iron Age house similar to those at Bosta on Great Bernera lies excavated. On a prime vantage point above *Bagh Ban* and facing across the Sound of Pabbay, there

is a small, but well preserved, galleried dun, *Dunan Ruadh* (G Red Fort NL613877). There is a stunning 270 degree panoramic view of the whole of the Bishops's Isles from this strategic viewpoint.

Small cross slab on mound

Dun Ruadh gallery and stairway
Iron Age house

Sound of Pabbay with Dun Ruadh on the right

Dun Ruadh is a well preserved Iron Age dun or small broch

Mingulay Bay from the south, it is very exposed and never had a pier

Mingulay (ON *Mikil-ey*, Muckle or Big Island) is the largest of the Bishop's Isles. The high cliffs, which reach 215m on the west side, with spectacular caves, stacks and precipices, are home to many breeding seabirds in summer. The 150m high natural arch at Gunamul and the immense geos are especially impressive from a boat. Rock climbers also favour these Lewisian Gneiss cliffs.

The main settlement of ruined blackhouses, field walls, cultivation strips and a burial ground lie above Mingulay Bay. A chapel, dedicated to St Columba, is now engulfed by sand. The large and incongruous Chapel House, built in 1898, is now ruinous but the Schoolhouse, built in the 1880s, is in good repair. There never was a pier because Mingulay Bay is subject to swell most of the time. Landing is best done on the rocks to the north or south of the lovely sandy beach.

There are good views from Macphee's Hill (224m) in the north, Hecla (ON *Hekle*, comb, or *Hekla*, cowl, 219m) in the south and the highest hill, Carnan (G Heap of Stones, 273m). Macphee's Hill is named after a boy who was abandoned on the island after a plague had wiped out the inhabitants. He survived for over a year on his own before the land was resettled. Mingulay was finally abandoned in 1912 after being populated for several thousand years. There are many prehistoric sites from the Iron Age and earlier.

Boat trips run daily from Castlebay to the Bishop's Isles. The spectacular western caves and cliffs can be seen close up on calm days. In summer hundreds of nesting Guillemots and Puffins may be seen, along with Basking Sharks, Minke Whales and Risso's Dolphins.

Builacraig and Bagh na h-Aoineig, Mingulay

150m high natural arch, Gunamul

Richard Jones

Barra Head is 190m high and often covered in mist

Berneray (ON *Bjornr-oy*, Bjorn's Island), or Barra Head, is the most southerly of the Western Isles. Its dramatic 190m cliffs are topped by Barra Head lighthouse, first lit in 1833 and automated in 1980, at *Sron an Duine* (G Fort Headland).

The remains of the Iron Age dun at the lighthouse protect a small area surrounded by rocks, right on the edge of the cliffs. Sadly this dun was partially destroyed during the building of the lighthouse. Barra Head was the final waypoint for sailing ships westbound for the USA and Canada, which is one of the reasons for the construction of the lighthouse.

Dun Briste (G Broken Fort, NL548806), is the north-west tip of the island, overlooking the Sound of Berneray. The landing place is on the northeast side below the old settlement. It is only exposed to the northeast, Shelter Rock and Maclean's Point protect it from the tide and swell otherwise. There is an ancient graveyard to the east of Maclean's Point, but nothing remains of the chapel which once stood there. A chalybeate (iron bearing) well lies halfway up the hill.

Midsummer sunset down the Sound of Berneray

Barra Head lighthouse

Sron an Duine Iron Age fort

Village Bay and Oiseval from Rueval, St Kilda

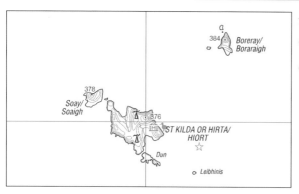

ST KILDA (ON *Skjoldr*, shield) is a fascinating and beautiful archipelago 66km (41mi) WNW of North Uist which was formed by volcanic action about 60 million years ago. It is one of the ultimate destinations for island lovers. The main island is *Hirta* (ON *Hirtir*, deer, G *Hiort*), which was populated from at least 1850BC until 1930.

Today the National Trust for Scotland owns the group. It is managed by NTS, Scottish Natural Heritage and the MoD in partnership. St Kilda is a UNESCO World Heritage Site in recognition of its natural and cultural heritage as well as the marine environment. A warden, researchers and visitors are present in summer. Missile Range radar staff may be present all year.

Bronze Age burial cists have been found in Village Bay as well as an Iron Age souterrain, suggesting that people were here at least 4,000 years ago. Norse brooches from a female burial as well as steatite pots have been found. Many of the placenames are Norse, in particular those of the hills and stacks.

Village Bay, on the east side, is well sheltered from the prevailing winds. The Street was built in 1860, and the ruined blackhouses behind about 1830, replacing earlier houses which were considered too primitive. The hillsides are dotted with nearly 1,300 *cleitan*. These small drystone sheds were variously used to wind dry and store birds, fish, dung, hay and peats, preserve eggs and to protect lambs. There are also a large number of walls and enclosures.

Chapels Three chapel sites are recorded but nothing now remains. Christ's Church was in the graveyard, St Columba's to the west of the village, and St Brendan's below Ruaival. A Viking female burial was also discovered, but the artefacts which were found have been lost. Two early

Village Bay from Conachair (426m) with Dun in the background

The Village Street, Hirta

Christian stone crosses are the only physical evidence. One is in the wall of house 16.

Hills The steep hills offer exhilarating walks which are rewarded by dramatic views, if the tops are clear. Hirta tends to produce its own weather. The main hills are Oiseval (290m), Conachair (426m), and Mullach Mor (361m).

The jagged island of Dun protects Village Bay from the south and west. It is home to huge numbers of Puffins in the Summer and has a ruined dun on its south eastern tip. Soay is separated from Hirta by the narrow Sound of Soay with Soay Stac and Stac Biorach in between.

Stacks About 7km (5mi) to the northeast, Boreray, Stac an Armin and Stac Lee rise steeply from the sea. They are part of the rim of the huge volcano that was here nearly 60 million years ago. Together these stacks host the world's largest gannetry with over 60,000 pairs nesting. St Kilda is one of the world's largest seabird colonies with well over 250,000 breeding pairs of all species.

Wren The St Kildan Wren, a subspecies, may be seen around the Village area, but seems to prefer the Puffin areas to breed. Their shrill calls make them easy to spot in the old stonework. They are larger than those from the

Mainland and breed on Hirta, Dun and Boreray. There is also a St Kildan subspecies of the Field Mouse which only lives on Dun.

A boat trip around Hirta and the stacks during the breeding season is an unforgettable spectacle. The jagged cliffs, lush grassy slopes, thousands of seabirds, and, above all, the sheer scale of the place can only be described as awe inspiring. The long trip over the open Atlantic offers the chance to see cetaceans such as Minke or Killer Whales, and various species of dolphins, as well as sea birds such as Gannets, Storm and Leaches Petrel and Manx Shearwaters.

The Street

WWI gun emplacement

Leaving St Kilda

Underwater, St Kilda is a sub-aqua diver's paradise, as the volcanic rocks erode into wonderful submerged shapes and caves. The clarity of the water means that visibility is often exceptional, while divers may be accompanied by curious Seals or Puffins.

Survival The St Kildans survived by using Nature's bounty to the full, harvesting thousands of Gannets, Puffins and Fulmars every year. They also kept the primitive Soay Sheep and later, Blackfaces. Although there would have been plenty of fish available, it

did not feature much in the people's diet. Perhaps they preferred it after avian processing.

To catch the birds the men had to be very agile climbers. They were on the craigs from a young age and developed particularly strong feet. Before a young man could marry, he had to show off his prowess by balancing on one foot atop the Lover's Stone. One leg was outstretched over the edge and the suitor had then to bend over and touch his toes with his fist.

Mortality There was a very high infant mortality rate which was previously thought to have been caused by typhus. Recent research has shown that the high consumption of

St Kildan "Parliament" on the late 1800s

One of the many cleits

Soay Sheep

Stac an Armin (191m) and Boreray (384m) from the Gap

seabirds, including their livers, resulted in a toxic overload of heavy metals. This was made worse by the fields and gardens being contaminated by discarded carcases. The islanders were also prone to imported diseases such as smallpox and measles.

Ultimately, the St Kildans decided that life was no longer tenable and they asked to be evacuated in 1930. Today many people visit by yacht, motorboat or cruise ship. Few leave disappointed and most have a yearning to return one day to this unique and fascinating volcanic archipelago.

Boat Trips to St Kilda are run by several operators but especially from Leverburgh in Harris and Uig in Lewis. Kilda Cruises, who have an booking office in Tarbert, run trips from April to September. Angus Campbell has two powerful offshore craft capable of reaching as far as Rockall. A trip to St Kilda is a magical experience, worth every penny of the seemingly expensive fare.

Stac an Armin (191m)

Boreray and Stac Lee

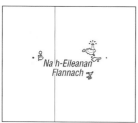

Na h-Eileanan Flannach

The Flannan Islands (after the 8th century St Flann) are about 33km (21mi) WNW of Gallan Head on Lewis. Also known as the Seven Hunters, they are bird paradise in summer, with many breeding seabirds, including Puffins, Fulmars, Gannets, Storm and Leaches Petrels. Minke, Killer and Pilot Whales, Risso's and other Dolphins are present.

The lighthouse was first lit in 1899. It has an especially large lamproom to house its equally impressive lens. The shore station was at Breasclete in the west of Lewis. But for the events soon to unfold, it would be a quite obscure light.

On 15th December 1900 SS *Archtor* noticed that the light was not in operation. A few days later the tender *Hesperus* visited to find all three keepers were missing. They were assumed to have been washed away by extremely large waves piling up at the West Landing.

The official explanation was less fanciful than many of the theories put forward. Robert Muirhead of the NLB reported, *"From evidence which I was able to procure I was satisfied that the men had been on duty up till dinner time on Saturday the 15 December, that they had gone down to secure a box in which the mooring ropes, landing ropes etc. were kept, and which was secured in a crevice in the rock about 110ft (34 m) above sea level, and that an extra large sea had rushed up the face of the rock, had gone above them, and coming down with immense force, had swept them completely away."*

The lighthouse was automated in 1971 and is now electrically powered by a large bank of photocells along the south side. The accommodation block is well appointed for visiting NLB staff.

On *Eilean Mor* (G, Big Island) below the lighthouse, there is a small stonebuilt chapel, dedicated to St Flann, and on the western headland a series of bothies (*Bothain Chlann 'ic Phaill*, (G McPhail's Bothies) attributed to the Clan MacPhail. There are remains of a house on the top of *Eilean Tighe* (G House Island).

The gannetry is on the south end of *Roareim*, and should

St Flann's Chapel (8th century) and the lighthouse (19th century)

The West Landing where the keepers may have been lost

The lamphouse is spacious to accommodate the large lens

not be closely approached to avoid disturbance. Between Roareim and *Eilean a'Ghobha* (G Blacksmith's Island) there are rock stacks and natural arches eroded into fantastical shapes which can be observed from a boat in settled weather.

Geology The islands are volcanic and consist of Gabbro and Dolerite which have intruded the basal Lewisian Gneiss. These rocks have eroded into fantastic shapes, but are hard on the hands. The soils are fertile and there is a rich covering of grass, with a carpet of wildflowers and lichen in summer.

Getting Ashore on *Eilean Mor* is possible at either the East or West Landings, though care must be taken on the slippery steps, many of which have been washed away. All of the other islands are easily accessible in fine weather.

Various boat operators run trips to the Flannans, which are very subject to weather and sea conditions. These mostly run from the west of Lewis.

The Flannans from Gallan Head in Lewis

The East Landing

The lighthouse on a midsummer night

Roareim has a fine stack and arch

Eilean Mor from Eilean Tighe

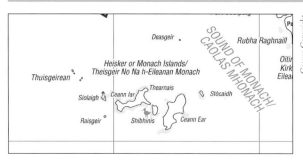

A small new light was installed in 1997 after the loss of the *Braer* in Shetland in 1993. In company with similar installations on Haskier to the west of North Uist and Gasker off North Harris, it marks the Deep Water Route recommended for large laden tankers.

In 2005 it was decided to fit a more powerful light here and in July 2008 the original tower was brought back into use. Despite being abandoned for 60 years the tower remains in good condition and required very little repairs.

Ceann Ear (G East Island) was also known as *Heisker nan Cailleach* due to the nunnery there which may have been established in the 13th century. At low tide *Ceann Ear*, *Shivinish* and *Ceann Iar* are joined by sand bars.

THE MONACH ISLANDS (G *Manach*, monks) are about 10km off the west of North Uist. They comprise a series of small sandy islands and low skerries. Legend has it that up to the 16th century a sandbank connected the islands to North Uist, until a huge storm swept the sand away. The last inhabitants left in 1948, but until 1810 there were around 100 people here.

The islands are also known as Heisker (ON *Heisker*, Bright Skerry) due, no doubt, to their appearance on a sunny day. The outermost is Shillay (ON, *Selr-oy*, Seal Skerry) or *Heisker nam Manach*, where the monks traditionally had to maintain a light. The lighthouse was established in 1864, but was discontinued in 1942 and not relit after WWII.

Nature Today the islands are a National Nature Reserve. The undisturbed machair has a particularly rich flora here. About 10,000 Grey Seals now come ashore here each autumn to have their pups and mate, making it one of

Shillay coastline on a rough day

Old lighthouse before cleaning up

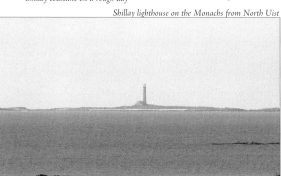

Shillay lighthouse on the Monachs from North Uist

the largest such colonies in the world. Their dung helps fertilise the machair.

Many Waders, Terns, Eider Ducks, Shelducks and Fulmars breed on the islands. There is a very large colony of Black Guillemots which especially like the storm beaches. Barnacle Geese also overwinter. Over 200 species of flowering plants grow here, making early summer a wonderful time to visit as the machair becomes a sea of colour.

Access From seaward on a dull day the Monachs present a forbidding air, with sea breaking on the many sandbanks, rocks and skerries. All of the area in the vicinity is

The lighthouse reflected in a rock pool

a maze of hazards, but navigable with care. The best anchorage is under the lighthouse at Shillay, where there is a jetty. Boat trips are run from North Uist occasionally.

Grey Seal mother and pup

Temporary 1997 lighthouse

Black Guillemots

Sound of Shillay with the lighthouse in the distance

Lisgeir Mhòr
RONA/
RÒNAIDH
Lòba Sgeir
Gealldruig Mhòr

Sula
Sgeir

Rona (ON *Hraun-oy*, rough island) is a small isolated island about 70km (44mi) NNE of the Butt of Lewis. The people of Ness knew it as *Ronaidh ant'Haf* (ON *Haff*, ocean) which is an apt description. The northern and southwestern peninsulas are quite rough, with bare rock and storm beaches, but the rest of the island is covered with luxuriant grass and wild flowers.

St Ronan The hermitage is one of the oldest remote Christian sites in Scotland and is said to have been founded by St Ronan in the 7th or 8th century. The oratory may be the oldest part. It has shell sand mortar and was once limewashed white inside. One small window high in the east gable provides some light.

The roofless chapel has one doorway and is sur-rounded by an oval earth and stone wall which encloses an ancient graveyard. There are a number of cross-inscribed and cross-shaped grave markers which may date from the 7th to 9th and from the 12th or 13th centuries. The best known one, said to be St Ronan's own, is in the Ness Heritage Centre, Lewis.

Population A complex group of domestic buildings to the west of the chapel was occupied until the early 19th century. There are sub-rectangular living rooms, small oval side chambers with corbelled roofs and porches as well as byres, a kiln and a barn. Extensive field walls and *feannagan*, or lazybeds, surround the settlement.

Up to five families lived here. Periodically people left the island for Lewis and

Fianuis and Sgeildige from the southwest

Feannagan or lazybeds surround the settlement

Sunset over Fianuis from Toa Rona

Approaching Rona from the east. Toa Rona (108m) is the highest point and has a small lighthouse

resettlement also came from there. There are several records of catastrophe when the residents were wiped out. Infections borne by incomers and rats from wrecked ships which ate the food were two. The saddest is the story that some fishermen landed and stole the only bull. This meant no calves and no milk, an important part of the diet.

Like the St Kildans the Rona people depended on seabirds for part of their diet. They are said to have caught Gannets on Sula Sgeir as well as Puffins and other auks on Rona. Unlike the St Kildans they were also fishermen and are said to have driven whales ashore on the rocks. They doubtless utilised the large Grey Seal population also. Thus, although isolated, they had access to a wide variety of resources.

Nature Reserve The island is a National Nature Reserve on account of its importance as a seabird and seal breeding area. There are large numbers of breeding Puffins, Guillemots, Kittiwake and Fulmars, as well as both Leaches and Storm Petrels. In autumn up to 8,000 Grey Seals come ashore to calve. The lush grass of summer is partly a consequence of their dung.

Landing is possible in several places, at Geodha a' Stoth in the east, Sgeildige in the northwest, or in several places on the south coast. A visit is well worthwhile as Rona has a character all of its own.

Wartime U-boats are said to have regularly stopped off at Rona to steal sheep and take fresh air. *U-90* regularly stocked up with fresh mutton during WWI in this way.

Cross slab in the Chapel

The Oratory interior

One of the domestic buildings

St Ronan's Chapel interior with entrance to the Oratory

Sula Sgeir from the southeast in winter

SULA SGEIR (ON *Sula Sker*, Gannet Skerry) is a small narrow rock, about 17km west of Rona. In summer it is home to large numbers of Gannets, Guillemots, Razorbills, Shags Fulmars, Eider Ducks and Puffins. Both Storm and Leaches Petrels also nest here.

Gugas In August, the Men of Ness come to harvest up to 2,000 *gugas*, the plump young Gannets which have not quite fledged. The birds are salted on the island, and are considered a delicacy by everyone from Ness. Indeed they grace tables all over the world. Despite the cull, the Gannet population remains stable at about 9,000 pairs.

The Gannetry covers the whole southern end of the island. During the breeding season the cacophony, smell and presence of the wheeling Gannets is most impressive.

Brenhilda Although seemingly very inhospitable to humans, there is a ruined stone bothy called *Tigh Beannaichte* (G Blessed House) on the east headland, Sgeir an Teampall. St Ronan's sister, Brenhilda, is alleged to have stayed here for some time, leaving him on Rona, only to be found dead in a bothy with a Shag's nest in her ribcage.

Her brother is said to have admired her beauty while they were climbing the hill on Rona. Apparently he especially remarked on her shapely legs as she ascended in front of him. As a result she decamped to Sula Sgeir where she eventually died.

Bothies There are a total of five bothies on Sula Sgeir, which are still used by the Men of Ness when they come to harvest the gugas. These circular structures are undoubtedly ancient, but it seems unlikely that they were ever occupied for long periods.

Geology The hard Lewisian Gneiss rock splits into long pieces, which are excellent for building bothies and cairns. The rough boulders and sharp rocks make for tough walking, but their hardness has resisted erosion for perhaps 3,000 million years. The sea has burrowed right through the southern part of the island

One of several bothies

Gannets and Guillemots

in a series of interconnected and spectacular caves. They may be explored by inflatable dinghy during calm weather.

There is a small lighthouse on the south end at *Sron na Lice*, the highest point of the island (74m). It is regularly damaged by the huge seas which break right over the rock during Atlantic storms.

Despite this there is a surprising amount of vegetation. The Thrift is especially luxuriant and colourful in June, which is probably the best month to visit. Scentless Mayweed, Orache, Scurvy Grass and Sea Spurrey are a few other salt tolerant plants which grow here, along with several lichens and even some grasses.

Approaching Sula Sgeir at dawn in midsummer

Landing There is a good anchorage at *Geodha a' Phuill Bhain*, where landing is not difficult in settled weather. It is sheltered from the east by the rocky islet of *Thamna Sgeir* (ON *Hamna Sker*, Harbour Skerry). Care should be taken to avoid disturbing the birds during the breeding season. A visit to Sula Sgeir is an experience not to be missed if the chance arises.

Guillemots & Gannets on Sula Sgeir

Sron na Lice in the mist from the south

View from inside a cave
One of the many spectacular caves

Geodha a' Phuill Bhain from the south

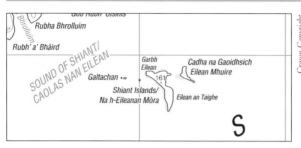

The Shiant Islands (G *Na h-Eileanan Seunta*, The Enchanted Islands) lie between Skye and Lewis at the south end of the Minch and are about 18km (11mi) east of Scalpay. The rocks here are volcanic and, at 60 million years, very young by Hebridean standards.

Geology The Dolerite columns on the north side of *Garbh Eilean* (G Rough Isle) are over 100m tall and about 2m across. Similar to those at Staffa and the Giant's Causeway, they were caused by the slow cooling of volcanic rocks deep underground. In some places the basalt is overlain by Jurassic mudstone, which weathers to form much more fertile soil than elsewhere in the Western Isles.

The previously inhabited and cultivated areas of *Airihghean a'Baigh* and *Airihghean na h-Annaid* on *Eilean Garbh* and most of the top of *Eilean Mhuire* (G The Virgin's Island) are unusually fertile land for this reason. *Feannagan* may still be discerned in these areas.

Apart from the 19th century house and adjacent ruins on *Eilean an Tighe* (G House Island) there is other evidence of human occupation. The islands were inhabited up until the late 18th century, when changes in land ownership and society made the old way of life no longer viable.

Chapels There are several possible chapel sites. The first may have been dedicated to St Columba and have been

sited on the west side of *Eilean Garbh*, perhaps at *Airihghean na h-Annaid*, as the name *Annaid* means Old Church. There was possibly a more recent church, dedicated to the Virgin, near the cottage.

Finds During excavations on the farmstead on *Eilean an Tighe* an interesting round stone with a cross surrounded by a circle was found. This type of stone is common in Ireland, but unusual in Scotland. It was perhaps buried by the builders for good luck, and probably came from a much earlier church site.

Another find was a gold torc dredged up by Scalpay scallop fishermen southwest of the islands. This object dates from around 1200BC and, while similar torcs have turned up elsewhere in UK, this is by far the furthest north. It is possible to speculate on the provenance of such a find, and whether it got there by shipwreck, or as a votive offering.

Seabirds The Shiants are a major seabird breeding site due to their location next to good feeding grounds and the lack of predators, except for Black Rats. Huge numbers of Puffins breed on *Garbh Eilean*, as well as Fulmars, Guillemots, Razorbills, Kittiwakes, Shags, Gulls and Great Skuas. St Kilda has more Puffins, the density on the Shiants is greater.

Sound of Shiant The Sound of Shiant or *Sruth na Fear*

Eilean Garbh in 1815 by William Daniell

Gorm is said to be inhabited by the *Blue Men of the Minch*, who must be treated with the greatest respect by mariners. The strong tides, uneven seabed and many hazards make the area dangerous in rough conditions. The offshore rocks and stacks to the west of the Shiants are called the *Galtachean* (which may derive from ON *Goltr*, boar). Their basalt columns are beautiful on a calm day, but fearsome when the sea is rough.

Landing The best landing is on the shingle and boulder beach at *Mol Mor* on the east side of the isthmus, between Eilean Tighe and Garbh Eilean.

Approaching the Shiants from Skye

Cross incised stone

Adam Nicholson

Dolerite columns of Garbh Eilean

NMS

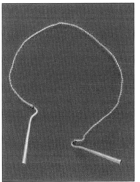
Golden torc

Eilean Tighe and Garbh Eilean from Eilean Mhuire

Feannagan (lazybeds) on Garbh Eilean

Eilean Garbh from Eilean an Tighe with Mol Mo

Rockall with the Hasselwood Rock in the background

ROCKALL (ON *Hrukka*, a fold or wrinkle or *Rok*, foaming sea) is a very remote volcanic plug located 300km (187mi) west of St Kilda at 57°35'N, 13°41'W. It is about 21m high and rises sheer out of the sea. It is situated on the Rockall Bank. Helen's Reef is one of several nearby skerries and is about 2km to the northeast. These reefs and the nearby Hasselwood Rock are normally only visible at very low tides.

Geology The Rockall Bank was formed about 55 million years ago as a result of volcanic activity. Rockall and the nearby shoals are formed of granite.

Landings In August 1810 the frigate *HMS Endymion* sailed to Rockall and plotted its position. The ship returned in July 1811, to survey the Rockall Bank. A landing was effected on 8th September, the first to be recorded.

On 18th September 1955 the rock was annexed for the British Crown by a party from *HMS Vidal*, who landed by helicopter. A plaque was affixed, which read, *"By authority of Her Majesty Queen Elizabeth II, by the Grace of God of the United Kingdom of Great Britain and Northern Ireland and of her other realms and territories Queen, Head of the Commonwealth, Defender of the Faith, and in accordance with Her Majesty's instructions dated the 14th day of September, 1955, a landing was effected this day upon this island of Rockall from HMS Vidal. The Union flag was hoisted and possession of the island was taken in the name of Her Majesty. [Signed] R H Connell, Captain, HMS Vidal, 18th September 1955."*

Shipwrecks have occurred here, the most serious being the *SS Norge* on 28 June 1904. This 3359GRT Danish

SS Norge which foundered on Helen's Reef in 1904 with great loss of life

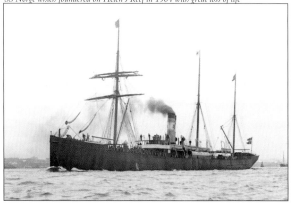

owned steamer was *en route* to New York with 727 passengers and 68 crew. It hit Helen's Reef in fog at 7:45am. The ship reversed off the rock, but was badly damaged and sank within 20 minutes.

Unfortunately the 8 lifeboats could only carry 251 survivors. As a result 635 people died and only 160 were saved. The Captain was exonerated, but the lessons were not learnt. A similar, but far greater, lack of lifeboats was to result in a much more severe loss of life only 8 years later when the SS *Titanic* sank, also in fog.

Other documented losses include a French or Spanish fishing vessel in 1686, from which survivors reached St Kilda, reported by Martin Martin. The brigantine *Helen* from Dundee, headed for Quebec, went aground on a rock here in 1824. The crew abandoned ship with the only boat, and left the passengers to their fate.

RAF Coastal Command picture taken in March 1943

Territorial Claims This isolated rock has been claimed by United Kingdom, Eire, Iceland and Denmark. It was formally annexed by Great Britain in the *Island of Rockall Act 1972* and is within the Exclusive Economic Zone claimed by UK. Negotiations regarding the exploitation of possible oil and gas reserves continue.

Basil Hall from "HMS Endymion" landing on Rockall in 1811

Royal Navy landing in 1955

Hirta, Soay and Stac Lee, St Kilda

Loganair Twin Otter in Flybe livery at Barra Airport

Travel The Outer Hebrides may appear to be remote, but are very easy to get to by both air and sea. There are connections by air from three Scottish airports. Ferries run from several ports, to which travel is facilitated by good roads as well as bus and rail links which tie in with the ferry schedules.

Sea The main ferry operator is Caledonian MacBrayne, known as *CalMac*. Roro ferries cover routes from Stornoway from Ullapool, Tarbert and Lochmaddy from Uig and Castlebay and Lochboisdale from Oban. Island Hopscotch and Island Rover tickets offer substantial savings.

Caledonian Macbrayne, Ferry Terminal, Gourock PA19 1QP Tel 0800 0665000 or 01475 650397 calmac.co.uk.

There are local offices at

Stornoway	Tel 01851 702361
Tarbert	Tel 01859 502444
Lochmaddy	Tel 01876 500337
Lochboisdale	Tel 01878 700288
Ullapool	Tel 01854 330304
Uig (Skye)	Tel 01470 220116

Air Direct daily services are operated into Stornoway Airport (SYY) from Edinburgh (EDI), Glasgow (GLA), Aberdeen (ABZ), Inverness (INV) and Benbecula (BEB) by Loganair. They also fly from Glasgow to Barra (BRR) and Benbecula.

Loganair Bookings 0344 800 2855 loganair.com For Loganair codeshares see their website.

Flybe Bookings Tel 0871 700 2000 flybe.com

Eastern Airways flights to Stornoway from Aberdeen. Bookings Tel 0870 366 9100 easternairways.com

British Airways codeshare Flybe has codeshare agreements with several airlines. For connecting flights to London (Heathrow, London City and Gatwick) and worldwide see ba.com

BA Bookings 0844 493 0787

MV "Loch Seaforth" arriving at Stornoway

Loganair Saab 340

Highlands and Islands Airports has live flight information at hial.co.uk

Air Discount Scheme (ADS) Anyone whose residence is in Colonsay, Orkney, Shetland, the Western Isles, Islay, Jura, Caithness and North West Sutherland can apply for membership. airdiscountscheme.com

Holiday Operators offer independent travel advice and bookings to the Western Isles. A wide range of specialist operators offering tours, cruises and activities. For the latest information see the current VisitHebrides brochure.

Hebridean Hopscotch is *"the only Outer Hebrides based provider of complete touring holidays with expert local travel advisors. You can come by air or sea, we're completely flexible on routes, accommodation and holiday duration. Just call us, then relax while we do all the work for you."*

Hebridean Hopscotch Holidays, 11 James Street, Stornoway Isle Of Lewis HS1 2QN Tel: 01851 706611 hebrideanhopscotch.com

Getting Out and About is all part of your visit. This Guide describes the huge number of places to explore, but the visitor must be able to reach them in the first place.

Distances can be deceptively long, it is 200km (130mi) from one end to the other! The roads are quiet, with little heavy traffic. Most are excellent, but many are still single track, so please take care.

The quiet roads, and generally flat country make for excellent cycling, but beware there are steep hills, and the wind can be strong. Many people take their bikes with them. Generally starting in Barra and heading northwards is the best option.

The Hebridean Way is a suggested cycling route which starts on Vatersay and ends at the Butt of Lewis. The total distance is c.185mi (296km).

MV "Clansman" docked at Castlebay

Many of the roads in the Outer Hebrides are single track

It is another 30mi (48km) to reach Stornoway from Ness. Side trips can easily add a further 125mi (200km).

Walking is also an option, but watch out for vehicles on the single track roads. Care should be taken on the main roads as traffic can be quite fast and there are no footpaths except in settlements. The many quiet side roads and peat tracks are very useful for creating circular countryside walks. Getting lifts is also no problem as people will often stop and ask if you really want to walk!

Local Travel The VICs in Stornoway, Tarbert, Lochmaddy, Lochboisdale and Castlebay stock the latest timetables of travel operators.

The Comhairle nan Eilean Siar (Western Isles Council) website cne-siar.gov.uk has all transport timetables.

Buses Local bus routes connect most of the main settlements, as well as with most inter island ferries and airports. There are no Sunday bus services. *"Please refer to the relevant tables for full details and do read the timetables carefully, as certain journeys do not operate every day, and parts of some routes run only on request. If in doubt, please check in advance with Stornoway Bus Station, Tel 01851 704327. In addition, you are strongly advised to check time and pick-up point for return journey."*

Inter Island Travel There are daily flights between

Stornoway, Benbecula and Barra run by Loganair. CalMac runs roro ferries between Harris and North Uist as well as between Eriskay and Barra.

Car & Bike Hire Most of the places and sites of interest mentioned in this guide are best reached by independent transport, since many are "off the beaten trail". A car is virtually essential to those with time limitations, while a bike allows a much more leisurely approach. The ideal is of course to combine the two.

There are car and bike hire outlets on all the main islands. It is essential to book in advance, especially during busy periods. Hebridean Hopscotch Holidays can handle all such bookings.

Taxis & Coach Tours Taxis are widely available, and are useful when catching ferries or flights. Minibus and coach tours are also run by several companies. Guiding is available from qualified Western Isles Tour Guides.

Tours are run by a variety of businesses throughout the Outer Hebrides. The best place to start is the visithebrides.co.uk website which lists over 20 options. As with other activities it is essential to contact operators to check availability and make bookings.

There is an extensive public transport network in the Outer Hebrides

Approaching Berneray ferry terminal

Petrol Stations Apart from in the main centres of population, filling stations tend to be few and far between. Most are closed on Sunday; some are open for long hours, others are not. It is best to keep your tank topped up, especially if you plan Sunday driving!

Activities Boat Trips, Wildlife cruises to islands, hillwalking and rambling, guided walks, sub aqua, sea kayaking, trout and salmon fishing, riding school, rock climbing and golf are some of the many organised activities on offer.

Trips to St Kilda are run by several operators from Leverburgh, Skye and Uig on Lewis. Regular excursions also go to Taransay and the Monachs. Details are included in the Places to Visit section, pages 213-214. Booking is essential. There may be occasional trips to the Flannans and the Shiants. Operators tend to be flexible in cases where bad weather causes cancellations, either offering alternative dates or refunds.

Yacht Charter is a very good option for experienced and qualified sailors. A two week charter is necessary to visit the remoter islands such as St Kilda. There is no better way to explore the many beautiful inlets and bays of the Outer Hebrides than by sailing boat with a group of friends. Whales, dolphins, Basking Sharks, Eagles, seabirds, otters and seals are frequently seen from yachts.

Road Safety is paramount in the isles, as everywhere.

1. Touring is not a race - take your time and enjoy it! Many of our roads are 'single track' which means that there are passing places to give way to oncoming traffic. If you are taking your time and enjoying the scenery, please be courteous and pull over to allow faster following traffic to pass.

2. Watch where you stop
The route is full of beautiful views, but please remember to carefully consider where you pull over as it is not safe nor responsible to stop in a spot that may affect passing traffic. Always park appropriately and never in passing places.

3. Speed
Although most rural roads may have a speed limit of 60mph always drive at a safe speed. The *"golden rule is that you must always be able to stop in the distance you can see to be clear ahead."* On winding narrow roads, the distance you can see to be clear ahead may be quite short. Also, always drive according to the weather conditions; in winter many stretches may become impassible in snow.

4. Share the road
Many hikers, cyclists and bikers also use these roads. Obey the Highway Code and give them plenty of room when passing. Check your mirrors and blind spots for any oncoming bikers and allow them to pass.

5. Share the road with animals
Sheep, cattle, deer and other animals are often encountered on these mostly unfenced roads. Take heed of any signs warning of animals, especially lambs. Hitting a Red Deer in the dark can be lethal. Do not sound your horn as this could frighten them and cause an accident!

Yacht charter is a good way to visit the outlying islands

WHAT TO SEE & DO IN THE OUTER HEBRIDES

The Outer Hebrides have a huge range of things to see and do. Whatever your interest, whether it be archaeology, history, nature, arts or culture there is something special for everyone. Gaelic remains the everyday language for many of the inhabitants, especially outside Stornoway.

Museums There are a number of museums, ranging from the newly renovated Museum nan Eilean, in Stornoway, to specialist village heritage centres. All are interesting and staffed by enthusiastic people who love to tell the story of their island or parish.

Nature enthusiasts will not be disappointed as the islands are a year round destination for bird watchers. The Outer Hebrides are also famous for wild flowers, including several rare orchids. Nature reserves include RSPB Balranald on North Uist and Loch Druidibeg NNR on South Uist.

Walkers will find the Outer Hebrides very welcoming, with a huge selection on offer, long distance and shorter. The Itineraries Section at the back of this book includes a variety of suggested routes. Alternatively there is a selection of walking books available. Tour guides also lead groups in many places.

Cycling Cyclists will find the quiet roads very enticing. Apart from one steep section in North Harris there are very few hills, though there are frequently strong headwinds. There is no better way to observe the life of the countryside than on

Kilda Cruises run trips to St Kilda - April to September

an ambling bike ride. The more energetic cyclist will find the 130mi (208km) route from Castlebay on Barra to Ness in Lewis an interesting route. Hebridean Hopscotch offers the *"Freedom of the Isles"* cycling holiday year-round, including bike hire, helmet, panniers, maps, B&B accommodation and ferry tickets.

Activities There are many to chose from, including walking to water sports, horse riding to hiking, fishing to surfing, there is a vast choice. Sea trips to St Kilda and other offshore islands are also on offer from several operators.

Coastline For many the prime attractions of the Outer Hebrides are the many stunningly beautiful beaches. There are no traditional seaside facilities and entertainments here, just miles and miles of amazing sandy strands. Those who prefer quiet coves or rugged cliffs will not be disappointed either, even in the winter.

Year-round Attractions The Outer Hebrides is a destination which will reward the visitor at any time of year and in any weather. That so many visitors come back time and again is testament to the place, but also to the welcome afforded by the inhabitants.

Accommodation This guide specifically does not cover information about accommodation, eating out or shopping as these are well covered by annual tourist guides or websites and subject to frequent change. The Outer Hebrides offers everything from five star hotels, self catering and bed & breakfast, to campsites.

Eating Out ranges from top class restaurants to very good pubs. An excellent range of local produce including prime Highland beef, lamb, and seafood as well as vegetables in season, is on offer. Few are disappointed.

Shopping The many small settlements have largely retained their local shops. In Stornoway these include butchers, bakers, fish shops, clothing shops, bookshops, hardware stores, newsagents and other interesting businesses.

Visitor Information Centres
visitouterhebrides.co.uk

The Visitor Information Centre in Stornoway is open all year, while those in Tarbert, Lochmaddy, Lochboisdale and Castlebay are seasonal. visitouterhebrides.co.uk is the Outer Hebrides Tourism Industry Association website.

Other information sources include visitor attractions, museums, local shops, accommodation providers and rural post offices. Books, maps and guides are available from VICs, local bookshops and visitor attractions, as well as online.

The Western Isles have a large range of Visitor Attractions, Tour Organisers, Activities, Shops and Services. For further information please see the current VisitHebrides brochure, or contact any of the businesses listed on these pages.

Stornoway Visitor Information Centre,
26 Cromwell Street, Stornoway HS1 2DD
Tel 01851 703088

Tarbert Visitor Information Centre,
The Pier, Tarbert, Isle of Harris HS3 3DG
Tel 01859 502011

Lochmaddy Visitor Information Centre,
Pier Road, Lochmaddy, Isle of North Uist
HS6 5AA Tel 01876 500321

Lochboisdale Visitor Information Centre,
Pier Road, Lochboisdale, Isle of South Uist
HS8 5TH Tel 91878 700286

Castlebay Visitor Information Centre,
Main Street, Castlebay, Isle of Barra HS9 5XD
Tel 01871 810336

Archaeology - Neolithic

Callanish, West Lewis

Archaeology - Standing Stones

Archaeology - Bronze Age

Bharpa Langass chambered cairn, North Uist

Dun Carloway broch, West Lewis

ARCHAEOLOGY - IRON AGE

Kisimul Castle, Barra

ARCHAEOLOGY - NORSE SITES

ARCHAEOLOGY & HISTORY
CASTLES & DUNS

ARCHAEOLOGY & HISTORY
LAND WARS

Archaeology & History
Churches

Best Beaches

St Clement's Church, Rodel, Harris

Boat Trips

Barra Fishing Charters, 4 Caolis, Vatersay, Isle of Barra HS9 5YL
Tel 01871 810679 barrafishingcharters.com
Sea Angling, Wildlife Spotting, Island Tours and Private Charter

Isle of Skye Yachts The Boat Shed, Ardvasar Isle of Skye IV45 8RS Tel 01471 844216
skyeyachts.co.uk
Yacht charters and RYA courses

Kilda Cruises, Angus Campbell, 4 Procropool, Isle of Harris HS3 3BG
Tel 01859 502060 kildacruises.co.uk *St Kilda was the highlight of our trip to Scotland. We highly recommend Kilda Cruises - professional and polite staff, fair price together with some great weather.*

Seilebost, West Harris

Cleits in Hirta

Sea Harris,Tarbert, Isle of Harris HS3 3DB Tel 01859 502007 seaharris.co.uk *Trips to St Kilda three times weekly from April to September, departing from Leverburgh harbour at 8am and returning around 7pm.*

Go to St Kilda from Skye, Derek Gordon, Uig, Isle of Skye IV51 9XX Tel 077899 14144 gotostkilda.co.uk *Distance Uig to St Kilda: 85 miles .journey time: 4 hours each way (3 hours 30 mins on good days). Approx 4 hours on Hirta. Cruise to Boreray and Sea Stacs.*

Lady Anne Boat Trips from Kallin Harbour, Grimsay, North Uist Tel 01870 602403 uistboattrips.com Trips to Monach Islands, Ronay, North Ford

Seatrek, 16 Uigen, Uig, Isle of Lewis HS2 9HX Tel 01851 672469 seatrek.co.uk Trips to St Kilda, Flannan Islands and round the Uig coast.

Taransay Day Trips, 5 Horgabost, Horgabost, Isle of Harris HS3 3HR Tel 01859 550260 From Horgabost Beach

Flannan Islands

DISTILLERIES

Abhainn Dearg Distillery, Carnish, Uig, Isle of Lewis HS2 9EX Tel 01851 672429 abhainndearg.co.uk Producer of single malt whisky since 2018. 106

Isle of Harris Distillers Ltd, Tarbert, Isle of Harris HS3 3DJ Tel 01859 502212 harrisdistillery.com Established in 2015, producer of *The Hearach* single malt and unique sugar kelp flavoured gin 115

MUSEUMS - MAIN

Museum nan Eilean, Lews Castle, Stornoway Isle of Lewis HS1 2NF Tel 01851 709266 cne-siar.gov.uk/museum Aspects of the history of the communities of Lewis and Harris from the first human settlement until more recent times........................ 212

MUSEUMS - SMALL & SPECIALIST

Dualchas (Barra Heritage and Cultural Centre) Castlebay, Isle of Barra HS9 5XD Tel 01871 810413 barraheritage.com Local history displays, art exhibitions and cultural events. 169

Bernera Museum, Breaclete, Bernera HS2 9LT Tel 01851 612285 tasglann.org.uk/en/heritage-groups/bernera Open in summer, displays on local subjects. Also runs the replica Iron Age house at Bosta. 100

Kildonan Museum, Kildonan, South Uist HS8 Tel 01878 710343 kildonanmuseum.co.uk Heritage and cultural amenity; museum, shop, Fèis room, cafe and archaeology room. 159

Museum nan Eilean, Sgoil Lionacleit, Benbecula HS7 5PJ Tel 01870 602864 cne-siar.gov.uk/museum Operates the exhibition area next the Library and supervises the Council's collection stored at Torlum.

Ness Historical Society, Cross, Ness, Isle of Lewis HS2 0TG Tel: 01851 810377
tasglann.org.uk/en/heritage-groups/ness
Over 500 artefacts illustrating the life of Ness: domestic life, social life, fishing and the sea....98

Taigh Chearsabhagh Museum & Arts Centre, Lochmaddy, Isle of North Uist HS6 5AA
Tel 01870 603970 taigh-chearsabhagh.org
"A place where people can meet, share ideas, learn new skills and experience cultural interpretation that is imaginative and stimulating." 132

Uig Heritage Centre, Crowlista, Uig, Isle of Lewis I IS2 9JG Tel 01851 672233
uigcommunity.com
"Collecting, preserving and promoting the rich culture and history of Uig. Open from May until early September, afternoons only."

MUSEUMS
OUTSIDE THE OUTER HEBRIDES

National Museum of Scotland, Chambers Street, Edinburgh EH1 1JF Tel 300 123 6789
nms.ac.uk Many artefacts from the Outer Hebrides are held including some Lewis chessmen.

British Museum, Great Russell Street, London WC1B 3DG Tel 020 7323 8299
britishmuseum.org
Holds most of the Lewis chessmen.

NATURE

Balranald RSPB Reserve, Hougharry, North Uist HS6 5DL Tel 01876 560287
rspb.org.uk 138

Loch Druidbeg National Nature Reserve, Scottish Natural Heritage, Stilligarry, South Uist HS8 5RS Tel 01870 620238
snh.org.uk 155

North Harris Eagle Observatory, Glen Meavaig, West Loch Tarbert, Harris HS3 3AW Tel 01859 502222
north-harris.org.................. 114

Lochmaddy, North Uist

SHOPPING, ARTS & CRAFTS
- STORNOWAY

An Lanntair, Arts Centre, Cafe & Shop, South Beach, Stornoway
Tel 01851 703307 lanntair.com
Exhibitions by local, national and international artists, cinema, cafe and shop. 75

Harris Tweed Hebrides, 25 North Beach Street, Isle of Lewis HS1 2XQ Tel 01851 700046 harristweedhebrides.com
An award-winning company, based at Shawbost, which revitalised the industry bringing fabric into 21st century fashion and design.

Roderick Smith Ltd, The Baltic Bookshop, 8-10 Cromwell Street, Stornoway
Tel 01851 702082
Excellent selection of local interest, Scottish and general books in the Western Isles' biggest bookshop, also a newsagent.

Charles MacLeod Ltd., Ropework Park, Stornoway Tel 01851 702445
charlesmacleod.co.uk Makers of Stornoway Black Pudding. Local lamb a speciality.

Lewis Chessmen

Harris Tweed

Sportsworld, Frances Street, Stornoway
HS1 2XD   Tel 01851 705464
sportsworldlewis.co.uk Fishing tackle, sales and
hire, fresh bait, sports gear. Top brands stocked.

Shopping, Arts & Crafts - West Lewis

Harbour View Gallery, Port of Ness, Lewis
Tel 01851 810735 abarber.co.uk
Original watercolours, prints and greetings cards
on sale from the studio and in shops.

Brenish Tweed, 5 Adabrock, Ness, Isle of Lewis
HS2 0TW
Tel 01851 810022 breanishtweed.co.uk
Lightweight lambswool, cashmere or Shetland
wool tweeds, also made to measure.

Borgh Pottery, 5 Penny House, Borgh, Lewis
Tel 01851 850345 borgh-pottery.com
Sue & Alex Blair, unique ceramics and gifts -
hand thrown studio pottery, irresistible shop.

Morven Gallery, Upper Barvas, Lewis
Tel 01851 840266 morvengallery.com
Original paintings, prints, ceramics, jewellery,
textiles, shop.

Willie Fulton in his studio

Gisla Woodcraft, Uig, Lewis
Tel 01851 672371 Scottish woods turned by
hand into many beautiful and useful items.

Shopping, Arts & Crafts - Isle Of Harris

Harris Tweed and Knitwear, 4 Procropool,
Drinishader, Harris HS3 3EB
Tel 01859 511217
harristweedandknitwear.co.uk
Harris Tweed weavers, wide selection of gar-
ments also knitwear and wool. 125

Isle of Harris Knitwear Company, Grosebay,
Harris HS3 3EF Tel 01859 551108
harristweedco.co.uk
Harris Tweed jackets and coats, designer knitwear, Hebrides local wool.

Seallam! Visitor Centre, Taobh Tuath, Harris
HS3 3JA Tel 01859 520258 seallam.com
People and landscape of the Hebrides, *Co Leis
Thu?* - genealogy research, books, CDs. 118

Skoon Art Cafe, 4 Geocrab, Harris HS3 3HB
Tel 01859 530268 skoon.com Original art
gallery, freshly made cakes, coffee and leaf tea.

Harris Tweed Isle of Harris, Caberfeidh,
Tarbert, Harris HS3 3DJ Tel 01859 502040
harristweedisleofharris.co.uk
Different, classy, stylish garments and accessor-
ies, large variety of Harris Tweed.

Finsbay Gallery, 1 Ardvey, Harris HS3 3JG
Tel 01859 530244 finsbaygallery.co.uk
Contemporary gallery, mainly Hebrides, exhib-
itions, originals and reproductions.

Willie & Moira Fulton, Ardbuidhe Cottage
Gallery & Studio, 3 Drinishader, Isle of Harris
HS3 3DX Tel 1859 511140 williefulton.com

The Mission House Studio Ltd, Finsbay, Isle of
Harris HS3 3JD Tel 01859 530227
missionhousestudio.co.uk Photographer Beka
Globe and Ceramic Artist Nickolai Globe.

SHOPPING, ARTS & CRAFTS
- NORTH UIST

Hebridean Smokehouse Ltd, Clachan, North Uist HS6 5HD Tel 01876 580209 hebrideansmokehouse.com Locally produced peat smoked salmon and sea trout. Buy from shop or by mail order. Tasting available..... 139

SHOPPING, ARTS & CRAFTS
- BENBECULA

MacGillivrays, Balivanich, Benbecula HS7 5LA Tel 01870 602525 macgil.co.uk "Aladdin's Cave" of quality souvenirs, clothing, tweed, books, crafts, fishing tackle, etc. 147

MacLennan's Supermarket, 2, Balivanich, Isle of Benbecula HS7 5LA Tel 01870 602308 maclennanssupermarket.co.uk An excellent independent, family-run supermarket first established in 1902.

SHOPPING, ARTS & CRAFTS
- SOUTH UIST

Hebridean Jewellery, Carnan, Iochdar, South Uist HS8 5QX Tel 01870 610288 hebridean-jewellery.co.uk Silver and gold jewellery, Pictish, Celtic and contemporary designs, established 1974..... 154

Salar Smokehouse Ltd, Lochcarnan, South Uist HS8 5PD Tel 01876 500293 salar.co.uk Distinctive, Flaky Smoked Salmon.

SHOPPING, ARTS & CRAFTS
- ISLE OF BARRA

A&C MacLean, Castlebay, Isle of Barra HS9 5XD Tel 01871 810291 Groceries, Fuel, Hardware, Gifts

VISITOR ATTRACTIONS

Arnol Black House, Arnol, Isle of Lewis HS2 9DB Tel 01851 710395 *Preserved 19th century blackhouse*. Nearby 39 Arnol dates from c.1900; small visitor centre and shop...........................92

Mission House Studio

Callanish Visitor Centre, Calanais, Lewis HS2 9DY Tel 01851 621422 callanishvisitorcentre.co.uk *"An excellent visitor centre, shop and cafe along with free parking, free entry and direct access to the stones."* 84

Dun Carloway Broch Centre Ionad an Duin Mhor, Carloway, Isle of Lewis HS2 9DY Tel 01851 643338 Free entry to the Visitor Centre and the Broch, open all year round. The Visitor Centre is open April to September. ...88

Gearrannan Blackhouse Village, 5a Gearrannan, Carloway, Isle of Lewis HS2 9AL Tel 01851 643416 gearrannan.com Self-catering accommodation close to Carloway Broch. Open all year. In summer, the village and its living museum are open for visitors. 90

Kisimul Castle, Castlebay, Isle of Barra HS9 5UZ Tel 01871 810313 On a small island, reached by small boat from jetty. Seasonal opening, under care of Historic Scotland. .. 170

Arnol Blackhouse

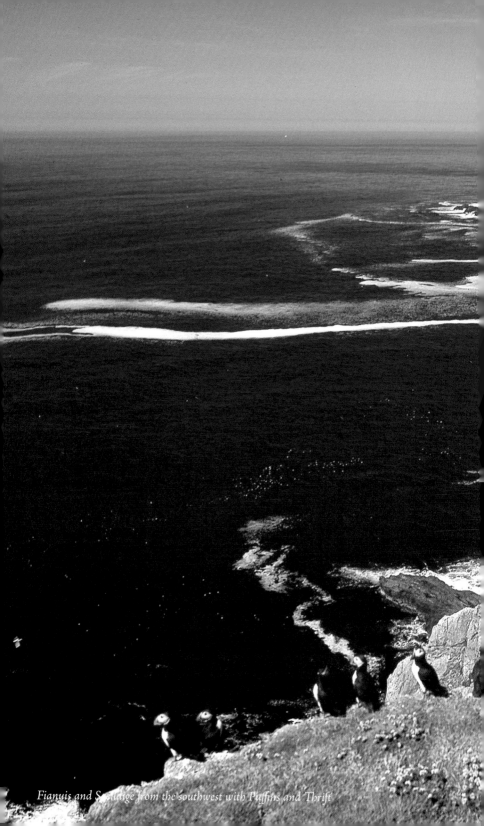

Fianuis and Sgeildige from the southwest with Puffins and Thrift

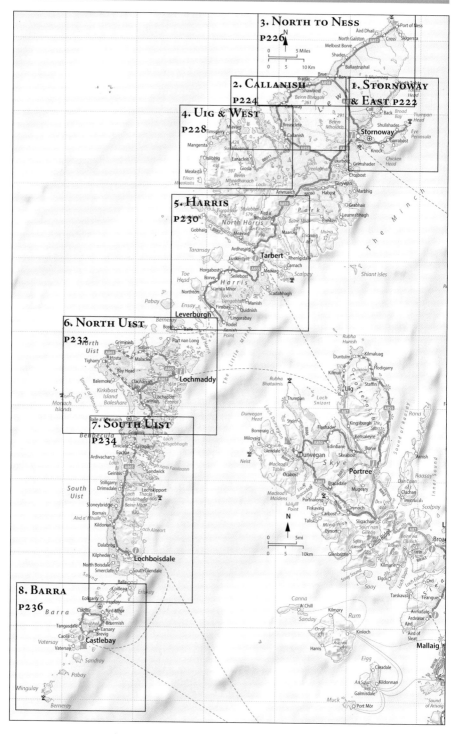

What to Do and See - Some Suggested Itineraries

What to Do and See in the Outer Hebrides This guide describes many places to visit throughout the area. The following itineraries will help visitors plan their time.

Maps This book makes extensive use of Ordnance Survey 1:250,000 maps. The 1:50,000 maps are best for in car use, while the 1:25,000 series is for walking or cycling.

Routes are circular where possible. Please note that most shops and services are closed on Sundays. In some areas shops, hotels, cafes and facilities are sparse, absent, or only open for limited times.

Roads and Distances Main roads are generally very good, except where sections are still single track. Plenty of time should be allowed because of this and to stop frequently to appreciate the stunning scenery. Approximate distances are included between the main centres (in miles only) in the table below.

Transport Although the itineraries here are designed for use with cars, they are also suitable for cyclists and those using public transport. Details of all Western Isles Transport Timetables are available online at the Comhairle nan Eilean Siar (Western Isles Council) website, cne-siar.gov.uk/travel.

Inter Island Ferries run between Harris and North Uist and also between South Uist and Barra. It is essential to book vehicles in advance for these crossings. CalMac Hopscotch tickets are very good value, see page 206.

DISTANCES IN MILES	Stornoway	Barvas	Port of Ness	Callanish	Timsgarry	Tarbert	Leverburgh	Lochmaddy	Balivanich	Lochboisdale
Stornoway	0	11	28	15.5	35	37	57	67	83	108
Barvas	11	0	17	18	38	46	66	72	95	118
Port of Ness	28	17	0	33	53	62	81	87	110	133
Callanish	15.5	18	33	0	20	39	59	64	87	110
Timsgarry	35	38	53	20	0	55	75	81	104	127
Tarbert	37	46	62	39	55	0	20	32	46	71
Leverburgh	57	66	82	59	75	20	0	10	26	51
Lochmaddy	67	72	87	64	81	32	10	0	19	42
Balivanich	83	95	110	87	104	46	26	19	0	31
Lochboisdale	108	118	133	110	127	71	51	42	31	0

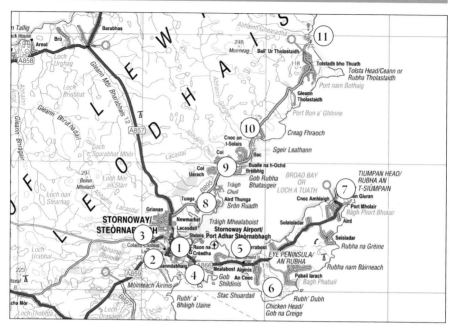

STORNOWAY (popn c.8,000) is the only major settlement in the Outer Hebrides. For those who prefer to stay in town and take advantage of its hotels, restaurants and shops, it is an ideal base. The oldest part is clustered around the northern shore of Stornoway Bay. The harbour dates from Norse times or earlier. Due to being on an island, it has a much greater range of shops and services than a similar sized mainland town.

The streets have evocative names, which reflect mainland influence. Most are English and include places, such as South Beach, or Bayhead, as well as famous people, including, Cromwell, Francis, Kenneth, Matheson and James Streets. There are no remains of any buildings from before the late 18th century.

An Lanntair hosts art exhibitions and live music, as well as a shop, cafe and cinema. The Museum nan Eilean, at Lews Castle, relates the history of life in the Outer Hebrides. Harris Tweed can be purchased as cloth or as garments; its history is explained at the Lewis Loom Centre. Locally made jewellery makes an attractive gift. The Baltic Bookshop and Hebridean Jewellery both stock a wide range of books of local and Scottish interest.

Stornoway is famous for its award winning black pudding, available from the makers, Charles Macleod Butchers. Stornoway Fish Smokers are well known for their kippers and smoked salmon.

STORNOWAY & NORTHEAST LEWIS			
1. Stornoway	72	8. Tunga	80
An Lanntair	75	Traigh Mealabost	80
Lewis Loom Centre	75	9. Coll	80
Point Street	72	Traigh Chuil	80
Stornoway Harbour	73	10. Gress	80
2. Lews Castle & Museum	75	St Olav's Church	80
3. War Memorial	76	Land Wars Memorial	80
4. Holm Point	77	Traigh Ghriais	80
5. The Braigh	78	Carn a' Mharc	80
Loch Branahuie	78	Sialabhig Mor	80
Braigh Na h-Aoidhe	78	11. Tolsta	80
St Columba's Church	78	Port Beag	81
Aignish Cairn	78	Tolsta Head	80
6. Chicken Head	78	Traigh Mhor	80
7. Tiumpan Head	78	Garry Beach	81
Loch an Duin	78	Bridge to Nowhere	81
Loch an t-Siumpain	78		

ORDNANCE SURVEY 1:50,000 and 1:25,000 maps of LEWIS	
OS Landranger Map 8	Stornoway & North Lewis
OS Explorer Map 459	Central Lewis & Stornoway

STORNOWAY & NORTHEAST LEWIS

1. Stornoway (page 72) The Inner Harbour, with its working fishing boats is always interesting. There are convenient free carparks at South Beach for a stroll around the town and an exploration of the many retail and culinary possibilities.

An Lanntair Arts Centre on South Beach is the local arts venue with a gallery, multipurpose theatre/cinema and an excellent cafe.

The Town Centre between South Beach and Bayhead hosts a wide variety of independent shops. Locally made Harris Tweed, jewellery and black pudding are all available.

Lewis Loom Centre (page 75) at 3 Bayhead is an eclectic but very interesting display on all aspects of wool, dyeing, spinning and weaving.

2. Lews Castle Grounds (page 74) There are extensive paths in the Castle grounds suitable for walking and cycling. The plantations include over 100 species of trees and shrubs. There are creative benches and seats, and several good viewpoints.

Museum nan Eilean (page 75) is now housed in a modern extension to Lews Castle. Some of the famous Lewis Chessmen may be seen here along with a wide variety of other artefacts.

3. Lewis War Memorial overlooks the town from the hill behind the hospital. It poignantly commemorates 1,151 Lewismen killed in WWI and the further 376 lost in WWII.

4 Holm Point (page 77) The memorial to those lost on HMS *Iolaire* in 1919 is at Holm Point, east of the town. It can be reached by walking round the north shore of the harbour or from a carpark near the monument (6km, 4mi, 2h).

5. The Braigh (page 78) is the local name for the beaches on the tombola linking Lewis to the Eye Peninsula. A walk along both beaches makes a pleasant afternoon.

Loch Branahuie and the south bay, Braigh Na h-Aoidhe, are good for wintering wildfowl.

St Columba's Church, Eaglais na-Aoidhe, dates from the 14th century with two interesting 15th century grave slabs (page 78).

Aignish Farm Raiders' Monument commemorates the events of 1888 when a riot broke out after the tenant was issued with an eviction notice which gave him 2 weeks to leave the rented farm.

6. Chicken Head (*Ceann na Circ*, page 78) on the southern side of Eye, makes a fine circular walk from Suardail or Pabail Iarach (8km, 5mi, 2h).

7. Tiumpan Head (page 78) is the most easterly point of Lewis. A circular walk round the headland takes in the lighthouse, Port Mholair, Loch an Duin, Cnoc Amhtaigh and Port nan Guiran. Look out for Risso's Dolphins (8km, 5mi,2h).

8. Tunga (page 80) overlooks a large area of saltflats northeast of Stornoway. They are very attractive to waders and waterfowl at all seasons.

Traigh Mealabost (page 80) is on the south side of the estuary and can be reached from Steinis. Care should be taken not to trespass onto the airport.

9. Coll overlooks a fine sandy beach (*Traigh Chuil*). Many peat tracks lead into the moorland here

10. Gress Land Wars Memorial (page 80) stands next to the river above the fine sandy beach of Traigh Ghriais. It commemorates events after WWI.

Carn a' Mharc is a Neolithic chambered cairn which can be reached via a peat track alongside Abhainn Ghriais (8km, 5mi, 2h).

St Olav's Church (*Teampall Amblaigh*, page 80) dates from the 12th century. Though oofless, it is the only intact Norse church in the Outer Hebrides.

Sialabhig Mor is just north of Gress c.1,000m southeast of the road. This beautiful sheltered sandy cove had geos, a small stack and a natural arch.

11. Tolsta (page 80) offers two beautiful sandy beaches. Garry Beach (*Traigh Geiradha*) is sheltered, with rock stacks, while Traigh Mhor is backed by extensive dunes. A lovely walk takes in both beaches, Tolsta Head and the small beach at Port Beag.

The "Bridge to Nowhere" was built in 1920 as part of a new road to Ness planned by Lord Leverhulme, cancelled on his death. The elegant 30m reinforced concrete structure is the start of the trail across the moor to Ness (17km, 11mi, 4h).

Tolsta Circular Walk starts at either of the carparks, or in North Tolsta village near the Post Office. It takes in both sandy beaches and Tolsta Head. The headland has a waymarked route around it. The low cliffs are quite spectacular with natural arches, stacks and geos. Dolphins are frequently seen close inshore here, especially in late summer 8km, 5mi, 2-3h for the whole circuit, 4km, 2.5mi, 1h headland only.

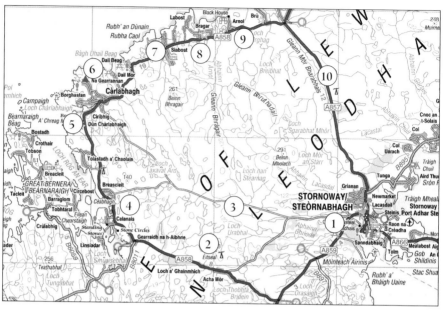

The Westside of Lewis

This circular route starts from Stornoway and runs clockwise, but it can be completed anticlockwise; begin at any point. Those with limited time should chose the main road which is mostly standard carriageway. The Pentland Road is all narrow single track with a few passing places.

Callanish Visitor Centre, with its interpretation displays and coffee shop, on the shore of East Loch Roag is the place to start a tour. The stone setting itself is about 300m up a steep and narrow road. Several other stone circles are prominent nearby.

Dun Carloway, the best preserved broch in the Outer Hebrides, stands on the side of a low hill 10km (6mi) further north. The restored blackhouse village of Gearrannan is about 4km (2.5mi) further on. Dalmore and Dalbeg are the first of several very attractive sandy coves which are situated along this coast. The latter, with its lochs and low cliffs, is especially photogenic. There is a restored Norse Mill and Kiln at Shawbost.

At Bragar a ruined broch sits on an islet in Loch an Duna. Nearby a large archway is made from the jawbones of a large Blue Whale. A preserved Blackhouse in the township of Arnol is now a museum in the care of Historic Environment Scotland. It clear-ly shows the way of life in the recent past. Across the road an early 20th century house gives a contrasting viewpoint of the past.

Return to Stornoway on the A857. It is 16km (10mi) across undulating moorland with many small lochans. There are innumerable peatbanks, some of which are still cut along this road.

Eating Out The Doune Braes Hotel is the only such establish-ment in this area and serves meals all day. There are cafés at the Gearrannan Blackhouse Village and at Callanish Visitor Centre.

Shopping The Callanish Visitor Centre has an interest-ing shop. The visitor centres at Dun Carloway and the Arnol Blackhouse also sell small ranges of books and other items. The Welcome Inn Filling Station at Barvas is the only shop on this itinerary. It has a very well stocked shop with a huge range of stock ranging from food and drink to car parts and tools.

ORDNANCE SURVEY 1:50,000 and 1:25,000 maps of LEWIS	
OS Landranger Map 8	Stornoway & North Lewis
OS Explorer Map 459	Central Lewis & Stornoway
OS Explorer Map 460	North Lewis

THE WESTSIDE OF LEWIS

1. From Stornoway take the first left at the Manor Roundabout onto the A859 to Tarbert. After c.1,400m the single track A858 bears right across the moor to Achmore (8mi,13km); alternatively keep on the main road and turn right at Tom Mhic Leoid.

2. Eithshal (NB305305, 223m, page 82) is a stiff climb up a concrete road to the summit. It is well worthwhile for the panoramic view (1km, 0.7mi, 1h).

3. The Pentland Road (page 82) follows the route of a planned light railway to Carloway. Birds such as Red and Black-throated Divers and Greenshank nest on the moorland and may be seen from the car. **Ancient Tree Stumps** found under peat banks can be seen scattered all along these side roads.

4. Callanish (NB213330, page 84) is one of the most spectacular Neolithic stone settings in the UK. The nearby Visitor Centre is well worth a visit. In addition to the main setting there are several small stone circles and standing stones; many are marked on the OS maps. A walking tour of the area is strongly recommended. The main sites are all signposted (10km, 6mi, 2h).

5. Dun Carloway (NB191412, page 88) This well preserved broch is about 200m up a short track from the carpark. There is a small Visitor Centre nearby. A walk around the township, perhaps including a bar meal at the Doune Braes Hotel is well worthwhile (4km, 2.5mi, 1h).

6. Gearrannan Blackhouse Village (NB194442, page 90) is signposted at Carloway. This restored street of thatched blackhouses offers unique self catering cottages, a hostel and a café.

Carloway to Dalbeg (page 90) From Gearrannan follow a trail along the coast to the attractive sandy bay of Dalmore and then on to sheltered Dalbeg. Loch Dalbeg is a good place to look for Otters. Return via the main road (12km, 7.5mi, 3h).

7. Shawbost Norse Mill (NB244463, page 90) is signposted off the A858. This horizontal axis mill and nearby kiln are restored to working order and typical of those in use for many centuries.

Shawbost Museum is part of *Ionad Na Sean Sgoil* (Old School Centre). Local artefacts, archives and displays on the history of the area.

Shawbost Beach is at the head of a pretty cove.

This 200m expanse of sand is separated from Loch a' Bhaile by a shingle ayre. There is a fine short circular walk from the Community Centre around the township taking in Siabost na Thuath, the beach and Siabost bho Dheas (3mi, 4km, 1-2h).

8. Bragar is a pretty little township, bypassed by the A858. All around there are ruins of blackhouses. There are many possible short circular walks to explore between nearby Shawbost and here.

Bragar Broch is situated on an islet in Loch an Duna, connected to the shore by a causeway. This is a very scenic location well worth exploring.

9. Arnol Blackhouse Museum (NB311493, page 92) is a restored example of a traditional farmhouse. The people and their stock were under one roof. There was no chimney and the roofs were thatched. **No39 Arnol** is across the road and dates from the mid 20th century. It is typical of the many such houses in the area which lie abandoned.

Arnol Circular Walk - follow a track down to the low, rugged coast from the Blackhouse Museum. Head west past the shingle storm beaches of Port Arnol and Port Mhor Bragar. Return via the broch and whalebone arch and the A838 (8km, 5mi, 1.5h).

Loch na Muilne RSPB Reserve is a short distance across the moor east of the Blackhouse. The star attraction in spring and summer is breeding Red-necked Phalaropes. Dunlin, Snipe and Golden Plovers also nest here. Whooper Swan and Greylag Geese stop here on migration.

Loch Arnoil is also part of an interesting circular walk. In contrast to Loch na Muilne it is fed by Ahainn Arnoil, with an estuary to the beach at Port Arnol. The shore here is a shingle storm beach with a small ayre protecting the loch. This is another good birdwatching place, but Otters are the main attraction. The best times are early morning and evening, especially when cubs are being fed.

10. Gleann Mor Bharabhais (Glen More Bravas) At the Barvas junction turn left along the A857 to return to Stornoway. This road crosses undulating moorland, dotted with countless lochs, many of which drain into Abhainn Bharabhais. There are many peatbanks which are still worked. The little sheds are *shielings* used by the peat cutters.

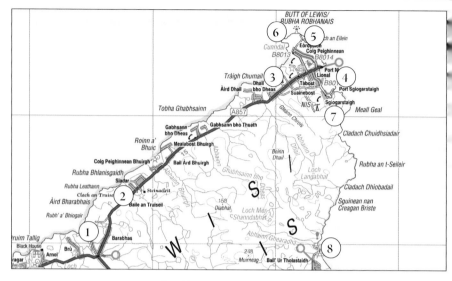

BARVAS TO NESS The A857 passes through a series of crofting townships in the 15mi (24km) from Barvas to Ness. There are many places of interest, including ancient sites, beautiful coastline and Ness, with its harbour, Heritage Centre and the Butt.

In summer the machair is awash with colourful wild flowers. Many species of birds may be seen or heard here, including the normally elusive Corncrake, which is locally common. Gannets and various cetaceans may be seen offshore.

Linear Tour From Stornoway, take the A857 to Barvas. The road passes through moorland and then a series of small villages. Crofting is practised; mostly only sheep are kept. The placenames are attractive, all derived from Old Norse. Many are signposted with Modern Gaelic orthography, hiding the Norse.

This coastline is low rocky cliffs with frequent small coves which shelter exquisite sheltered beaches. At Barvas, and from Dell to Eoropie, there are wide sandy beaches backed by extensive dunes and machair.

The suggested walks include visits to all of the main places of interest. If time is short they can all be curtailed to include just the main sights. Not to be missed are Port of Ness, the Butt of Lewis and the Eoropie or Swainbost beaches.

Comunn Eachdraidh Nis (Ness Historical Society) was founded in 1977 and has amassed a significant archive of documents, photographs, recordings and artefacts about the area. A visit is strongly recommended, it is open on weekdays all year.

Shopping Those interested in retail therapy will not find any chain stores or shopping centres here. However aficionados of art and pottery will not be disappointed. There are several general stores; a number of old fashioned country shops still exist.

Galleries The Morven Gallery at Barvas, has exhibitions from April to September by numerous recognised artists. Wonderful coffee, leaf teas and homemade cakes are available in the cafe. At Borgh Pottery Sue Blair crafts hand thrown pottery. Harbour View Gallery overlooks the harbour at Port of Ness. It is the studio of Anthony Barber whose work is primarily on the Highlands and Islands.

Eating Out The Cross Inn, at Ness, is the most northerly hotel on Lewis. Borve Country House, is opposite the pottery.

ORDNANCE SURVEY 1:50,000 and 1:25,000 maps of LEWIS

OS Landranger Map 8   Stornoway & North Lewis
OS Explorer Map 460   North Lewis

North Lewis & Ness

1. Barvas (page 90) is 11mi (18km) from Stornoway via the A837. This is the first of several scenic crofting townships on the way to Ness.

Barvas Beach & Machair Turn off the A857 to Lower Barvas and park at the end of the track. A fine sandy beach which is popular with surfers, is backed by extensive dunes and machair. The Cladh Mhuire cemetery has an ancient chapel ruin.

Circular Walk Start from Barvas Beach and follow the coast to Port Arnoil. Return via tracks across the moor to Brue and thence the starting point. This walk is best in summer (10km, 6mi, 2h).

2. Shader (page 94) Park at Clach an Truiseil, a tall standing stone (NB377538, signposted). Follow a track down to the shore to the tiny beach at Siorrabhaig then along the shore to a ruined chapel, Teampull Pheadair. Another track goes back to the main road near the school. Cross the road to visit Clach Stein Lin standing stone and Steinicleit, a ruined chambered cairn with good views, before returning to the start (6km, 4mi, 1.5h).

3. Traigh Dail, Traigh Chrois & Traigh Chumil (page 97) are a series of lovely pristine sandy coves sheltered by low cliffs. They are accessible by tracks from North Dell and Swainbost. All of them are delightful to visit, whether in a severe northwesterly winter storm or on a midsummer evening.

Traigh Swainbost & Eoropie Sands are more open, backed by dunes and machair, resplendent with wild flowers in summer. For a longer walk, park at Eoropie and follow the beaches and headlands southwest to Dell Sands, either return on the road or by the dunes. There are multiple tracks to access the shore and by which to return (up to 12km, 8mi, 3h).

4. Ness is the most northerly part of Lewis. There is a different feel from the rest of the island. Traditionally the Men of Ness have been seamen with a distinctly Norse heritage. Some were fishermen but most went deep sea, many as ships' Captains. The roads are lined with houses and with a seaward aspect.

Port of Ness (page 96) is a very attractive small harbour with a tendency to silt up with sand.

Buail a' Muigh is 300m of beautiful sandy beach south of the harbour. There is a fine walk south along the coast from here to Skigersta with its small,

exposed, harbour (6km, 4mi, 1h).

Ness Heritage Centre is based in the former Cross Primary School. On display are local artefacts and old photographs. Extensive archives on crofting, fishing, wars, boats, etc. may be consulted. The famous pierced cross-slab from Rona is here.

Taigh Dhonnchaidh Arts & Music Centre (Duncan's House), 44 Habost *is committed to being a centre of excellence for the promotion and enhancement of the Gaelic language, music and the arts."*

Teampall Mholuaidh may date from the 14th century and is associated with many myths and legends. The annual sacrifice of ale to the sea-god, Shony, is particularly interesting.

5. Dun Eistein (page 99) is an ancient fort which can be reached by a footbridge northeast of Five Penny Ness. This fortress was held by the Morrisons for centuries until it was captured and sacked by the MacLeods. A pleasant circular walk along the cliffs starts at Port of Ness (4km, 2.5mi, 2h).

6. The Butt of Lewis (NB520666, page 98) is the most northerly point on the Outer Hebrides. On a very clear day Cape Wrath and the mountains of Sutherland may be seen on the eastern horizon, usually during a winter anticyclone. There are particularly interesting rocks on this coast. The Butt is an excellent seawatching site for seabirds during migration times. Whales and dolphins are sometimes seen offshore from here.

Circular Walk Park at the lighthouse and follow the wild coast to Roinn a' Roidh and Luchruban. There is a large natural arch on the north side of Cunndal. Return via Eoropie on the public road, stopping to look at the many *feannagan* in the fields. Port Stoth was the main landing place for the lighthouse in former times (4km, 2.5mi, 1h).

7. Ness to Tolsta This moorland and coastal walk follows the route of a road proposed in the 1920s. Park at the Skigersta road end and follow the peat track southwards. The route passes peat cuttings, shielings and many small lochs. Claddach Chuidshader (NB553587) is a particularly attractive cove with a small sandy beach. From here the trail becomes much rougher as it traverses remote moorland. The "Bridge to Nowhere" at Tolsta marks the destination (16km, 10mi, 6h).

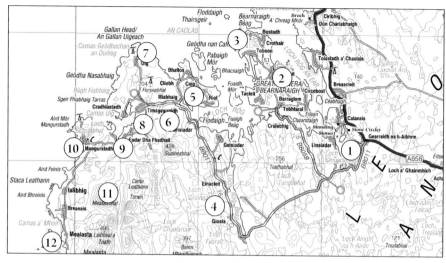

West Lewis The Uig area is perhaps the most beautiful of all in Lewis, with its golden sands, clear blue sea and machair, backed by hills of over 500m. The approach by single track road over undulating moorland makes arrival at the west end of Glen Valtos all the more impressive.

Linear Tour From Garynahine, it is about 32km (20mi) along

West Lewis	
1. Ceann Hulavig	86
2. Great Bernera	100
Breicleat	100
3. Camas Bosta	100
4. Gisla	102
5. Miavaig	102
Valtos Peninsula	102
Traigh na Berie	102
Glen Valtos	103
6. Aird Uig	103
Forsnaval	107
7. Uig	104
Timsgarry	104
8. Ardroil	106
Carnish	106
Abhainn Dearg Dist	107
9. Mangersta	106
10. Mealsival	107
11. Breanish	107
12. Mealista	107

the B8011 to Timsgarry. The first stop is the outlying small Callanish stone circle, Ceann Hulavig, about 1mi from the junction. There are fine views down Loch Roag from here.

Gisla is in a pretty location facing Little Loch Roag. The hydro electric power station is the only one on the Outer Hebrides.

At Miavaig a side road turns to the right and meanders around the Valtos peninsula. The township names of Cliff, Berie, Riff and Uigen are echoed by the equally beautiful surroundings, especially the beaches of Camas na Clibhe and Traigh na Berie.

The B8011 traverses the glacial valley of Glen Valtos before reaching Uig. A side road leads to Aird Uig and Gallan Head with its old radar base and modern communications mast. There is a fine panorama from Forsnaval (205m).

From Crowlista to Carnish, Uig Bay presents different aspects as light, weather, tide and season changes. There is a special beauty in this landscape which has to be savoured to be understood.

As the road winds westwards over wild and stony moorland, there are further surprises. These include Mangersta Sands and the nearby headland of Ard Mor Mangersta. The remote settlements of Islivig and Brenish are passed before reaching the end of the road at Mealista. From here, Hushinish in Harris is less than 16km (10mi) away over trackless rocky hills and moorland.

The summit of the highest hill on Lewis, Mealsival (574m), can be reached from Islivig, while there is a series of lovely changeable sandy and shingly beaches at Camas a' Mhoil, Mol Forsgeo, Mol Tiacanish and Camas Chala Moil.

Stay Timsgarry is 35 miles from Stornoway. To appreciate this area it is essential to stay at least a couple of nights. Baile-na-Cille at Timsgarry and Auberge Carinish are especially recommended.

Eating Out Loch Croistean Coffee Shop and Restaurant is on the B8011 south of Miavaig. Auberge Carinish, and Gallan Head Restaurant are both excellent, booking required.

ORDNANCE SURVEY 1:50,000 and 1:25,000 maps of this area

| OS Landranger Map 13 | West Lewis & North Harris |
| OS Explorer Map 458 | West Lewis |

West Lewis

1. Ceann Hulavig (NB230304) is one of the small Callanish stone circles. It overlooks the B8011 on a small hillock overlooking Loch Roag with fine views over Callanish c.1mi (1.5km) from Garynahine.

2. Great Bernera (page 100) is reached via the B8059 and a concrete bridge, first on Lewis.

Breicleat has a Community Centre and Museum with many interesting artefacts as well as a café. The local shop and Post Office also has fuel pumps.

Walk From Breacleit follow a signposted path to a restored Norse mill and on to the old lobster pond at Loch Risay (3km, 2mi, 1h).

3. Camas Bosta (NB 137402, page 100) is a beautiful sandy beach with a replica Iron Age house. From here head west across the beach and follow the low cliffs to the headland of Siaram Bosta. Follow the coast to Tobson, returning via the small hill of Shelaval (87m) Loch a' Sgail (5km, 3mi, 2h).

4. Gisla is a pretty little settlement near the head of Little Loch Roag. The hydro electric power station here was the first in the Outer Hebrides. It was commissioned in 1960 and generated 720kW.

5. Miavaig is a very sheltered harbour at the western head of Loch Roag. Seatrek operate boat trips to St Kilda and the Flannans from here.

Valtos is a delightful small peninsula north of Miavaig. The beaches are some of the best in the Outer Hebrides. Cliff Beach or Camas na Clibhe is a 700m arc of sand sheltered by cliffs. Traigh na Berie or Valtos Beach is a 1500m wide arc of perfect white shell sand backed by dunes and machair (page 102). The campsite here is in a lovely situation.

Berie Broch is above the beach beside Loch na Berie, while there is a dun on an islet on Loch Baravat. A series of ruined Norse mills stand on the burn which runs down from Loch Baravat (4km, 2.5mi, 2).

6. Glen Valtos is a steep-sided valley cut by a melting glacier which once occupied Uig Bay. The floor of the valley has exceptionally rich grassy areas.

7. Aird Uig (page 103) was the base which served RAF Aid Uig, a radar and communications site on Gallan Head. Many of the buildings are now houses; one is an excellent restaurant. A walk around Gallan Head including outside the base fence affords fine views. There is a ruined chapel at An Bheannaich (4km, 2.5mi, 1h).

8. Uig Sands (p158) are enclosed by a vast bay which stretches in an arc from Crowlista round to Carnish. At low tide practically the whole area is exposed white sand. A whole day could be spent between Timsgarry and Carnish, exploring the beach, dunes, machair and headlands (8km, 5mi, 3h).

Timsgarry has a shop, filling station and wonderful views over Uig Bay backed by the mountains of Harris. The cemetery from where ghosts are said to roam is next to Baile na Cille Guest House. Dun Borranish is on an islet to the south.

9. Ardroil Dunes cover much of the east side of Camas Uig. It was here that the Lewis Chessmen were discovered in 1831. There is a fine campsite here and lovely sand dunes to explore. This is an excellent starting point for exploring Uig Sands.

Carnish overlooks Uig Sands from the west. There is a beautiful panoramic view from the promontory above the settlement (1000m, 1h).

Abhainn Dearg Distillery is in a shed next to the turnoff to Mealista on the site of a former Salmon hatchery. The whisky may be sampled and purchased on site.

10. Mangersta (p106) The Mangersta Sands are bounded on both sides by low, rugged cliffs. The little cove of Sheilavig is to the south, Ard More Mangersta is to the north. The wild rocky terrain, jagged cliffs and the beach backed by dunes make this a dramatic place to explore, allow plenty of time.

11. Mealsival (NB023270, 574m, p107) is the highest hill in Uig. Park at Islivig and follow a peat track up towards Loch Sandavat, then strike straight up the north saddle of the hill, avoiding the rocky outcrops on the west face. There are fine panoramic views over Uig and the mountains 6km, 4mi, 2h).

12. Breanish (p107) has abundant remains of a WWII Chain Home Low radar station. There are also remains of another Norse mill in a burn at the side of the road in the village.

Mealista is at the end of the road. Park at Mol Forsgeo before the gate. A gentle stroll along the shore from Camas a' Mhoil past Mol Forsgeo to Camas Chala Mhoil and back is very pleasant on a summer evening. During a winter storm huge waves break spectacularly on these storm beaches (6km, 4mi, 2-3h).

HARRIS is separated from Lewis by high mountains and the deep inlets of Loch Resort in the west and Loch Seaforth in the east. Most of the area is wild, rocky and remote, but the west coast has a series of expansive and enchantingly beautiful beaches. The main settlement is Tarbert.

The Golden Road twists its way slowly up the rugged and heavily indented east coast. It passes through a series of interestingly named townships, many with resident artists or Harris Tweed weavers. The views over the Minch to Skye are stunning.

ORDNANCE SURVEY 1:50,000 and 1:25,000 maps of this area	
OS Landranger Map 13	West Lewis & North Harris
OS Landranger Map 14	Tarbert & Loch Seaforth
OS Landranger Map 18	Sound of Harris
OS Explorer Map 455	South Harris
OS Explorer Map 456	North Harris & Loch Seaforth

HARRIS

1. Loch Seaforth (page 112) is the eastern boundary between Harris and Lewis. This long, narrow, sea loch stretches over 15mi (24km) inland.

2. Clisham (799m, page113) Park off the A859 at Abhainn Mharaig and strike uphill, following the burn at first. At about 600m keep to the left of the craigs. Return by the same route, again keeping to the west of the craigs (540m, 5km, 3mi, 2h).

3. Rhenigidale is one of the remotest townships in the Outer Hebrides. It is accessed by a side road off the A859 which passes through a wild landscape.

4. West Loch Tarbert (*Loch a Siar*) stretches from Tarbert to Taransay.

Bunavoneader (page113) was a whaling station from the 1890s until 1922. Ruins of buildings and a slipway are all that remains.

North Harris Eagle Observatory is reached via a 1.5mi (2km) track north from Meavaig (NB101063).

Amhuinnsuidhe Castle has elegant public rooms and well-appointed bedrooms. It is on one of the finest sporting estates in Scotland.

Hushinish (page 114) Park near the jetty and follow the coast north to Traigh Mheilen, with its beautiful sandy beach. Skirt the coast to Cravadale and Loch na Cleavag, return by a track (8km, 5mi, 3h).

5. Ardhasaig is on the A859 north of Tarbert with beautiful views to the Harris mountains and down West Loch Tarbert.

Tarbert (page 115) is the main village and ferry port on Harris, with hotels, interesting shops, cafés, bars, a filling station and a bank.

Harris Distillery (page 115) opened in 2015. It produces *Na Hearadh* malt whisky and *The Dottach* gin.

Rhenigidale Trail starts at Urgha east of Tarbert. A path follows Laxdale Lochs to Maraig, then the side road south to Rhenigidale, before resuming the postman's path back to Urgha (350m, 18km, 11mi, 6h).

6. Scalpay (page 115) Park at Kennavay near a sheepfold and walk to the lighthouse at Eilean Glas. Return northwest along the coast and then up the summit of Ben Scoravick (104m, 5km, 3mi, 2h).

7. West Harris Beaches are the jewel in the crown of the Outer Hebrides, stretching for 8mi (13km).

Luskentyre (page 116) Turn off the A859 south of Tarbert and follow a side road round the coast. The lovely beach of Traigh Rosamol faces the Sound of Taransay (3km, 2mi, 2h).

8. Seilebost (page 116) forms the west shore of Corran Seilebost and faces Luskentyre across a beautiful bay (2km, 1.5mi, 1h).

Horgabost & Traigh Iar (page 116) are on opposite sides of Aird Nisabost. From Traigh Iar walk along the beach, then climb to the Clach Mhic Leoid standing stone for a fine view. Head east to Traigh Nisabost with its fine dunes then return along the main road (3km, 2mi, 1h).

9. Traigh Scarista & Traigh an Taoibh Tuath (p118) form a huge area of sand at low tide, backed by salt marshes and Ceapabhal (339m).

Seallam! Visitor Centre has displays on the natural and cultural history of the Outer Hebrides and is home to Co Leis Thu?, a major genealogical archive.

36 Northton (p118) is home to the unique and unmissable Croft 36 roadside shop and catering business which delivers ready to eat meals.

Walk From Northton take a track across the machair to the ruined Rubh'an Teampall. A path goes towards the summit of Ceapabhal (365m) for a wonderful vista (8km, 5mi, 2h).

10. Leverburgh (*An t-Ob*, page 119) is a thriving village and port for the roro ferry to North Uist.

11. Rodel (p120) From the church take a track towards Borosdale, then head south over moorland to Renish Point, from where there is a fine view of Loch Rodel (50m, 6km, 4mi, 2h).

Roinebhal (460m, p120) dominates the south end of Harris. The summit can be reached via a track leading to Lingerabay Quarry. The upper flanks are of gleaming white Anorthosite. Take care near the cliffs of Coire Roinebhal (400m, 5km, 3mi, 3h).

12. The Sound of Harris is strewn with islets, reefs and sandbanks. The ferry takes a tortuous route through the hazards. This is one of the best places in the Outer Hebrides to observe seabirds.

13. Golden Road follows the rugged east coast of Harris from Rodel to Miavaig. There are interesting businesses to visit, including **the** Mission House Studio (sculpture & photography), Isle of Harris Knitwear Co, Skoon Art Cafe, Harris Tweed & Knitwear and Willie & Moira Fulton (painting).

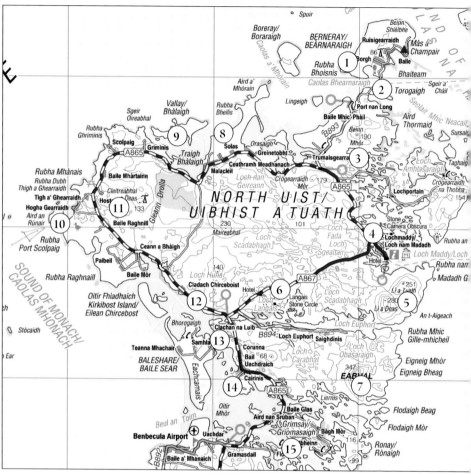

NORTH UIST has much to interest the visitor, with outstanding archaeology, many lochs amid wild moorland and spectacular beaches on the west. It is especially noted for Otters, wild flowers, Corncrakes and waders.

NORTH UIST			
1. Berneray	134	8. Greinetobht	136
2. Port nan Long	133	Corran Aird	136
Dun Sticir	133	9. Vallay Strand	136
3. Dun Torchuill	133	10. Balranald RSPB Res	138
4. Lochmaddy	130	11. Cleitreabhal	137
5. North & South Lee	131	12. Clach Mor a' Che	138
6. Langass	140	Claddach Kirkibost	138
Bharpa Langass	140	13. Hebridean Smokehouse	139
Pobull Fhinn	140	14. Teampall na Trionaid	142
7. Eaval	130	15. Grimsay	143

Circular Tour This can be started from Lochmaddy, Berneray or from the south depending on which ferry was taken. From Lochmaddy take the A865 northwest and then the B893 to Berneray, via Port na Long. For the anticlockwise experience take the A689 from Lochmaddy. Regardless of the direction, there are many fine views over the moorland, lochs, hills, beaches and saltmarshes. North Uist will not disappoint nature lovers.

ORDNANCE SURVEY 1:50,000 and 1:25,000 maps of this area	
OS Landranger Map 18	Sound of Harris
OS Landranger Map 22	Benbecula & South Uist
OS Explorer Map 453	Benbecula & South Uist
OS Explorer Map 454	North Uist& Berneray

NORTH UIST

1. Berneray (page 134) is joined to North Uist by a causeway. The ferry from Leverburgh on Harris docks here. Berneray is a beautiful island with a vast sandy beach stretching the length of the west coast, backed extensive sand dunes and machair.

Walk From the carpark inland from Borve, strike west across the machair and head north or south along the beach (up to 10km, 6mi, 3-4h).

2. Port nan Long is a pretty little inlet with salt-marsh and fine views over Caolas Berneray.

Dun Sticir (NF897777) is an example of a broch which remained in use until Medieval times.

3. Dun Torchuill (NF889738) may be the most spectacular broch on North Uist. It is situated on an islet and joined to the shore by a causeway

4. Lochmaddy (page 130) is situated at the head of an excellent natural harbour.

Taigh Chearsabhagh Museum and Arts Centre, housed in the oldest building in the village, is an essential visit. A vibrant and stimulating exhibition and outreach programme run throughout the year.

Walk An evening stroll around Lochmaddy, exploring the 19th century buildings, old harbour and rugged coastline is very pleasant (4km, 2.5mi, 2h).

5. North Lee & South Lee (262m & 281m, page 131) overlook Lochmaddy from the east. The approach is either a long tramp across the moor from the A867 west of Lochmaddy, or by small boat for a more shorter excursion (10km, 6mi, 4-5h).

6. Bharpa Langass (NF838658, p140), the most intact Neolithic chambered cairn in the Outer Hebrides, is 200m from a carpark on the A687.

Pobull Fhinn stone setting is 400m east of Langass Lodge overlooking Loch Langass and Eaval.

Circular Walk From the signposted carpark follow the path to Bharpa Langass cairn, then down to Pobull Fhinn stone circle. Return via the road with lovely views throughout, (3km, 2mi, 1h).

7. Eaval (page 142) The highest hill on North Uist is prominent. It is reached across the moorland from the Claddach Chairinis road end (NF856590) which turns east just before the causeway to Grimsay. A long, hard tramp (12km, 8mi, 4h), alternatively get dropped off and picked up later by a boat from Kallin Harbour on Grimsay much nearer the hill.

8. Corran Aird a Mhorain (page 136) is a long sand spit which almost encloses Traigh Iar. The machair here is especially beautiful in early summer.

Walk Park at Greinetobht and then follow the track across the machair to Corran Aird a' Mhorain. From here the Udal and the headland of Aird a' Mhorain can be reached. Return via Traigh Iar and the machair (10km, 6mi, 3-4h).

9. Vallay Strand is another huge area of sand which is exposed at low tide. A ford leads across it to the interesting island of Vallay. Great care needs to be taken with tide times to avoid being stranded.

10. Balranald RSPB Reserve (NF718698, page 138) occupies much of the western tip of North Uist. The varied habitats are home to many species of waders and waterfowl as well as Corncrakes. The wild flowers on the machair attract butterflies and bumblebees. A waymarked trail starts at the visitor centre (6km, 4mi, 2-4h).

11. Cleitreabhal a Deas (133m, NF749717) is a fine viewpoint with a panoramic scene extending as far as St Kilda and covers the west side of the Uists. There is a Neolithic chambered cairn, with an Iron Age wheelhouse built in to it as well as a nearby standing stone, all presided over by a radio mast.

12. Clach Mor a' Che (page 138) is a 2.7m high monolith which stands on the shore overlooking Kirkibost Island. Nearby, Dun na Carnaich is another ruinous Neolithic chambered cairn.

Claddach Kirkibost Centre, in a renovated old school, is community-run. It provides services including a nursery, a well-regarded café, a gift shop, food production and sales under the Hebridean Kitchen brand, internet access and meeting facilities, as well as a programme of walks and talks.

13. Hebridean Smokehouse (p139) at Clachan produces and sells a delicious range of peat smoked Salmon and Sea Trout. It is an essential stop for all lovers of seafood.

14. Teampall na Trionaid (NF813607) at Carnish was a religious and educational centre established c.1200AD by Somerled's daughter.

15. Grimsay (p143) is joined to North Uist by a causeway. This quiet little island has a busy fishing harbour from which boat trips run in the summer.

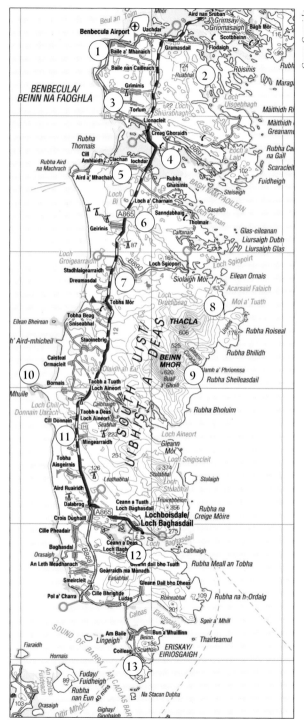

South Uist is long and thin, with a rugged east coast, and hills reaching 620m. In contrast the Atlantic coast is one long sandy beach, backed by fertile machair. It is joined by causeways, in the north to Benbecula and in the south to Eriskay.

Linear Tour Visitors can arrive from the north, via Lochboisdale or from Eriskay. Most of the roads on South Uist are single track with passing places which means that progress is slow. There are numerous side roads leading to the east and west which merit exploration.

South Uist has secret attractions for hillwalkers. The hills of Hecla (606m) and Beinn Mhor (620m) hide a series of majestic corries on their eastern flanks.

ORDNANCE SURVEY 1:50,000 and 1:25,000 maps of South Uist	
OS Landranger Map 22	Benbecula & South Uist
OS Landranger Map 31	Barra & South Uist
OS Explorer Map 453	Benbecula & South Uist

BENBECULA & SOUTH UIST

1. Balivanich, the main settlement on Benbecula, developed after the arrival of the RAF in WWII and continued with the development of a missile range. **Walk** The west coast of Benbecula (page 144) is a series of fine beaches backed by dunes and machair. Low rocky headlands separate the sandy bays. Try a coastal walk from Balivanich to Liniclate, returning mostly by side roads (up to 16km, 10mi, 3-4h).

2. Rueval and Rossinish (page 146) The hill of Rueval offers fine views over Benbecula. It can be accessed by a path from the Market Stance (144m, 5km, 3mi, 1h). For Rossinish follow the moorland track eastwards (a further 10km, 6mi, 3h return).

3. Borve Castle is just a ruin in a field now, but was once the base of the Clanranalds.

Liniclate has a large community school with a library and an outpost of the Museum nan Eilean.

4. South Ford is crossed by a causeway. This is a good place to look for Otters in the gloaming.

5. Iochdar (page 154) A walk along quiet roads and the low shoreline of the South Ford, North Bay, Ardivachar Point and the north end of Loch Bee (up to 8km, 5mi, 2h).

6. Loch Bee dominates the north end of South Uist with many fingers. The parking place south of the Lochcarnan turning has fine views over Loch Bee to the hills of Hecla and Ben Mhor.

Loch Carnan is accessed by a narrow side road that winds itself through remote and wild country, ending almost at Loch Skipport. With few inhabitants this quiet road makes for a tranquil day.

7. Our Lady of the Isles stands on the slopes of Rueval below a military radar site. There are lovely views of the west side of South Uist from here.

Loch Druidibeg (page 155) From the carpark on the B890 follow the Nature Trail to visit the Reserve. Greylag Geese and Eriskay Ponies will be seen and Corncrakes perhaps heard (8km, 5mi, 2h).

Howmore Chapels are just south of Loch Druidbeg. There are two ancient ruined chapels and two churches, the oldest dating from the 13th century.

8. Ushenish (page 155) is an isolated headland with a lighthouse that can be accessed from Loch Skipport at the end of the B890 (16km, 8mi, 4h).

Hecla (606m) can also be climbed as part of this walk via Beinn Scalabhat, returning directly via Loch Fada (extra 606m, 8km, 5mi, 3h).

9. Coire Hellisdale (page 155) is one of several glacial valleys on the eastern flanks of Ben Mhor. From the road end on the north side of Loch Eynort follow a track east, then head for Bealach Crosgard and Gleann Liathdail. The "secret" valleys of Hellisdale and Corrodale, with their spectacular cliffs, are to the north (300m, 16km, 10mi, 8h).

10. Rubha Ardvule (p158) From Bornish follow the track across the machair to this prominent headland formerly used by the military. Lovely sandy beaches stretch in both directions. Side roads and tracks allow quiet walks around the machair lochs all over this area (5-10km, 3-6mi, 1-3h).

Dun Vulan broch is on the south side of the headland. It is one of many archaeological sites on the west side of South Uist. Ruined duns stand on islets on several lochs in this area.

11. Kildonan Centre includes a museum, craft shop, café and an archaeology room. A special room is dedicated to Margaret Fay Shaw, the folklorist and Gaelic scholar who was married to John Lorne Campbell. They lived on Canna for many years.

Flora MacDonald's Birthplace is signposted at Milton, across the road from the Kildonan Centre.

Reineaval (page 159) There is a well preserved chambered cairn on the north side of Reineval (70m). A path leads from Mingarry, just south of Kildonan Museum. Beinn Mhuilinn (126m) has a communications mast and is an excellent viewpoint (5km, 3mi, 1h).

12. Lochboisdale (p160) There is a fine view over Lochboisdale from Beinn Ruigh Choinnich which overlooks the village (280m, 6km, 4mi, 2h). Truirebheinn (357m) is a further 2km to the north. The isolated chambered cairn at Loch a Bharp is well preservedb and reached by a tramp across a bog with many burns and lochs (4km, 2.5mi, 2h).

13. Eriskay Circuit (p164) In Haun, go west to the beach below the cemetery, turn left and follow the shore to Coilleag a' Prionnsa and the ferry terminal. Go on up the hill and turn right to the sheltered harbour of Acairseid. Return by the road, not missing The Am Politician bar where "Polly" bottles can be seen and the story of MV *Politician* is told. The church at Gaun is also very interesting, with unusual artefacts of war (6km, 3mi, 2h).

Barra, the most southerly of the Outer Hebrides, is one of the most attractive islands. It has much to offer, whether on a first day visit or a week long trip. Pristine sandy beaches, rugged hills, archaeological sites and abundant wildlife are all on offer.

Perhaps most important is the welcome from the people, the Barraghers, most of whom have Gaelic as their first language. Barra is a beautiful place, but it is also very warm and friendly.

ORDNANCE SURVEY 1:50,000 and 1:25,000 maps of Barra
OS Landranger Map 31   Barra & South Uist
OS Explorer Map 452   Barra & Vatersay

Barra

1. Castlebay (page 168) nestles around the head of its attractive and sheltered bay, backed by Heaval. The ferry from Oban docks here and most of the services are also based in the village.

Kisimul Castle (p170) dominates Castlebay. Originally a Norse fort, it is open during the season, access being by small boat from a slipway.

Dualchas (Barra Heritage & Cultural Centre), near the school, is open seasonally. It has a café, local history displays, archives and old photos. Art exhibitions and events are also held periodically.

Walk Start at the harbour and follow the shore road first to Ledaig on the east side, and then to the War Memorial via Nask on the west side of the bay, a fine evening stroll after dinner (4km, 2.5mi, 2h).

2. Heaval (383m, page 169) Follow the A888 east out of Castlebay to a quarry at the top of the hill (102m). Strike up the slope to the Virgin & Child statue and the summit of Heaval for a spectacular view. Return by the same route or head southwest towards The Glen (383m, 6km, 4mi, 3h).

3. Loch Tangusdale or St Clair's Loch is on the road northwest of Castlebay. Dun Mhic Leoid is a small castle on an islet on the loch.

Halaman Bay faces the Atlantic Ocean. This beautiful arc of pristine sand is backed by dunes and machair, protected by rocky headlands.

Ben Tangaval (333m, p172) overlooks Halaman Bay. A fine circular walk round Halaman Bay, Ben Tangaval & Doirlinn Head, offers fine views over Barra and the Bishop's Isles (333m, 8km, 5mi, 3h).

4. Borve is a fertile little valley with working crofts. The machair to the west of the road is especially resplendent with wild flowers in early summer.

Allasdale (p172) has another exceptional exposed sandy beach. A circular walk starting from the beach takes in Dun Cuier, Dun Bharpa chambered cairn, Beinn Mhartainn & Borve. Rejoin the road at the Blackhouse Museum and return via Craigston and Borve beach, (245m, 6km, 4mi, 3h).

5. Greian Head (p173) offers fine views of the west coast of Barra as well as a 9-hole golf course. A track leads to the top from Grein, near the church.

6. Cocklestrand or Traigh Mhor (p174) is a very unusual beach since it doubles as Barra Airport. Loganair Twin Otters provide links to Glasgow and Benbecula with a tide dependent schedule. The beach is also a source of wonderful Cockles.

Aird Mhor (p176) is the terminal for the ferry which runs across the Sound of Barra to Eriskay.

7. Eoligarry (p174) is a beautiful area of machair with two beautiful beaches, Traigh Cille Bharra to the east and Traigh Scurrival to the north.

Cille Bharra overlooks Eoligarry and may date from the 12th century. Inside is a replica of a stone with runes on one side and a Celtic cross on the other.

Dun Scurrival (p175) is one of the best preserved of many brochs on Barra. It sits on top of a 50m hillock from which there are marvellous views.

Walk Park south of the Airport Terminal and go west across the machair to the south end of Traigh Eais. Head north and climb Ben Eoligarry (102m) for excellent views, before descending to Dun Scurrival. Return via Cille Bharra, Saltinish and Eoligarry Jetty (102m, 8km, 5mi, 3h).

8. The East Coast of Barra (p176) is quite different to the west. It has a rugged, rocky coast backed by moorland and hills which are beautiful in late summer when the Heather is in bloom.

9. Vatersay (p180) is joined to Barra by a causeway. With beautiful beaches, interesting archaeology and machair wild flowers in summer it is a good visit.

Vatersay Walk Park near the Community Hall start on Vatersay Bay and walk through the village Bagh a Deas with views to the Bishop's Isles. Return via Beinn Ruilibreac and Bagh Siar (10km, 6mi, 3h).

The Bishop's Isles (page 182) are a string of uninhabited islands south of Vatersay. Boat trips run to the Bishop's Isles from Castlebay, principally to Mingulay. They explore the spectacular cliffs, natural arches and caves on the west of the island. Seabirds, especially Gannets and Puffins, as well as cetaceans or Basking Sharks may be seen.

10. Sandray (p182) has huge sand dunes above its startlingly white beach. Most of the abandoned settlement is now buried under the dunes.

11. Pabbay (p182) has an even more impressive sandy beach, Bagh Ban. There is also a famous Pictish symbol stone and a small galleried dun.

12. Mingulay (p184) is the largest of the Bishop's Isles and the most frequently visited. The west cliffs and caves are especially impressive, whether from a boat or from above. Mingulay Bay is also very interesting with its ruined village and seals.

13. Berneray (p185) has a lighthouse on Barra Head and interesting archaeological sites.

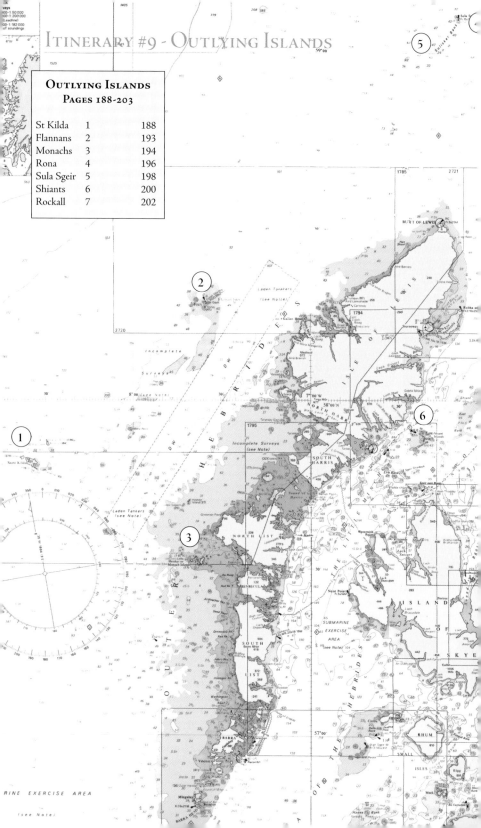

ITINERARY #9 - OUTLYING ISLANDS

HEBRIDEAN OUTLIERS

THE HEBRIDEAN OUTLIERS are a diverse series of islands, ranging from the iconic and much visited St Kilda to the isolated and hard to reach Rona and Sula Sgeir. The pinnacle of Rockall is the remotest of all. Some are relatively easy to reach on regular day trips from Harris or Lewis, while others are much more of an expedition.

All except for Rockall are easy to land on given fine weather and local knowledge. Details of some boat operators are in the "What to Do and See" section. St Kilda is the easiest of the outliers to reach, but involves a long trip over the open Atlantic Ocean in a fast boat.

1. St Kilda (page 188) is about 60nm (69mi) from West Loch Tarbert and 35nm (41mi) from North Uist. This wild and beautiful archipelago can be reached in boat trips from Tarbert in Harris and Uig on Lewis. It is the remains of a huge volcano which erupted about 60 million years ago.

The main island, Hirta, was inhabited until 1930. Today a military base, National Trust personnel and thousands of visitors make up the population. The stacks of Boreray, Stac an Armin and Stac Lee are to the northeast and host the world's largest gannetry. Vast numbers of other seabirds also breed here.

2. The Flannan Islands (page 192) lie about 18nm (21mi) WNW of Gallan Head on Lewis or 36nm (42mi) from Tarbert. They are volcanic and home to thousands of breeding seabirds. It is possible to get ashore in fine weather on all of the islands. The east landing on Eilean Mor is the best, but only when there is no easterly sea running.

3. The Monach Islands (page 139) are about 5nm (6mi) west of North Uist. They are low-lying and covered by sand dunes. In autumn up to 10,000 Grey Seals come ashore to have their pups and breed. The islands are surrounded by a maze of rocks and shoals. Boat trips are run from Kallin Harbour on Grimsay.

4. Rona (page 196) is about 38nm (44mi) NNE of the Port of Ness. Landing is possible at a number of places. A trip here requires fine weather and much planning but is well worth the effort. Rona and Sula Sgeir can also be reached from Orkney or

the North of Scotland. Rona is 80nm (78mi) from Stromness. The island is mostly covered with luxuriant grass and wild flowers. In summer thousands of Puffins and other seabirds breed here, while in autumn about 8,000 Greys Seals haul out to give birth and breed.

5. Sula Sgeir (page 198) is 9nm (11mi) west of Rona and best visited on the same trip. This long, thin, rocky island is home to 9,000 pairs of Gannets. In late summer the men of Ness harvest about 2,000 gugas, unfledged Gannet chicks, which are a delicacy. Landing is easy in the sheltered Geodha a' Phuill Bhain.

6. The Shiant Islands (page 200) are situated in the Little Minch, between Scalpay and Rubha Hunish on Skye. They are formed largely of Dolerite, which forms spectacular columns on the west of Garbh Eilean. Thousands of Puffins and other seabirds nest here. Boat trips run regularly to the Shiants during the summer from Tarbert.

7. Rockall (page 202) is 163nm (187mi) west of St Kilda, or 223nm (156mi) from West Loch Tarbert. This volcanic pinnacle rises 21m out of the sea. Dangerous nearby reefs include Helen's Reef and the Hasselwood Rock. Despite its remote location it is sometimes possible to land here in very settled conditions.

Offshore Wildlife Landing on these remote, mostly uninhabited islands in the middle of the ocean, is a unique experience. The voyages to them present very good opportunities to observe cetaceans and oceanic birds.

Minke Whales, Short-finned Pilot and Killer Whales are often sighted. White-sided, White-beaked Risso's and Bottle-nose Dolphins may also be seen, as well as Basking Sharks. Pelagic birds include Storm and Leaches Petrels, Manx and Sooty Shearwaters. Gannets, gulls and skuas often pass boats closely.

Visiting Offlying Islands is a serious undertaking which can provide lasting memories. Apart from the commercial trips mentioned, sailors also visit in their own vessels or with yachts hired from Skye and elsewhere.

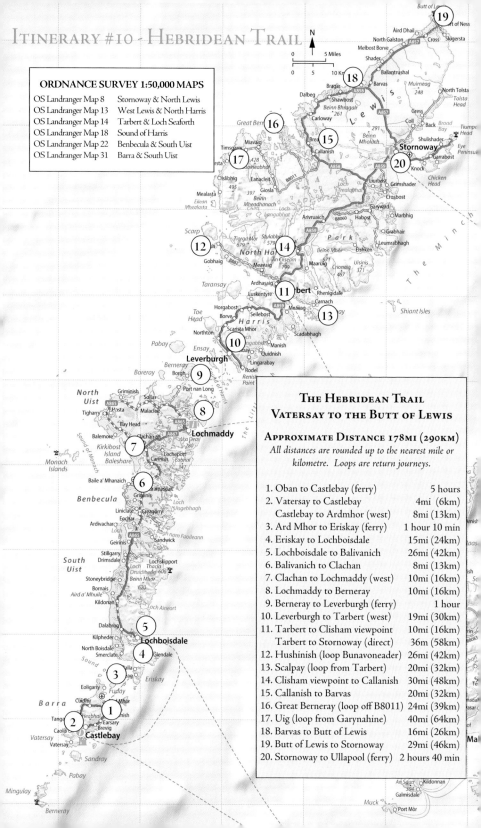

ORDNANCE SURVEY 1:50,000 MAPS

OS Landranger Map 8	Stornoway & North Lewis
OS Landranger Map 13	West Lewis & North Harris
OS Landranger Map 14	Tarbert & Loch Seaforth
OS Landranger Map 18	Sound of Harris
OS Landranger Map 22	Benbecula & South Uist
OS Landranger Map 31	Barra & South Uist

THE HEBRIDEAN TRAIL
VATERSAY TO THE BUTT OF LEWIS

APPROXIMATE DISTANCE 178MI (290KM)
*All distances are rounded up to the nearest mile or
kilometre. Loops are return journeys.*

1. Oban to Castlebay (ferry) — 5 hours
2. Vatersay to Castlebay — 4mi (6km)
   Castlebay to Ardmhor (west) — 8mi (13km)
3. Ard Mhor to Eriskay (ferry) — 1 hour 10 min
4. Eriskay to Lochboisdale — 15mi (24km)
5. Lochboisdale to Balivanich — 26mi (42km)
6. Balivanich to Clachan — 8mi (13km)
7. Clachan to Lochmaddy (west) — 10mi (16km)
8. Lochmaddy to Berneray — 10mi (16km)
9. Berneray to Leverburgh (ferry) — 1 hour
10. Leverburgh to Tarbert (west) — 19mi (30km)
11. Tarbert to Clisham viewpoint — 10mi (16km)
    Tarbert to Stornoway (direct) — 36m (58km)
12. Hushinish (loop Bunavoneader) — 26mi (42km)
13. Scalpay (loop from Tarbert) — 20mi (32km)
14. Clisham viewpoint to Callanish — 30mi (48km)
15. Callanish to Barvas — 20mi (32km)
16. Great Berneray (loop off B8011) — 24mi (39km)
17. Uig (loop from Garynahine) — 40mi (64km)
18. Barvas to Butt of Lewis — 16mi (26km)
19. Butt of Lewis to Stornoway — 29mi (46km)
20. Stornoway to Ullapool (ferry) — 2 hours 40 min

The Hebridean Trail
Vatersay to the Butt of Lewis

The Hebridean Trail runs for about 178mi (290km) from Vatersay to the Butt of Lewis. It can be undertaken by bicycle or car, starting at either Castlebay or Stornoway. A number of side loops are suggested.

1. Castlebay (page 168) The ferry from Oban arrives at Castlebay at variable times of day.

2. Vatersay (page180) The trail starts at the south end of Vatersay. Cyclists could start at Bagh a' Deas (South Bay). *Vatersay to Castlebay 4mi (6km)*

Castlebay (page 168) is the main settlement on Barra. From here, there is a choice of the west route with its spectacular bays or the east route with a steep climb over the shoulder of Heaval. *Castlebay to Ardmhor (west) 8mi (13km)*

3. Ardmhor (page 176) is the ferry terminal for Eriskay. Bottle-nosed Dolphins may be seen here. *Ardmhor to Eriskay 1 hour 10 min*

4. Eriskay (page 164) is a picturesque little island joined to South Uist by a causeway. *SS Politician* ran aground here, and inspired the film *Whisky Galore*. *Eriskay to Lochboisdale 15mi (24km)*

5. Lochboisdale (page 160) is 3mi (4km) east of Daliburgh. In summer the lochans here are covered with White Water Lilies. *Eriskay to Lochboisdale15mi (24km)*

6. Balivanich (page 144) South Uist is relatively flat with beautiful machair backed beaches on the west coast and mountains to the east. Benbecula is joined to the South and North Uists by causeways. *Lochboisdale to Balivanich 26mi (42km)*

7. Clachan (page 136), at the south end of North Uist offers the spectacular west route to Lochmaddy or a shorter east one. Langass chambered cairn and Pobull Fhinn standing stones are worth a short diversion. *Clachan to Lochmaddy (west) 10mi (16km)*

8. Lochmaddy (page130) is attractively situated and home to the Taigh Chearsabhagh Arts Centre. *Lochmaddy to Berneray Ferry Terminal 10mi (16km)*

9. Berneray (page 134) should be explored if there is time before the ferry. It has a lovely 3mi (4km) beach all along its west coast. The Sound of Harris ferry crossing is great for birdwatchers. *Berneray to Leverburgh 1 hour*

10. Leverburgh or An t' Ob (page 120) is at the southern end of Harris. From here either take the spectacular west coast route past the wonderful Harris beaches, or the equally interesting east coast "Golden Road" northwards. Either way the little St Clement's Church and harbour at Rodel should be visited. *Leverburgh to Tarbert (west) 19mi (30km)*

11. Tarbert (page 114), the main village and ferry terminal on Harris, offers a number of options. *Tarbert to Stornoway (direct) 36m (58km)* *Tarbert to Callanish 39mi (63km)*

12. West Loch Tarbert (page 114) offers a very fine route to the remote beach of Hushinish with good chances to see Golden or White-tailed Sea Eagles. *Hushinish from Bunavoneader return 26mi (42km)*

13. Scalpay (page 115) is joined to Harris by a bridge. This small fishing community has the oldest lighthouse in the Western Isles. *Scalpay (loop from Tarbert) 20mi (32km)*

14. Clisham (799m, page 113) is the highest point in the Outer Hebrides and overlooks the dramatic view over Ardvourlie. The climb from Ardhasaig is the only steep part of the whole route. *Tarbert to Clisham viewpoint 10mi (16km)*

Lewis The trail enters Lewis at the head of Loch Seaforth, passing pretty Balallan, before turning west to Achmore and Garynahine. *Clisham viewpoint to Callanish 30mi (48km)*

The Pentland Road is a very scenic diversion from Achmore. It follows the path of a proposed railway line to Breascleit across open moorland. *Achmore to Breascleit (direct 8mi (13km), via the Pentland Road 14mi (22km)*

15. Callanish (page 84) The spectacular standing stones overlooking Loch Roag at Callanish are an essential stop. From here there are alternatives. *Callanish to Barvas 20mi (32km)*

16. Great Bernera (page 100) Take the B8011 towards Uig at Garynahine, then the B8059 across the moor to Great Bernera. Camas Bosta at the north end is one of the loveliest beaches of all. *Great Berneray (loop off B8011) 24mi (39km)*

17. Uig (page 102) Uig Bay vies with the Harris beaches for sheer scale and beauty. The road continues for another 8mi (12km) to Mealista. *Uig (loop from Garynahine) 40mi (64km)*

18. Barvas (page 90) From Callanish the A858 passes Dun Carloway broch and the Blackhouse Museum at Arnol before reaching Barvas. *Barvas to Butt of Lewis 16mi (26km)*

19. Ness and the Butt of Lewis (page 98) The A857 continues northeast to Ness and the Butt of Lewis, the most northerly point of Lewis. *Barvas to Butt of Lewis 16mi (26km)*

20. Stornoway (page72) Follow the A857 to Stornoway and catch the ferry to Ullapool. *Butt of Lewis to Stornoway 29mi (46km)* *Stornoway to Ullapool (ferry) 2 hours 40 min*

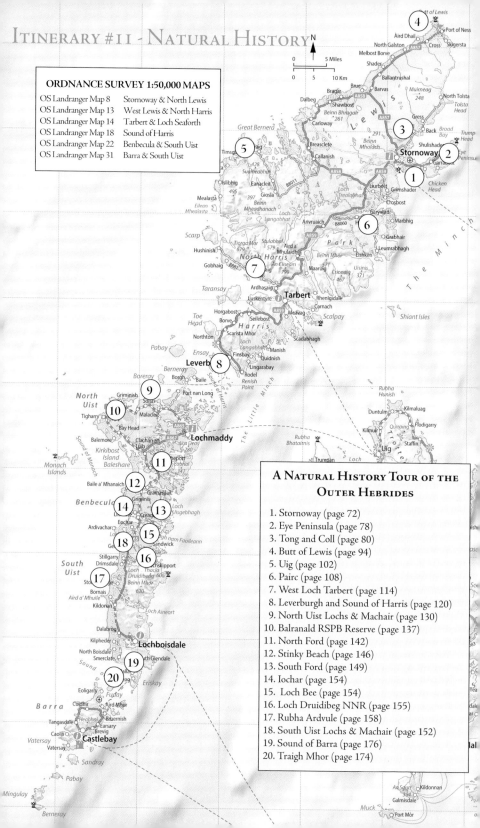

ORDNANCE SURVEY 1:50,000 MAPS

OS Landranger Map 8   Stornoway & North Lewis
OS Landranger Map 13   West Lewis & North Harris
OS Landranger Map 14   Tarbert & Loch Seaforth
OS Landranger Map 18   Sound of Harris
OS Landranger Map 22   Benbecula & South Uist
OS Landranger Map 31   Barra & South Uist

A NATURAL HISTORY TOUR OF THE OUTER HEBRIDES

A NATURAL HISTORY TOUR OF THE OUTER HEBRIDES

1. Stornoway (page 72) The Lews Castle woodlands are unique in the Outer Hebrides with breeding Rooks and Herons as well as many passerines. Dippers nest beside the River Creed. The Woodland Centre has a good cafe and interpretation panels. Gob Steinis, to the west of the airport, usually has a large Arctic Tern colony. In winter Stornoway Harbour often has Iceland or Glaucous Gulls while Corncrakes breed in and around the airport.

2. Eye Peninsula (page 78) The Braigh is the isthmus joining the Eye Peninsula to Lewis. Loch Branahuie holds many breeding waterfowl in summer, while in migration times it attracts a wide range of ducks. In winter the bays hold rafts of Long-tailed Ducks and Red-breasted Mergansers. Tiumpan Head has substantial numbers of breeding seabird. Risso's and other dolphins are often seen from here in late summer. Arctic Terns as well as Great and Arctic Skuas nest on the moorland nearby. The small lochs are all good for breeding and migrant waders and waterfowl.

3. Tong and Coll (page 80) The extensive saltmarshes at the estuary of the River Laxdale are very popular with waders at all seasons. Dippers may be seen on some of the streams, especially the River Gress. Red-throated Divers breed on the inland lochs, while skuas nest on the moorland.

4. Ness and the Butt of Lewis (page 94) The northern extremity of Lewis is prime bird watching territory. Loch Stiapavat and its surrounding marsh is one of the prime birdwatching sites in Lewis all year round. Unusual species often turn up here. The Butt itself is an excellent sea watching site all year round, both for migrant birds and for cetaceans such as Orca or Risso's Dolphin. Seabirds nest along the cliffs in several places.

5. Uig (page 102) Both Golden and White-tailed Sea Eagles may be seen in this remote area. Red and Black-throated Divers nest on inland lochs. Terns breed in several sites near the coast.

6. Pairc (page 108) The remote moorland of Pairc is famous for its breeding Golden and White-tailed Sea Eagles as well as Red and Black-throated Divers.

7. West Loch Tarbert and North Harris (page 114) is prime raptor country and has its own Eagle Observatory in Glen Miavaig.

8. The Sound of Harris (page 120) ferry crossing offers great opportunities to watch seabirds at all seasons. Seals and Otters may also be seen.

9. North Uist Lochs & Machair (page 130) The eastern side of North Uist is a maze of lochs which are home to a good population of Otters. Red and Black-throated Divers breed on many of the lochs. Hen Harrier, Merlin and Short-eared Owls all breed and may be seen almost anywhere.

10. Balranald RSPB Reserve (page 137) 640ha of beaches, sand dunes, machair, marsh and lochs. Corncrake and Corn Bunting breed here along with many waders and waterfowl. There is a small visitor centre; the 3mi (4km) trail takes 2 hours.

11. North Ford (page 142) has a huge area of sand exposed at low tide. There are vantage points on the causeway, on Grimsay and various roads.

12. Stinky Bay (page 146) on the southwest of Benbecula often has large piles of rotting seaweed which attract a wide range of birds especially during the migration periods.

13. South Ford (page 149) is one of the best places to seek waders and wildfowl.

14. Iochar (page 154) The road to Hebridean Jewellery passes lochans, salt marsh and fields before reaching the beach at Bagh a Tuath. There are many excellent viewpoints for waders.

15. Loch Bee (page 154) is a large expanse of fresh water which exits to the sea at Clachan near Iochar. There are good vantage points here as well as from the layby on the main road further south.

16. Loch Druidibeg National Nature Reserve (page 155) can be viewed from the main road but is better seen from the B890 to Loch Skipport. There is a signposted nature trail.

17. Rubha Ardvule (page 158) is a good sea watching site, especially in autumn when there is a strong westerly wind. The beaches to the north and south are good for waders during migration times. Terns breed around Loch Ardvule and many waders nest around the lochs.

18. South Uist Lochs & Machair (page 152) A walk around any of the side roads and tracks which crisscross the area will reveal a good selection of birds at all times of year. The many small lochs, streams and marshy areas attract large numbers of waders and waterfowl.

19. Sound of Barra (page 176) A pod of Bottlenose Dolphins frequents this area. They are most often seen from the ferry to Eriskay.

20. Traigh Mhor (page 174), or the Cocklestrand is Barra's airport. There are good vantage points to watch for waders on a rising tide. The Eoligarry area is famous for its Corncrakes.

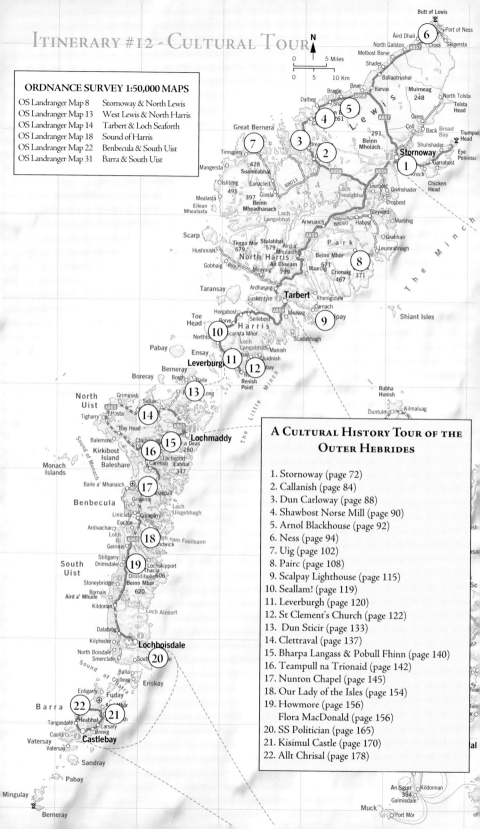

N

0   5 Miles

0   5   10 Km

ORDNANCE SURVEY 1:50,000 MAPS

OS Landranger Map 8   Stornoway & North Lewis
OS Landranger Map 13   West Lewis & North Harris
OS Landranger Map 14   Tarbert & Loch Seaforth
OS Landranger Map 18   Sound of Harris
OS Landranger Map 22   Benbecula & South Uist
OS Landranger Map 31   Barra & South Uist

A CULTURAL HISTORY TOUR OF THE OUTER HEBRIDES

A Cultural History Tour of the Outer Hebrides

1. Stornoway (page 72) The new Museum nan Eilean, at Lews Castle, is an excellent place to start a tour of the cultural history of the Outer Hebrides. The Baltic Bookshop on Cromwell Street stocks a wide range of local books, while An Lanntair Arts Centre features many artists.

Land Wars Cairns at Gress and Aignish commemorate the "Land Wars" of the 1880s and after WWI when local crofters fought the landowners and the authorities for rights to land.

2. Callanish (page 84) is 15mi (24km) west of Stornoway. This remarkable Neolithic stone setting and associated smaller circles is one of the most impressive in the UK. The nearby Visitor Centre tells the story.

3. Dun Carloway (page 88), the best preserved Iron Age broch in the Western Isles, has a small visitor centre and is 5mi (8km) north of Callanish.

4. Shawbost Norse Mill (page 90) is about 5mi (8km) further northwest. The mill and kiln are both restored with traditional thatched roofs. There is a small museum nearby.

5. Arnol Blackhouse (page 92) is an example of the traditional thatched houses once universal here. The house, barn and byre are all in one. An open hearth burns in the middle of the main room. People and animals used the same doorway.

6. Ness (page 94) is the most northerly point on Lewis and has a wealth of places to visit. The Ness Heritage Centre tells the story. Clach an Truiseil is the tallest monolith in the Western Isles, while there are several interesting chapel sites. Dun Eistean on a large rock stack has a ruined fort on it. The Butt of Lewis lighthouse dates from 1862.

7. Uig (page 102) The Lewis Chessmen were found here in 1831 buried in a sand dune. The Brahan Seer was born in the area c.1600. Uig is home to the only distillery in the Western Isles.

8. Pairc (page 108) The Pairc Deer Raid took place in 1887 to draw attention to the ongoing clearances. It is commemorated by a large cairn.

9. Scalpay Lighthouse (page 115) is the site of the oldest one in the Outer Hebrides. First lit in 1789, the present tower dates from 1824. The island is joined to Harris by a causeway.

10. Seallam! Visitor Centre (page 119) at Northton on the west of Harris has exhibitions on local history and natural environment. It is also the starting point for anyone of Hebridean ancestry who is researching their family tree.

11. Leverburgh or An t' Ob (page 120) was established in the 1920s as a fish landing port to supply the national chain of Mac Fisheries chip shops. The enterprise was abandoned in 1925 after the death of Lord Leverhulme.

12. St Clement's Church (page 122) at Rodel is 4mi (6km) south of Leverburgh. It dates from the 16th century and is the only intact medieval building in the Western Isles. It was built by Alasdair Crotach MacLeod to house his rather magnificent tomb. Unusually, the tower features a number of Sheela na gigs, some of which are explicit.

13. Dun Sticir and Dun Torchuill (page 133) are good examples of Iron Age brochs built on islets in lochs and reached by causeways. There are many others throughout the islands.

14. Clettraval and Unival (page 137) are hills on the west side of North Uist with ruinous chambered cairns. There are fine views on clear days.

15. Bharpa Langass & Pobull Fhinn (page 140) By far the best preserved chambered cairn in the Outer Hebrides, Bharpa Langass sits prominently on Beinn Langass. Pobull Fhinn is a fine small stone circle overlooking Loch Langass.

16. Teampull na Trionaid (page 142) was established c.1200 and was an important seat of learning in medieval times.

The Battle of Carinish took place here in 1601 when 40 MacLeods from Skye came to steal cattle but were routed by the MacDonalds.

17. Nunton Chapel (page 145) may date from the 14th century. At Balivanich the ancient Teampall Chalium Cille stands roofless and atmospheric.

18. Our Lady of the Isles (page 154) was erected in 1957 to guard over South Uist and prevent any ill effects from the new Royal Artillery Range.

19. Howmore (page 156) Two churches and two chapels stand in an ancient graveyard here.

Flora MacDonald (page 156) is said to have been born at nearby Milton. A cairn commemorates the site of the house.

20. SS Politician (page 165)was wrecked off Eriskay in 1941 while on her way to the USA. She was carrying 21,000 cases of malt whisky and inspired the novel and later film *Whisky Galore*.

21. Kisimul Castle (page 170) stands on a small island in Castlebay. It probably dates from Norse times. Now maintained by Historic Scotland it is open to visitors seasonally.

22. Allt Chrisal (page 178) overlooks the vatersay causeway and includes Neolithic, Bronze and Iron Age houses.

White Water Lilies, Lochboisdale, South Uist

Harris from Dunvegan, Skye

During the research for this book large numbers of books, periodicals, guides, maps and other publications were consulted as well as many individuals and websites. The author wishes to thank everyone who has been of assistance during his years of wanderings in the Western Isles, as well as those who did the essential job of proof reading.

The following bibliography is a distillation of some of the books on the area. Some are essential reading, others

depend on personal interests. One of the best starting places is Hamish Haswell-Smith's book on the Scottish Islands, but then the author is a fellow sea-lover.

Many locally-produced leaflets, guides and small books are available produced by VisitScotland, Scottish Natural Heritage and other bodies or individuals. In particular the walks leaflets by the above bodies are excellent. Bill Lawson produces a good series of little

books on local history, chapels and genealogy, while the various heritage centres and museums also do useful local guides.

Apart from the Baltic Bookshop in Stornoway, and MacGillivrays in Balivanich, many shops throughout the isles also stock local books. The VICs and museums are also good sources of local publications, some of which are free, while others may be charged.

ESSENTIAL BACKGROUND READING

Travels in the Scottish Islands, The Hebrides	Kirsti MacDonald Jareg	MacD Books	2016
Love of Country	Madeleine Bunting	Granta	2016
Scotland the Best	Peter Irvine	Harper Collins	2016
The Scottish Islands	Hamish Haswell-Smith	Canongate	1996
West Over Sea	DDC Pochin Mould	Acair	1953
A Description of the Western Isles of Scotland circa 1695	Martin Martin	Birlinn	1698
The Archaeology of Skye and the Western Isles	Ian Armit	Edinburgh University Press	1996
Facing the Ocean - The Atlantic and its Peoples	Barry Cunliffe	Oxford	2001
Scotland's Hidden History	Ian Armit	Tempus	1998
The Ancient Monuments of the Western Isles	ed Denys Pringle	HMSO	1994
The Making of the Crofting Community	James Hunter	John Donald	1976
Island Going	Robert Atkinson	Birlinn	1949
An Island Odyssey	Hamish Haswell-Smith	Canongate	1999

GENERAL BOOKS ON THE WESTERN ISLES

Isles of the West	Ian Mitchell	Canongate	1999
The Western Isles - A Postcard Tour, 1 Barra to North Uist	Bob Carnley	MacLean Press	1992
The Western Isles - A Postcard Tour, 2 Harris & Lewis	Bob Carnley	MacLean Press	1993
Lewis & Harris	Francis Thompson	Pevensey	2007
Lewis - The Story of an Island	Christine Macdonald	Acair	1998

Benbecula	Ray Burnett	Mingulay Press	1986
Uists & Barra	Francis Thompson	Pevensey	2008
Road to the Isles, Travellers in the Hebrides 1770-1914	Derek Cooper	MacMillan	1979
Hebridean Island Hopping	Martin Coventry	Birlinn	2010
Riddoch on the Outer Hebrides	Lesley Riddoch	Luath	2008

HISTORY & ARCHAEOLOGY

The Stone Circles of Britain, Ireland and Brittany	Aubrey Burl	Yale	2000
The Extraordinary Voyage of Pytheas the Greek	Barry Cunliffe	Allen Lane	2001
The Illustrated Life of Columba	John Marsden	Floris Books	1991
Iron Age Britain	Barry Cunliffe	English Heritage	1995
Towers in the North	Ian Armit	Tempus	2003
The Lewis Chessmen	Neil Stratford	British Museum Press	1997
Somerled and the Emergence of Gaelic Scotland	John Marsden	Tuckwell Press	2000
The Papar in the North Atlantic	ed Barbara E Crawford	St Andrews	2002
The Lords of the Isles	Raymond Campbell Paterson	Birlinn	2001
Polly The True Story Behind Whisky Galore	Roger Hutchinson	Mainstream	1990
North Uist	Erskine Beveridge	Birlinn	1911
Lewis & Harris: History & Prehistory	Francis Thompson	Luath	2004
Lewis in History & Legend Vol1 (West Side)	Bill Lawson	John Donald	2008
Lewis in History & Legend Vol2 (East Side)	Bill Lawson	John Donald	2011
Harris in History & Legend	Bill Lawson	John Donald	2002
North Uist in History & Legend	Bill Lawson	John Donald	2004
Barra & Skye: Two Hebridean Perspectives	ed Arne Kruse	Scot Soc Northern Studies	2006
Stornoway In World War Two	Mike Hughes	Islands Book Trust	2008

GUIDE BOOKS

Ancient Lewis & Harris	Christopher Burgess	Comhairlenan Eilean Siar	2007
Ancient Barra	Keith Branigan	Comhairlenan Eilean Siar	2007
Ancient Uists	ed Anna Badcock	Comhairlenan Eilean Siar	2008
The Western Seaboard – Illustrated Architectural Guide	Mary Miers	Rutland Press	2008
The Western Isles, Innsegall	J Barber & DA Magee	John Donald	1989
Calanais, The Standing Stones	Patrick Ashmore	Urras nan Tursachan	1995
Argyll and the Western Isles	Graham Ritchie & Mary Harman	HMSO	1996
The Island Blackhouse	Alexander Fenton	Historic Scotland	1978
Scotland Highlands and Islands Handbook	Alan Murphy	Footprint	2001
The Chapels in the Western Isles	Finlay MacLeod	Acair	1997

HISTORY - SCOTTISH CONNECTION

Reflections on the History of Stornoway & Lewis	Sandy Matheson	Islands Book Trust	2008
Go Listen to the Crofters	AD Cameron	Acair	1986
From the Land (As an Fhearann)	ed M MacLean & C Carrell	Mainstream	1986
The Lewis Land Struggle	Joni Buchanan	Acair	1996
Who Owns Scotland Now?	Auslan Cramb	Mainstream	1996
Historic Stornoway	EP Dennison & R Coleman	Historic Scotland	1997
The Hebrides at War	Mike Hughes	Canongate	1998
The Companion to Gaelic Scotland	ed Derick S Thomson	Gairm	1994
Times Subject to Tides - The Story of Barra Airport	Roy Calderwood	Kea Publishing	1999

PLACENAMES

Scottish Place-Names	WFH Nicholaisen	John Donald	2001
The Celtic Placenames of Scotland	WJ Watson	Birlinn	1926
Place Names of the Highlands & Islands of Scotland	Alexander MacBain	Grimsay Press	1922
Scottish Hill Names	Peter Drummond	Scot Mountaineering Trust	1991
Place-names of Lewis and Harris	Duncan MacIver	Stornoway	1934
Reading the Gaelic Landscape	John Murray	Whittles Publishing	2014
Orkney Farm Names	Hugh Marwick	Kirkwall Press	1952
Place-Names of Shetland	Jakob Jakobsen	Edinburgh	1936

NATURAL HISTORY

Title	Author	Publisher	Year
Birdwatching in the Outer Hebrides	Cunningham, Dix & Snow	Saker Press	1995
The Outer Hebrides - The Shaping of the Islands	Stewart Angus	White Horse Press	1998
The Hebrides	JM & IL Boyd	Collins	1990
Scottish Birds - Culture and Tradition	Robin Hull	Mercat Press	2001
The Landscape of Scotland, A Hidden History	CR Wickham-Jones	Tempus	2001
Plants and People in Ancient Scotland	Camilla & James Dickson	Tempus	2000
Scotland After the Ice Age	ed KJ Edwards & IBM Ralston	EUP	2003
Collins Bird Guide	Mullarney, et al	HarperCollins	2000
Guide to Sea & Shore Life	Gibson, Hextall & Rogers	Oxford	2001
Whales, Dolphins and Porpoises	Mark Carwardine	Dorling Kindersley	1995
Guide to Whale Watching	Mark Carwardine	New Holland	2003
Sea Mammals of the World	Folkens, Reeves et al	A&C Black	2002
Marine Fish & Invertebrates	FE Moen & E Svensen	KOM	2004
Butterflies & Moths	Sterry & Mackay	Dorling Kindersley	2004
Moths of Britain and Ireland	Waring & Townsend	British Wildlife Publishing	2003
Dragonflies and Damselflies	Brooks and Lewington	British Wildlife Publishing	2004
Wild Flowers of Britain & Ireland	Blamey, Fitter & Fitter	A&C Black	2003
Wild Flowers of Britain & Northern Europe	Blamey & Grey-Wilson	Cassell	2003
Scottish Wild Plants	Lusby & Wright	Mercat Press	2001
Flora Celtica	Milliken & Bridgewater	Birlinn	2003
Orchids of Britain & Ireland	Anne & Simon Harrap	A&C Black	2005
Flora of the Outer Hebrides	PJ Pankhurst & J Mullin	Pelagic Publishing	2012

ACTIVITIES

Title	Author	Publisher	Year
The Hebrides: 50 Walking Routes	Peter Edwards	Cicerone	2015
Cycling in the Hebrides	Richard Barrett	Cicerone	2012
Riddoch on the Outer Hebrides	Lesley Riddoch	Luath Press	2008
Fisher in the West	Eddie Young	Stornoway Gazette	1994
70 Lochs - A Guide to Trout Fishing in South Uist	John Kennedy	John Kennedy	1997
Trout Fishing in Lewis	N MacLeod, E Young	Western Isles Publ Co	1993
Walking in the Hebrides	Roger Redfern	Cicerone	1998
25 Walks The Western Isles	June Parker	HMSO	1996
Walks Western Isles	Luke Williams	Hallewell	2007
Walking on Harris and Lewis	Richard Barrett	Cicerone	2010
Sea Kayaking Around the Outer Hebrides	Sullivan, Emmott & Pickering	Pesda Press	2010

OUTLYING ISLANDS

Title	Author	Publisher	Year
An Isle Called Hirte	Mary Harman	MacLean Press	1997
Mingulay	Ben Buxton	Birlinn	1995
Sea Room An Island Life	Adam Nicolson	Harper Collins	2001
St Kilda	David Quine	Colin Baxter	1995
Sula, The Seabird-Hunters of Lewis	John Beatty	Michael Joseph	1992
St Kilda The Continuing Story of the Islands	ed Meg Buchanan	HMSO	1995
Rona - The Distant Island	Michael Robson	Acair	1991

PHOTOGRAPH BOOKS

Title	Author	Publisher	Year
Hebrides	Peter May and David Wilson	Quercus	2013
Nis Aosmhor - The Photographs of Dan Morrison		Acair	1997
A Poem of Remote Lives - Images of Eriskay 1934	Werner Kissling	Neil Wilson	1997
The Hebrides	Angus & Patricia macDonald	John Donald	2010
The Unknown Hebrides	John MacPherson	John Donald	2005
The Outer Hebrides	Malcolm MacGregor	Frances Lincoln	2007
The Outer Hebrides, The Butt of Lewis to Mingulay	Colin Nutt	Ness	2011

SEA AND BOATS

Title	Author	Publisher	Year
The West Highland Galley	Denis Rixson	Birlinn	1998

The Yachtsman's Pilot to the Western Isles	Martin Lawrence	Imray Laurie Norie & Wilson	1996
Birlinn, Longships of the Hebrides	John MacAuley	White Horse Press	1996

STORIES AND FOLKLORE

Stories from South Uist told by Angus MacLennan	trans John L Campbell	Birlinn	1997
Tales from Barra told by the Coddie	Intro & Notes JL Campbell	Birlinn	1992
The Furrow Behind Me told by Angus MacLennan	trans John L Campbell	Birlinn	1997
The Voice of the Bard	Timothy Neat with John MacInnes	Canongate	1999
Seal-Folk and Ocean Paddlers	JM MacAuley	White Horse Press	1998
The Finlay J MacDonald Omnibus	Finlay J MacDonald	Warner	1994
Whisky Galore	Compton MacKenzie	Penguin	1947

NOVELS

The Blackhouse	Peter May	Quercus	2011
The Lewis Man	Peter May	Quercus	2012
The Chessmen	Peter May	Quercus	2013

MAPS

Throughout this book OS coordinates are quoted to aid in finding sites of interest, many of which are not signposted. Ordnance Survey 1:50,000 Landranger and Pathfinder 1:25,000 series cover the Outer Hebrides, and are indispensable to all serious walkers and explorers. The latest maps have the newer Gaelic place names. Also useful is the Ordnance Survey 1:250,000 Travelmaster sheet number 3 "Western Scotland and the Western Isles". Admiralty Chart no 2635 gives an overview of the whole West Coast of Scotland and also indicates the detailed charts of the area.

OS Landranger Map 8	Stornoway & North Lewis	Ordnance Survey	2010
OS Landranger Map 13	West Lewis & North Harris	Ordnance Survey	2010
OS Landranger Map 14	Tarbert & Loch Seaforth	Ordnance Survey	2008
OS Landranger Map 18	Sound of Harris	Ordnance Survey	2009
OS Landranger Map 22	Benbecula & South Uist	Ordnance Survey	2008
OS Landranger Map 31	Barra & South Uist	Ordnance Survey	2009
OS Explorer Map 452	Barra & Vatersay	Ordnance Survey	2007
OS Explorer Map 453	Benbecula & South Uist	Ordnance Survey	2007
OS Explorer Map 454	North Uist & Berneray	Ordnance Survey	2007
OS Explorer Map 455	South Harris	Ordnance Survey	2007
OS Explorer Map 456	North Harris & Loch Seaforth	Ordnance Survey	2007
OS Explorer Map 457	South East Lewis	Ordnance Survey	2007
OS Explorer Map 458	West Lewis	Ordnance Survey	2010
OS Explorer Map 459	Central Lewis & Stornoway	Ordnance Survey	2007
OS Explorer Map 460	North Lewis	Ordnance Survey	2007

MAPS AND BOOKS

This book includes 1:250,000 Ordnance Survey based maps throughout to help navigation. Each area also has a smaller scale map to locate and describe it. The 1:250,000 OS Road Map 1 "North Scotland, Orkney & Shetland" is very good for navigation and route planning.

Many sites of interest have OS grid references of the style (XX123456). The UK is divided into 100km squares, each with a two letter code. These in turn are divided into 1km squares.

Grid references are given with eastings followed by northings. It is assumed that visitors who are walking or cycling will be using the 1:50,000 Landranger Series or 1:25,000 Explorer Series maps. OS maps of the North Highlands are listed in the Bibliography.

Maps, GPS and compass should be carried when heading into remote regions. Digital offline OS maps are very useful on handheld devices because mobile phone signals are very patchy in most places. The use of a phone or GPS to geotag digital images will be found useful later when identifying images.

Local information centres and shops stock books related to the area as well as small booklets, brochures and other publications. VisitScotland produces information about accommodation, attractions, services and activities annually. The visithebrides.co.uk website is also an excellent source.

visithebrides.co.uk
visitscotland.com

INDEX

Callanish standing stones in the West of Lewis

CHARLES TAIT
GUIDE BOOKS

Charles Tait Guide Books

Orkney Guide Book, 4th ed (656p)
ISBN 9780951785980 (£24.95)
Orkney Peedie Guide, 4th ed revised (144p)
ISBN 9781909036000 (£9.95)
Outer Hebrides Guide Book, 3rd ed rev (256p)
ISBN 9780951785997 (£12.95)
Shetland Guide Book, 2nd ed (176p)
ISBN 9780951785942 (£12.95)
North Highlands Guide Book, 1st ed (400p)
ISBN 9780951785966 (£14.95)
Isle of Skye Guide Book, 1st ed (256p)
ISBN 9780951785973 (£12.95)
North Coast 500 Guide Book, 1st ed (256p)
ISBN 9781909036604 (£12.95)
Scapa Flow Guide Book, 1st ed (144p)
ISBN 9781909036024 (£9.95) - 2018

Charles Tait Miniguides

Orkney Miniguide, 1st edition (64p)
ISBN 9781909036116 (£4.95)
Heart of Neolithic Orkney Miniguide, 1st ed (64p)
ISBN 9781909036123 (£4.95)

Charles Tait Dorset Guide Books

Dorset Guide Book, 1st ed (384p)
ISBN 9781909036314 (£14.95)
West Dorset Guide, 1st ed (128p)
ISBN 9781909036321 (£6.95)
Purbeck Guide Book, 1st ed (96p)
ISBN 9781909036338 (£6.95)

Charles Tait Photographer & Travel Writer

Charles Tait has been publishing guide books since 1991, with nearly 100,000 sold. All are photographed, researched, written and designed by the author and lavishly illustrated by his photographs, with maps, old prints and other images. His strict policy of only writing about places he has visited gives this series an authenticity often lacking elsewhere. The guides have a common layout and are authoritative, yet easy to read and use.

Kelton, St Ola, Orkney KW15 1TR
Tel 01856 873738   charles.tait@zetnet.co.uk   charles-tait.co.uk